# NO ENEMIES, NO HATRED

# No Enemies, No Hatred

## SELECTED ESSAYS AND POEMS

## LIU XIAOBO

EDITED BY

PERRY LINK, TIENCHI MARTIN-LIAO, and LIU XIA

WITH A FOREWORD BY

VÁCLAV HAVEL

THE BELKNAP PRESS OF HARVARD UNIVERSITY PRESS

Cambridge, Massachusetts    London, England

Originally published as *Ich habe keine Feinde, ich kenne keinen Hass,*
copyright © S. Fischer Verlag GmbH, Frankfurt am Main 2011.

First Harvard University Press paperback edition, 2013

*Library of Congress Cataloging-in-Publication Data*

Liu, Xiaobo, 1955–
    No enemies, no hatred : selected essays and poems / Liu Xiaobo ; edited by Perry
Link, Tienchi Martin-Liao, and Liu Xia ; with a foreword by Václav Havel.
        p.   cm.
    Includes index.
    ISBN 978-0-674-06147-7 (cloth : alk. paper)
    ISBN 978-0-674-07232-9 (pbk.)
    I. Link, E. Perry (Eugene Perry), 1944–   II. Martin-Liao, Tienchi.   III. Liu, Xia,
1959–   IV. Title.
    PL2879.X53A2   2012
    895.1ʹ452—dc22        2011014145

# CONTENTS

# FOREWORD

Václav Havel

IT WAS MORE THAN THIRTY YEARS AGO that we, a group of 242 private citizens concerned about human rights in Czechoslovakia, came together to sign a manifesto called Charter 77. That document called on the Communist Party to respect human rights, and said clearly that we no longer wanted to live in fear of state repression. Our disparate group included ex-Communists, Catholics, Protestants, workers, liberal intellectuals, artists, and writers who came together to speak with one voice. We were united by our dissatisfaction with a regime that demanded acts of obedience on an almost daily basis. After Charter 77 was released, the government did its best to try to break us up. We were detained, and four of us eventually went to jail for several years. Surveillance was stepped up, our homes and offices were searched, and a barrage of press attacks based on malicious lies sought to discredit us and our movement. This onslaught only strengthened our bonds. Charter 77 also reminded many of our fellow citizens who were silently suffering that they were not alone. In time, many of the ideas set forth in Charter 77 prevailed in Czechoslovakia. A wave of similar democratic reforms swept across Eastern Europe in 1989.

In December 2008, a group of 303 Chinese activists, lawyers, intellectuals, academics, retired government officials, workers, and peasants put forward their own manifesto titled Charter 08, calling for constitutional government, respect for human rights, and other democratic reforms. Despite the best efforts of government officials to keep it off of Chinese computer screens, Charter 08 reached a nationwide audience via the Internet, and the number of new signatories eventually reached more than 10,000.

As in Czechoslovakia in the 1970s, the response of the Chinese government was swift and brutal. Dozens, if not hundreds, of signatories were called in for questioning. A handful of perceived ringleaders were detained. Professional promotions were held up, research grants denied, and applications to travel abroad rejected. Newspapers and publishing houses were ordered to blacklist anyone who had signed Charter 08. The prominent writer and dissident Liu Xiaobo, a key drafter of Charter 08, was arrested, and in December 2009 he was sentenced to eleven years in prison.

Despite Liu's imprisonment, his ideas cannot be shackled. Charter 08 has articulated an alternative vision of China, challenging the official line that any decisions on reforms are the exclusive province of the state. It has encouraged younger Chinese to become politically active, and boldly made the case for rule of law and constitutional multiparty democracy. And it has served as a jumping-off point for a series of conversations and essays on how to get there.

Perhaps most important, as in Czechoslovakia in the 1970s, Charter 08 has forged connections among different groups that did not exist before. Prior to Charter 08, "we had to live in a certain kind of separate and solitary state," one signatory wrote. "We were not good at expressing our own personal experiences to those around us."

Liu Xiaobo and Charter 08 are changing that, for the better.

Of course, Charter 08 addresses a political milieu that is very different from Czechoslovakia in the 1970s. In its quest for economic growth, China has seemed to embrace some features far removed from traditional Communism. Especially for young, urban, educated white-collar workers, China can seem like a post-Communist country. And yet China's Communist Party still has lines that cannot be crossed. In spearheading the creation of Charter 08, Liu Xiaobo crossed the starkest line of all: Do not challenge the Communist Party's monopoly on political power, and do not suggest that China's problems—including widespread corruption, labor unrest, and rampant environmental degradation—

might be connected to the lack of progress on political reform. And for making that very connection in an all too public way, Liu got more than a decade in prison.

*Shortened version of the article by Václav Havel, Dana Němcová,*
*and Václav Malý, "A Nobel Prize for a Chinese Dissident" (2010)*

# INTRODUCTION

LIU XIAOBO is one of those unusual people who can look at human life from the broadest of perspectives and reason about it from first principles. His keen intellect notices things that others also look at, but do not see. It seems that hardly any topic in Chinese culture, politics, or society evades his interest, and he can write with analytic calm about upsetting things. One might expect such calm in a recluse—a hermit poet, or a cloistered scholar—but in Liu Xiaobo it comes in an activist. Repeatedly he has gone where he thinks he should go, and done what he thinks he should do, as if havoc, danger, and the possibility of prison were not part of the picture. He seems to move through life taking mental notes on what he sees, hears, and reads, as well as on the inward responses that he feels.

Luckily for us, his readers, he also has a habit of writing free from fear. Most Chinese writers today, including many of the best ones, write with political caution in the backs of their minds and with a shadow hovering over their fingers as they pass across a keyboard. How should I couch things? What topics should I not touch? What indirection should I use? Liu Xiaobo does none of this. With him, it's all there. What he thinks, you get.

He was awarded the Nobel Peace Prize in 2010. For about two decades, the prize committee in Oslo, Norway, had been considering Chinese dissidents for the prize, and in 2010, after Liu Xiaobo had been sentenced to eleven years in prison for "incitement of subversion"—largely because of his advocacy of the human-rights manifesto called Charter 08—he had come to emerge as the right choice. Authorities in Beijing, furious at the award, did what they could to frustrate celebrations of it. Police broke up parties of revelers in several Chinese cities after the award was announced on October 8, 2010. The Chinese Foreign Ministry pressured world diplomats to stay away from the Award Ceremony in Oslo on December 10. Dozens of Liu Xiaobo's friends in China were barred from leaving the country lest they head for Oslo. Liu Xiaobo's wife, Liu Xia, although charged with nothing, was held under tight house arrest. Liu himself remained in prison, and none of his family members could travel to Oslo to collect the prize. At the Award Ceremony, the prize medal, resting inside a small box, and the prize certificate, in a folder that bore the initials "LXB," were placed on stage on an empty chair. Within hours authorities in Beijing banned the phrase "empty chair" from the Chinese Internet.

Liu was the fifth Peace Laureate to fail to appear for the Award Ceremony. In 1935, Carl von Ossietzky was held in a Nazi prison; in 1975, Andrei Sakharov was not allowed to leave the USSR; in 1983, Lech Wałesa feared he would be barred from reentering Poland if he went to Oslo; and in 1991, Aung Sang Suu Kyi was under house arrest in Burma. Each of the latter three prize-winners was able to send a family member to Oslo. Only Ossietzky and Liu Xiaobo could do not even that.

Liu was born December 28, 1955, in the city of Changchun in northeastern China. He was eleven years old when Mao Zedong closed his school—along with nearly every other school in China—so that youngsters could go into society to "oppose revisionism," "sweep away freaks and monsters," and in other ways join in Mao's Great Proletarian Cultural Revolution. Liu and his parents spent 1969 to 1973 at a "people's commune" in Inner Mongolia. In retrospect Liu believes that these years of upset, although a disaster for China as a whole, had certain unintended benefits for him personally. His years of lost schooling "allowed me freedom," he recalls, from the mind-closing processes of Maoist education; they gave him time to read books, both approved and unapproved. Moreover, the pervasive cynicism and chaos in the society around him taught him perhaps the most important lesson of all: that he would have to think for himself. Where else, after all, could he turn? In this general experience Liu resembles several others of the most powerfully independent Chinese writers of his generation. Hu Ping, Su Xiaokang, Zheng Yi, Bei Dao, Zhong Acheng, Jiang Qisheng, and many others survived the Cultural Revolution by learning to rely on their own minds, and for some this led to a questioning of the political system as a whole. Mao had preached that "rebellion is justified," but this is hardly the way he thought it should happen.

Chinese universities began to reopen after Mao died in 1976, and in 1977 Liu Xiaobo went to Jilin University, in his home province, where he earned a B.A. in Chinese literature in 1982. From there he went to Beijing, to Beijing Normal University, where he continued to study Chinese literature, receiving an M.A. in 1984 and a Ph.D. in 1988. His Ph.D. dissertation, entitled "Aesthetics and Human Freedom," was a plea for liberation of the human spirit; it drew wide acclaim from both his classmates and the most seasoned scholars at the university. Beijing Normal invited him to stay on as a lecturer, and his classes were highly popular with students.

Liu's articles and his presentations at conferences earned him a reputation as an iconoclast even before he finished graduate school. Known as the "black horse" of the late 1980s, seemingly no one escaped his acerbic pen: Maoist writers like Hao Ran were no better than hired guns, post-Mao literary stars like Wang Meng were but clever equivocators, "roots-seeking" writers like Han Shaogong and Zheng Yi made the mistake of thinking China had roots that were worth seeking, and even speak-for-the-people heroes like Liu Binyan were too ready to pin hopes on "liberal-minded" Communist leaders like Hu Yaobang (the Party chair who was sacked in 1987). "The Chinese love to look up to the famous," Liu wrote, "thereby saving themselves the trouble of thinking." In graduate school Liu read widely in Western thought—Plato, Kant, Nietzsche, Heidegger, Isaiah Berlin, Friedrich Hayek, and others—and began to use these thinkers to criticize Chinese cultural patterns. He also came to admire modern paragons of nonviolent resistance around the world—Mohandas Gandhi, Martin Luther King Jr., Václav Havel, and others. Although not formally a Christian, or a believer in any religion, he began to think and write about Jesus Christ.

Around the same time, he arrived at a view of the last two centuries of Chinese history that saw the shock of Western imperialism and technology as bringing "the greatest changes in thousands of years." Through the late nineteenth and early twentieth centuries, China's struggles to respond to this shock cut ever deeper into China's core. Reluctantly, Chinese thinking shifted from "our technology is not as good as other people's" in the 1880s and early 1890s to "our political system is not as good as other people's" after the defeat by Japan in 1895 to "our culture is not as good as other people's" in the May Fourth movement of the late 1910s. Then, under the pressure of war, all of the ferment and struggle ended in a Communist victory in 1949, and this event, said Liu, "plunged China into the abyss of totalitarianism." Recent decades have been more hopeful for China, in his view. Unrelenting pressure from below—from farmers, petitioners, rights advocates, and, perhaps most important, hundreds of millions of Internet users—has obliged the regime, gradually but inexorably, to cede ever more space to civil society.

The late 1980s were a turning point in Liu's life, both intellectually and emotionally. He visited the University of Oslo in 1988, where he was surprised that European Sinologists did not speak Chinese (they only read it) and was disappointed at how naïve Westerners were in accepting Chinese government language at face value. Then he went to New York, to Columbia University, where he encountered "critical theory" and learned that its dominant strain, at least at Columbia, was "postcolonialism." People expected him, as a visitor from China, to fit in by representing the "the subaltern," by resisting the "discursive hegemony" of "the metropole," and so on. Liu wondered why people in New York were telling him how it felt to be Chinese. Shouldn't it be the other way around? Was "postcolonialism" itself a kind of intellectual colonialism? Liu wrote in May 1989 that "no matter how strenuously Western intellectuals try to negate colonial expansionism and the white man's sense of superiority, when faced with other nations Westerners cannot help feeling superior. Even when criticizing themselves, they become besotted with their own courage and sincerity."

His experience in New York led him to see his erstwhile project of using Western values as yardsticks to measure China as fundamentally flawed. No system of human thought, he concluded, is equal to the challenges that the modern world faces: the population explosion, the energy crisis, environmental imbalance, nuclear disarmament, and "the addiction to pleasure and to commercialization." Nor is there any culture, he wrote, "that can help humanity once and for all to eliminate spiritual suffering or transcend personal limits." Suddenly he felt intellectually vulnerable, despite the fame he had enjoyed in China. He felt as if his lifelong project to think for himself would have to begin all over from scratch.

These thoughts came at the very time that the dramatic events of the 1989 pro-democracy movement in Beijing and other Chinese cities were appearing on the world's television screens. Commenting that intellectuals too often "just talk" and "do not do," Liu decided in late April 1989 to board a plane from New York to Beijing. "I hope," he wrote, "that I'm not the type of person who, standing at the doorway to hell, strikes a heroic pose and then starts frowning in indecision."

Back in Beijing, Liu went to Tiananmen Square, talked with the demonstrating students, and organized a hunger strike that began on June 2, 1989. Less than two days later, when tanks began rolling toward the Square and it was clear that people along the way were already dying, Liu negotiated with the attacking military to allow students a peaceful withdrawal. It is impossible to calculate how many lives he may have saved by this compromise, but certainly some, and perhaps many. After the massacre, Liu took refuge in the foreign diplomatic quarter, but later came to blame himself severely for not remaining in the streets—as many "ordinary folk" did, trying to rescue victims of the massacre. Images of the "souls of the dead" have haunted him ever since. The opening line of Liu's "Final Statement," which he read at his criminal trial in December 2009, said, "June 1989 has been the major turning point in my life." Liu Xia, who visited him in prison on October 10, 2010, two days after the announcement of his Nobel Prize, reports that he wept and said, "This is for those souls of the dead."

The regime's judgment of Liu's involvement at Tiananmen was that he had been a "black hand" behind a "counterrevolutionary riot." He was arrested on June 6, 1989, and sent for a bit more than eighteen months to Beijing's elite Qincheng Prison, where he was kept in a private cell, but not severely mistreated. "Sometimes I was deathly bored," he later wrote, "but that's about it." Upon release he was fired from his teaching job at Beijing Normal University.

He resumed a writing career, but now wrote less on literature and culture and more on politics. He could not publish in China, but sent manuscripts to Hong Kong publications such as *The Open Magazine* and *Cheng Ming Monthly,* as well as U.S.-based magazines such as *Beijing Spring* and *Democratic China.* In May 1995 the government arrested him again, this time for seven months. No reason was specified for the arrest, but it came in the same month that he released a petition called "Learn from the Lesson Written in Blood and Push Democracy and Rule of Law Forward: An Appeal on the Sixth Anniversary of Tiananmen."

On August 11, 1996, barely half a year after his second stint in prison, Liu joined with Wang Xizhe, a well-known dissident from the southern city of Guangzhou, to publish a statement on the sensitive topic of Taiwan's relations with mainland China. Earlier that year the Chinese military had fired missiles into the Taiwan Strait, in an apparent attempt to intimidate Taiwanese voters on the eve of presidential elections in which the issue of a formal declaration of independence from the mainland was at stake. In their statement, Liu and Wang wrote, "Is the government of the People's Republic of China the only legitimate [Chinese] government? In our view, it is both legitimate and not completely legitimate." Less than two months later, on October 8, 1996, Liu was arrested again and sent for three years to a reeducation-through-labor camp in Dalian, in his home province of Jilin. (Wang fled the country right after the declaration was issued and has since settled in the United States. He has never been back to China.)

The story of Liu Xiaobo's courage from the mid-1990s on cannot be separated from his wife, Liu Xia. Four years younger than he, Liu Xia is a poet and art photographer whom Liu Xiaobo has known since the 1980s and with whom he was living after his release from prison in January 1996. During his labor-camp incarceration, Liu Xia was allowed to visit him once a month, and, not missing a single month, made the 1,100-mile round-trip from Beijing thirty-six times. Shortly after Xiaobo entered the camp, Liu Xia applied to marry him. Camp authorities, puzzled at her request, felt that they needed to check with her to be sure she knew what she was doing. She reports answering them by saying, "Right! That 'enemy of the state'! I want to marry him!" A wedding ceremony inside the camp was impossible, and regulations forbade Xiaobo from exiting the camp, so the two married by filling out forms. On April 8, 1998, it was official.

It was during the three years at the labor camp that Liu Xiaobo seems to have formed his deepest faith in the concept of "human dignity," a phrase that has recurred in his writing ever since. It was also the camp environment that gave rise to many of his best poems, including most of those that appear in this book. Many of the camp poems are subtitled "to Xia," or "for Xia," but that does not make them love poems in the narrow sense. They span a variety of topics—massacre victims, Immanuel Kant, Vincent Van Gogh—that the poet addresses with Liu Xia standing beside him, as it were, as his spiritual companion. Liu Xia has prepared a book of her art photographs, which are deeply probing in what they suggest about China's moral predicament in contemporary times, and she subtitles her book "accompanying Liu Xiaobo."

On October 8, 1999, Liu Xiaobo returned from the reeducation camp, unreeducated. He resumed his writing career with no alteration of range or viewpoint, and lived primarily off his manuscripts, for which he was paid the equivalent of about US$60 to $90 per one thousand Chinese characters. In November 2003 he was elected chair of the writers' group Chinese PEN, and served in that post until 2007. During those years the rise of the Internet in China began to make a huge difference for Liu Xiaobo as well as for China as a whole. Finding ways to evade the government's "Great Firewall," Liu now could access information, communicate with friends, organize open letters, and edit and submit his manuscripts all much easier than before. He also watched with great satisfaction as the numbers of Chinese Internet users passed 100 million in 2006, giving rise to what he saw as "free assembly in cyberspace" and "power of public opinion on the Internet" that have turned into autonomous forces pushing China in the direction of democracy. In October 2006 Liu took over editorship of the Internet magazine *Democratic China* from his friend Su Xiaokang, who had been editing it from Delaware, and greatly expanded its reach inside China.

Charter 08, which was conceived in conscious admiration of Czechoslovakia's Charter 77 of the 1970s, and which became the main piece of evidence against Liu Xiaobo at his criminal trial, did not originate with Liu Xiaobo. A number of his friends had been working on a draft for several months in 2008 before he chose to join them. I do not know why he at first stood aside, but my surmise is that he felt the project was unlikely to get anywhere. When he did join, though, his efforts were crucial, and became increasingly so in the weeks and days immediately before the charter was announced. He insisted that the charter not be a "petition" to the government; it was a way for citizens to address fellow citizens about shared ideals. He persuaded his friends to remove certain confrontational phrases so that a wider range of people would feel comfortable endorsing the charter, and this judgment was vindicated when more than twelve thousand people eventually signed. He personally did more than anyone else to solicit signatures, but his most courageous move in the days before the unveiling of the charter was to agree to present himself as its leading sponsor. He was already known as the most prominent "dissident" inside China; taking primary responsibility for this text would only put him more in the government's spotlight and at greater risk for punishment.

He was not the only person punished for Charter 08. In the days right before and after it was unveiled, several others who had worked on drafting it saw their homes raided, or received from the police "invitations to tea" (i.e., interrogation) of the kind one is not at liberty to decline. Then came a nationwide campaign to suppress the charter itself. But even in this context, the eleven-year prison sentence that Liu received surprised many observers for its severity. Liu himself said of the ruling, which arrived on Christmas Day 2009, only that it "cannot bear moral scrutiny and will not pass the test of history." In his "Final Statement" he thanked his captors for the civil treatment he had received during his detention and declared, "I have no enemies." Then he appealed the ruling—not because he expected it could possibly be changed, but because he wanted "to leave the fullest possible historical record of what happens when an independent intellectual stands up to a dictatorship."

When the police came to remove Liu from his apartment late at night on December 8, 2008, they took him to a police-run hostel at an undisclosed location in Beijing for six months of "residential surveillance." (Chinese law says that "residential surveillance" happens at a person's residence, but for Liu this was not the case. He was allowed two monitored visits with Liu Xia during this time, but those occurred at a third location, neither his home nor the secret place where he was being held.) On June 23, 2009, he was formally arrested and charged with "incitement of subversion of state power," after which he was held at the Beijing Number One Detention Center. He continued to be held there after his trial in December 2009, and on May 24, 2010, was transferred to Jinzhou Prison in his home province of Liaoning. (By custom, notable Chinese criminals are sent home for punishment.) Liu Xia has been granted occasional, but closely monitored, visits at the prison.

We know very little of his prison conditions. Chinese Human Rights Defenders has reported that—as of late 2010—he was sharing a cell with five other inmates (although veterans of Chinese prisons suspect that these five, real inmates or not, are there to report on him). The other five are allowed weekly visits from family members, but Liu is allowed only monthly visits. Whether or not these visits can be from his wife depends on his behavior, on hers, and on the political "sensitivity" of the times. (A Nobel Prize and an Arab Spring are the kinds of things that generate great sensitivity.) Liu eats low-quality prison food. His cell mates are allowed to pay the prison to get specially prepared, better food, but Liu is denied this option. He has chronic hepatitis and stomach problems, but receives only cursory medical attention. He gets two hours each day to go outdoors. He can read books that Liu Xia has brought to him, but only if they are books published and sold in China. There is a television set in his cell, and the prison authorities control which programs he can watch—but not, of course, how he understands them.

Liu Xiaobo has published many hundreds of articles and, if one counts collections of essays and poems, seventeen books. To peruse this large oeuvre and select essays that reflect the breadth of his interests and the range of his erudition is no easy task, and I am grateful to his longtime friends Hu Ping and Tienchi Martin-Liao for doing this work so well. The essays selected here are drawn mostly from Liu's later and more political work done between 2004 and 2008. The poems, which have been personally selected by Liu Xia, are drawn from the 1990s, especially the labor-camp years of 1996–1999.

I owe a tremendous debt to the thirteen translators for their observance of deadlines, their efficient follow-up, and, most importantly, their spirit of collaboration. Everyone in the project admires Liu Xiaobo, and our shared goal was that he not sound like fourteen different people. We have sought to produce an English-language "voice" for him that is not only consistent throughout the book but captures the eloquence of his Chinese. Readers of Chinese who compare our translations with the original texts will note that we have not pursued word-to-word, or sometimes even sentence-to-sentence, literalness. Such an approach can produce a stilted flavor that is quite absent from the originals when they are read in Chinese. Instead, we have aimed for what we think Liu Xiaobo would likely have written had he been thinking in English. Anyone who knows both Chinese and English knows that to have precisely the "same thought" in two such different languages can seldom be more than a gentle fiction. This fact makes the translator's work an art, not a science. In the end, though, we feel that the effort to translate tone and spirit, not just words, produces a better kind of fidelity.

*Perry Link*

# NO ENEMIES, NO HATRED

# PART I

## POLITICS WITH CHINESE CHARACTERISTICS

# LISTEN CAREFULLY TO THE VOICES
# OF THE TIANANMEN MOTHERS

## Reading the Unedited Interview Transcripts of
## Family Members Bereaved by the Massacre

◆　　◆　　◆　　◆　　◆

*Late at night on June 3, 1989, a 17-year-old boy named Jiang Jielian was shot and killed by People's Liberation Army troops in Beijing. Later his mother, Ding Zilin, a retired professor of philosophy at People's University, joined with Zhang Xianling, who had lost a 19-year-old son, and Huang Jinping, who had lost a husband, to form and lead a group called the "Tiananmen Mothers." They took it as their mission to seek out family members of others who had been killed or wounded in the Tiananmen Massacre of 1989. Their effort required patience and persistence—the Chinese government had made it clear that any victim of the massacre was by definition a "counterrevolutionary rioter," so families who provided information to the group might face further trouble from the government. Still, after a decade of work, the Tiananmen Mothers had compiled enough material to publish a booklet,* Witnessing the Massacre and Seeking Justice, *in which they listed the names, along with photographs and capsule histories, of 155 who died in the massacre. The booklet also included twenty-five accounts of the arduous work involved in seeking out family members of victims. An expanded version of the booklet was later published in Hong Kong under the title* In Search of the Victims of June Fourth, 1989–2005 *(Open Magazine Press, 2005).*

*Liu Xiaobo, who regards himself as a student of Ding Zilin, was an early and stout supporter of the Tiananmen Mothers. What follows is an excerpted version of a long essay that Liu wrote in 2004 on the eve of the fifteenth anniversary of the massacre. Two months before Liu wrote it,*

*Ding Zilin, Zhang Xianling, and Huang Jinping had been seized in their homes and held in detention for several days, apparently because (although Party officials never specified the reason) they had publicized their work with the families of victims.—Ed.*

READING THE RECOLLECTIONS of bereaved family members allows me to see in detail the cruelty of the executioners, and, even more clearly, the brightness of humanity that shone in the midst of great terror.

Immediately after the massacre in Beijing on June 4, 1989, Chinese authorities exploited their monopoly of the mass media in order to blur the difference between black and white. They constantly repeated how cruelly so-called thugs had treated the martial-law troops and tried their best to hide the truth about how the troops had wantonly slaughtered ordinary people. But despite the government-imposed lockdown on alternate sources of information, the troops' cruelty could be gleaned in some accounts that appeared at the time. One of these told of what happened near Xidan when troops used tanks to chase and crush students and civilians. Several eyewitnesses had reported this outrage at the time, but now, thanks to the bereaved families who are speaking out in these transcripts, we have fuller and more vivid testimony.

It is obvious from the transcripts that troops opened fire blindly in all directions and killed a great number of innocent civilians. Around 10 p.m. on the evening of June 3, troops moving from west to east along Fuxing Boulevard had already begun spraying bullets back and forth into residential compounds, with no regard for life. Around 11 p.m., when a detachment of infantry scouts was passing the bridge at Muxidi, an order suddenly rang out and soldiers hit the ground. Then one of the officers among them rose to one knee, raised his submachine gun, and fired blindly all along the road while many people fell in pools of blood. The startled crowd broke in all directions. Students who tried to stop these blind killings themselves were shot.

Because the gunfire was so blind, many people died inside their homes. Among the 182 documented dead in the transcripts, some were people who had never joined the protests, never confronted the troops, and never even gone out to watch the excitement. Yet bullets, fired randomly, took their lives. A woman named Ma Chengfen, who had been a veteran of the People's Liberation Army, was shot and killed while sitting on a staircase chatting with a neighbor. A 66-year-old worker named Zhang Fuyuan was shot in the backyard of his relative's home. Another victim was an old lady from Wanxian in Sichuan who had been working in Muxidi as a nanny in the 22nd-floor home of the head of a government ministry. She was shot dead after she went down to the 14th-floor balcony to see what was going on. In the same building the son-in-law of a deputy inspector was killed in his kitchen.

Perhaps most shocking of all, passersby who simply encountered martial law troops along the street were sometimes chased down and killed by soldiers who had been carried away by their mission to kill. One group of seven, five men and two women, who were walking near Nanlishi Road were chased down in this way. Three of them, Yang Ziping, Wang Zhengsheng, and An Ji, were killed. Two of the others were wounded.

These transcripts show, too, how martial-law troops could be so cruel as to impede help for the wounded and dying. Zhang Xianling, one of the original Tiananmen Mothers, reports an instance in which a young man rushed out to take a photo just as the troops began firing and was struck by a bullet. People who saw the boy fall wanted to help him, but soldiers would not let anyone go near. One old lady went to her knees to beg them. "He's a kid," she said. "*Please* let us go help him!" A soldier answered by pointing his gun at her and roaring, "He's a thug! I'll shoot anyone who takes one step." Later two ambulances arrived, and soldiers stopped them. When a doctor got off and tried to negotiate, the troops refused and the ambulances had to turn around. In short, they killed people and wouldn't let others help: how cruel is that?

Readers of the transcripts can also learn how the shameless murderers sought to cover up the evil they were doing. They hid bodies of the dead. Many people disappeared on June 4, 1989, and even today it is hard to know how many are living and how many died. After Zhang Xianling's son Wang Nan was shot, martial law troops buried his body in a lawn in front of the gate to No. 28 Middle School (now known as Chang'an Middle School) near Tiananmen. However, because he had been wearing a military uniform and a soldier's belt, the soldiers later feared he might be one of their own, so they dug up his body and sent it to a hospital. When Zhang Xianling was finally able to locate her son's body, the troops at first wouldn't let her take it home. "You can't have it," a soldier barked at her. "Get out or you'll be arrested." The mother later learned that there actually had been three unidentified dead bodies in that pit. The two others had already been sent to a crematorium—as "unknown corpses." "During our search," Zhang Xianling observed, "we ran across people from a dozen or so other families who were looking for their loved ones, be they dead or alive, but were looking in vain. They may well have been looking for some of those 'cremated unknown.'"

Guilt feelings stab at my heart like daggers as I read these transcripts, because it is clear that not one of the people whose lives were so cruelly snuffed out that night was among the "elite." None of the conspicuous activists—like me—were killed. The victims ranged from a 66-year-old senior citizen to a child barely 9. There were people in their thirties and forties, the prime of life, a youngster of 17, another who was 20-something . . . But they were all just ordinary students and civilians, people who apparently wanted to live ordinary lives and to enjoy every-day sorts of happiness, and on that blood-soaked night they had made the mistake of acting on impulses of sympathy or of justice, and it had cost them everything.

Some of the dead had been participants in the 1989 movement. They had stayed in the square until the last moment, as if waiting for the bullets of evil to take their lives. For example:

> Cheng Renxing, a 25-year-old student at People's University, was just about to withdraw from the square when a random shot felled him. He collapsed at the base of the flag pole that faces Tiananmen.

> Dai Jinping, a 27-year-old M.A. student at Beijing Agricultural University, was shot to death around 11 p.m. on June 3, 1989, right beside the Mao Zedong Memorial Hall.

> Li Haocheng, a student in the Chinese Department at Tianjin Normal University, had been among 5,000 students and faculty from his school who traveled to Beijing to protest. Early on the

morning of June 4, as martial law troops entered Tiananmen Square, Li stood at the southeast corner of the square taking a photo to document the moment. A flash of his camera, then he fell and died.

Wu Xiangdong, a 21-year-old university student who had been part of the 1989 movement from the beginning, had already written a farewell note to his family: "The fate of a nation rests with each single person. If this costs my life, then so be it . . ." It did cost his life.

Others had originally been bystanders to the protests, but then, moved by the moral intuition that is native to human beings, they came to the aid of the protesters during their hour of peril. When the massacre began, some of these people rushed straight into the most dangerous scenes. Here are some examples:

On the evening of June 3, Jiang Jielian, a 17-year-old high school student, defying the tearful admonitions of his mother, who had locked all the doors of their residence, jumped out of a bathroom window and ran toward the blood-stained Chang'an Boulevard to join a mass of people who were trying to dissuade the martial law troops from advancing. His dissuasion failed, and a bullet took his life.

Wang Nan, a 19-year-old student in senior high school, felt an urge to "record the true facts of history." He ran toward Tiananmen Square carrying a camera. But before he could use his camera to document anything, his own life itself was spent as a piece of evidence of the barbaric massacre.

Yan Wen, a 23-year-old student at Peking University, also wanted to record events for history. He headed with some classmates for Muxidi. A bullet struck him in the thigh, crushed a main artery, and led to uncontrollable bleeding. He stopped breathing fairly quickly.

Still other cases were of people who braved danger trying to rescue the dying and assisting the wounded. Here are a few examples.

At 7 a.m. on June 4, Yang Yansheng, 30 years old, went out of his way to help a wounded stranger. Troops delivered a bullet to his liver, where it exploded, and he died.

Du Guangxue was a 24-year-old worker, a passionate young man who had visited the protesters at Tiananmen many times. At midnight on June 3 he heard that people had died at the square, so he hopped onto his bicycle to see what he could do, and was shot to death while biking past Xinhuamen.

Zhou Deping, age 25, was an M.A. student in electrical engineering at Tsinghua University. During the evening carnage of June 3, 1989, he volunteered to a group of his Tsinghua classmates to go to Tiananmen Square to check out what other classmates were facing. He headed off on his bicycle and never returned.

Sun Hui was a 19-year-old chemistry major at Peking University. He, too, volunteered to go look for a group of classmates who had said they were going to withdraw from the square but who failed to appear back on campus. Sun was shot to death while riding his bicycle near the overpass at Fuxingmen.

The transcripts tell of the deaths of three people who, had cameras been able to record their images, would have given us three more heroes to stand alongside the famous "tankman" who stood before a row of tanks.

Duan Changlong, age 24, was a recent graduate in chemical engineering from Tsinghua University. After that night in which bullets flew in every direction, and as bad news kept pouring in, he spent his day visiting emergency wards trying to save the wounded. In the evening he went to the area near the National Minority Palace to try to persuade the martial law troops to stop confronting the people. As he ran toward a military official, he apparently never imagined that a bullet would come flying out of the official's revolver to greet him.

Wang Weiping, age 25, was a graduate of the Beijing University of Medicine and was about to begin an assignment in the OBGYN department of People's Hospital. On June 4 she threw herself into the volunteer effort to save the lives of the wounded. Eye-witnesses report that she seemed utterly without fear, as bullets flew and flames burst forth on every side, while she concentra-ted solely on the people, one after another, who were lying in pools of blood. As she was applying dressing to a wound of one of them, she lifted her head slightly, was struck in the neck by a bullet, collapsed wordlessly, and that was that.

Yuan Li, age 29, worked in the Automation Research Institute in the Ministry of Electrical Engineering. Watching as troops shot recklessly in every direction, and no longer able to endure the sight of the slaughter of innocent civilians, he stepped forward, raised his right arm, and shouted, "I was a graduate student at Tsinghua University . . ." Before he could finish, a shot rang out and his life disappeared into the black night.

Killings are only part of the story of the suffering of these "name-less" heroes. Among people who were sent to prison for their roles in the protests, the ones who got heavy sentences—ten years or more—were predominantly people of this kind, not famous intellectual leaders. Wang Yi, a student at the Beijing College of Broadcasting, was sentenced to eleven years for blocking a military vehicle. Chen Lantao, a youngster from Qingdao, got eighteen years merely for making a protest speech in public once the massacre had begun. The Sichuan poet Liao Yiwu re-ports that the ordinary Tiananmen prisoners with whom he was locked up included many who were serving terms of ten years or more. There are uncountable others all across the country, and many remain behind bars today.

Among the well-known figures during the demonstrations—people who have high opinions of themselves and sometimes even look down on their ordinary followers—not one died or was wounded on June 4, and very few got prison sentences of more than ten years. Some of the elite were forced into exile and others were sent to prison, but all es-caped the knives of the butchers. They also managed to make names for themselves, of greater or lesser size, and to attract the concern of others. Among the "black hands" who were accused of "causing turmoil behind the scenes," only Wang Juntao and Chen Ziming got sentences of as long as thirteen years, and even those two were released on medical parole in the mid-1990s. I myself was one of the "black hands"; I have been incarcerated three times since 1989, but my total time of lost freedom, adding the three terms together, still amounts to less than six years.

In raising this topic I am not trying to encourage a competition over whose "sacrifice" was greatest. I am just trying to remind myself, as one of those "influential" figures, of the true facts of the Tiananmen Massacre. How was it that university students and high-level intellectuals led the 1989 movement, but when the dust settled all the people who were massacred, went out to rescue the wounded, or received heavy sentences were common people? Why is it that we scarcely hear the voices of the people who paid the heaviest prices, while the luminaries who survived the massacre can hardly stop talking? Why is it that, in the wake of the massacre, the blood of ordinary people has gone to nourish the reputations of opportunists large and small, people who run around presenting themselves as the leaders of a "people's movement"? Fifteen years have passed since the massacre, and yet that spilled blood, except for establishing the place of a few "heroes" at home and abroad, has resulted in almost no advance within this cold-blooded nation of ours.

What is the meaning of "suffering" and "sacrifice"? What have we bought with lost life and blood? Everyone knows that, in this land of ours, the gap between winners and losers is normally as wide as heaven and earth. But does the moral high ground that results from suffering caused by a big massacre also have to apportioned so unevenly—as starkly as the difference between heaven and earth? China's great writer Lu Xun (1881–1936) observed, after another massacre in Beijing in 1926:

> Time just flows along. The streets are peaceful again. In China
> a few brief lives count for nothing. At most, they provide sub-
> ject matter for the after-dinner chat of idlers who mean no
> harm, or for other idlers who do enjoy their malevolent gossip.

The so-called elites of our country have made no progress at all since Lu Xun's day. It is hard to find any shame or guilt in us. We have yet to learn how to draw spiritual meaning from our encounters with suffering, how to live in human dignity, or how to feel concern for the suffering of actual, ordinary people.

Take me, for instance: a self-styled elite intellectual in the 1980s and an eye-catching leader in the 1989 protest movement. What have I ever done for the massacre victims? This question has been weighing heavily on me. After the massacre, during my eighteen-month stay in Qincheng Prison, I wrote a "confession." In doing that I not only sold out my personal dignity, but betrayed the blood sacrifices of the massacre victims. Moreover the confession left me, after I got out of prison, with a bit of a bad reputation, and for that a number of people offered me their support. Did I deserve support? Compared to whom? What about all the ordinary people who lost their lives? What about those wounded who, right now, cannot live independent lives? And what about the nameless who still languish in prison? What support has any of them got? Liao Yiwu, whose four-year prison sentence resulted in part from two long poems called "Massacre" and "Requiem," ended one those poems with the line "And who are the lucky survivors?—They are bastards one and all!"

To look squarely at the suffering of the ordinary people whose misery is recorded in the transcripts makes me feel that I am not qualified even to be called a "survivor." It is true that I was one of the last people to leave Tiananmen Square on June 4th, but I did nothing to volunteer myself during the bloody terror of the massacre's aftermath, nothing to show that a kernel of my humanity had survived. After I left the square, I did not go to Beijing Normal University campus to check on the students from my alma mater who presumably had also left the square. Still less did I consider going out into the streets to minister to dead and wounded whom I did not know. Instead I fled to the relative safety of the foreign diplomatic housing compound. It is no wonder that the ordinary people who lived through the butchery might ask: "When great terror engulfed the city of Beijing, where were all those 'black hands'"?

Fifteen years after Tiananmen, we can do nothing about the persistent cold blood in the veins of the massacre's perpetrators, but at least we can ask the "heroes" of the movement, the people who have all those battle decorations pinned on our chests, this question: When we think about the victims who harvested nothing, indeed whose "gains" were only negative numbers, do we feel no personal responsibility, no guilt? Should we not observe minimal standards of human decency and, with that same passion with which we cherish freedom, be sure that the moral resources that derive from the loss of human life—which are the only resources people have in challenging totalitarian power—are properly apportioned? When we look at those "Tiananmen mothers" who so tirelessly persist in seeking justice for victims, can elite survivors like us not show a bit more compassion, and a better sense of equality and justice, by being sure that moral credit goes to those people who suffered far more than we did, and to whom such credit in the first place rightly belongs?

Let us offer our thanks to these bereaved family members, who have given to Chinese history portraits of the ordinary people who died in the massacre.

*Originally published on the website of New Century News, www.ncn.org*
*Translated by Paul G. Pickowicz*

# YOUR SEVENTEEN YEARS

*Two years after Tiananmen*

*Foreword:* Though your father warned you not to go, you snuck out the bathroom window. When you fell, flag in hand, you were only seventeen. I lived. I am now thirty-six. In the face of your death, living is a crime, and writing this poem for you is an even greater shame. The living must hold their peace, and listen to the voices from the grave. I am not worthy to write poetry for you. Your seventeen years are more precious than any work of words or hands.

I, alive
and with my share of infamy
have not the courage, nor the right
to come bearing flowers or words
before your seventeen-year-old smile

I know
seventeen years cannot hate or begrudge

And I have learned, from your seventeen years
that a life is a simple and unembellished thing
like a horizonless desert
requiring no water

requiring no adornment of tree or flower
to withstand the ravages of the sun

When your seventeen years collapsed upon the road
the road disappeared
your seventeen years rest peacefully as pages
between covers of mud
seventeen years in this world
yearn after nothing
but white, immaculate Age

When your seventeen years ceased to breathe,
miraculously they did not cease to hope
when bullets pierced the mountains
and the oceans writhed in pain
when all flowers became a single color
your seventeen years did not cease to hope
could not cease to hope
seventeen years of unfinished love
were returned to a white-haired mother

The mother who kept your seventeen years
locked up at home
the mother who beneath a five-starred flag
severed the ties of noble blood
which bound her own family
woke when you fixed her with your final gaze
bearing your seventeen-year-old bequest
she has crossed and recrossed every graveyard
every time she was about to fall
the spectral breath of a seventeen-year-old
propped her up
and sent her on her way

Surpassing age
surpassing death

your seventeen years
will last forever

Beijing, June 1, 1991, at night

*Translated by Isaac P. Hsieh*

# STANDING AMID THE EXECRATIONS OF TIME

*Ten years after Tiananmen*

To me, standing amid the execrations of Time
that day seems so strange

1

Ten years ago this day
dawn, a bloody shirt
sun, a torn calendar
all eyes upon
this single page
the world a single outraged stare
time tolerates no naïveté
the dead rage and howl
till the earth's throat
grows hoarse

Gripping the prison bars
this moment
I must wail in grief
for I fear the next
so much I have no tears for it
remembering them, the innocent dead,

I must thrust a dagger calmly
into my eyes
must purchase with blindness
clarity of the brain
for that bone-devouring memory
is best expressed
by refusal


2

Ten years ago this day
soldiers stand at attention
poses dignified and correct, trained
to uphold a hideous lie
dawn is a crimson flag
fluttering in the half-light
people crane and stand on tiptoe
curious, awed, earnest
a young mother
lifts her baby's hand
to salute that sky-eclipsing lie

And a white-haired mother
kisses the image of her son
delicately pries his fingers apart
and washes the blood from his nails
she can find no soil, not even a handful
in which her son may rest
she has no choice
but to hang him on the wall

Now she walks among unmarked graves
hoping to expose the lie of a century
from her sealed throat she exhumes
that long-stifled name
lets her freedom and dignity be

a denunciation of amnesia
police listen on the wiretap
and dog her footsteps


3

The world's largest square
has been given a new face

When the peasant Liu Bang became
Han Gaozu, founder of a dynasty
he invented a tale about his mother and a dragon
to inflate his family history
this ancient pattern continues
from the Ming Tombs to the Memorial Hall
butchers lie in state
in resplendent underground palaces
across millennia, tyrants and autocrats
exchange tips on dagger technique
while their entombed vassals
offer obeisance

In a few months' time
amid glorious pomp
murder weapons will roll once again across this square
and the corpse in the Hall
and the butchers dreaming their imperial dreams
will look on with approval
while beneath the earth the Emperor of Qin
reviews his clay troops

Still that old ghost
mulls his past glories
while his heirs glut themselves
upon his legacy
with his blessing they wield scepters of bone

and pray the next century
will be even better

Amid tanks and flowers
salutes and daggers
amid doves and bullets
jackboots and expressionless faces
a century concludes
in blood-reek and darkness
and a new era begins
without a glimmer of life

      4

Refuse to eat
refuse to masturbate
pick a book out of the ruins
and admire the humility of the corpse
in a mosquito's innards
dreaming blood-dark dreams
peer through the steel door's peephole
and converse with vampires
no need to be circumspect
your stomach spasms
will give you the courage of the dying
retch out a curse
for fifty years of glory
there has never been a New China
only a Party

In the labor camp, Dalian, June 4, 1999

*Translated by Isaac P. Hsieh*

*Editor's Postscript: In the 1950s the Communist Party promoted a song called "Without the Communist Party There Would Be No New China." In 1989, student protesters at Tiananmen sang the song, clearly intending a sarcastic second-level meaning of "without the Communist Party, there would be no (such disaster as) 'New China.'" (Authorities could not stop them from singing it, because its first-level meaning was unobjectionable.) In the last two lines of this poem, Liu Xiaobo seems to push the students' meaning one step further.*

# TO CHANGE A REGIME BY CHANGING A SOCIETY

◆　◆　◆　◆　◆

*This essay is one of six that were adduced at Liu Xiaobo's trial on December 23, 2009, as evidence of his guilt of "the crime of inciting subversion of state power." The phrase "to change a regime" was directly quoted several times.*—Ed.

CHINA HAS NOW OFFICIALLY SEEN more than twenty years of "reform." Yet because of the Communist Party's continuing jealous grip on power, and because popular movements within society remain diffuse, there is no prospect that any organization will be able to muster a political force sufficient to bring regime change any time soon. There is also no sign within the ruling elite of an enlightened figure like Mikhail Gorbachev or Chiang Ching-kuo, who in the late 1980s and early 1990s helped turn the USSR and Taiwan toward democracy. For these reasons China's transition toward a modern, free society must necessarily be gradual and tortuous, and the amount of time it will take might well be more than anyone estimates.

Resting beneath the mighty Communist regime is a civil society that remains weak. It doesn't have much courage and is not very sophisticated. As a civil society it is still in a nascent stage, and this is why we must not expect it, in the near term, to produce a political organization that might replace the Communist regime. Given this situation, any plan, program, or action that aims at quick changes in

China's political system or in its current regime is little more than a mirage.

But none of the above should cause us to abandon hope for a free China in the future. The hope has a realistic basis because it is plain that in post-Mao China it is no longer possible, as it once was, for a single great dictator to block the entire Chinese sky. The sky now bears a distinct pattern of two shades, darkness and light, and both are always present. The relation between rulers and ruled is no longer one in which the people are held in regimented silence except when permitted, on cue, to shout "Long Live Somebody!" Today, the ossified language of the regime and the people's rising awareness of their rights exist side by side; oppression from the authorities above and resistance from the people below also exist side by side. The political system remains autocratic, but people in society are no longer ignorant; officials are as tyrannical as ever, but a "rights-defense" *(weiquan)* movement is having effects in many places; the regime can still send a person to prison for what he or she writes, but the chilling effect on other writers is much less than it was before; the regime's "enemy mentality" is quite the same as before, but it no longer has the effect of turning "politically sensitive" people into isolated figures whom the rest of society shuns like lepers.

The one-person dictatorship of the Mao era rested on the following four conditions:

1. A comprehensive nationalization of the economy that erased the very possibility of economic independence for citizens. The regime became, in effect, "nanny" to every citizen. There was little choice but to accept this nanny from cradle to grave.

2. An all-encompassing political organization that made personal freedom impossible. This organization was the sole basis of every person's legal status. People were made to be utterly dependent on it. If one ventured outside it, the simplest task became a difficult chore. To live outside of it entirely was tantamount to living as an alien in one's own homeland.

3. A culture of violence that the ruling authority imposed throughout society. Unbridled arbitrary rule by the dictator, combined with an "enemy mentality" in society, produced an

atmosphere in which citizens were in effect used as soldiers and even came to resemble them. Monitoring became so ubiquitous and vigilance so unrelenting that virtually every set of eyes—be they in the workplace, the neighborhood, or even among family and friends—turned into the tools of state supervision.

4. A tyranny of the mind that arose from an ideology that claimed to explain everything and to possess all virtue, and which was reinforced by huge mass movements. An extreme personality cult of the great leader narrowed the source of public thinking until one master brain was deciding what everyone else should think. Anyone who strayed from the ideology could be labeled "deviant," and this was a fate that led not merely to political, economic, and social demotion but to extremes of personal insult, public humiliation, physical abuse, and mental torture—or, in the officially approved phrase of the time, "attack to the point of collapse and stench." Victims of such persecution normally buckled under its weight. Most agreed to perform rituals of self-humiliation.

But in recent times the Chinese people have been making great strides toward a society that is far more pluralist than it was during the Mao years. It is no longer possible for society to be utterly dominated by official power. The steady growth of private capital has eaten away at the regime's onetime economic monopoly; increasingly diverse concepts of value are challenging the monopoly on "thought"; the expanding rights-defense movement is eroding the power of government officials to act on caprice; and advances in public courage have made the specter of political terror ever less frightening.

Three of the four pillars of totalitarian rule that I have sketched above have suffered considerable decay and collapse, especially in the years since the 1989 Tiananmen Massacre. Personal dependence on the regime for livelihood is steadily giving way to economic independence. Now that ordinary people can live more directly from their own efforts, they have a stronger material base for autonomous choice, and this trend has brought a new plurality of interests to the whole of society. The total dependence of citizens on "the organization" for personal identity has also been replaced by greater (if still limited) freedoms. The days when venturing outside the organization turned the simplest task into a chore are gone forever. Chinese society is seeing more and more freedom to move, to migrate, and to choose one's own work.

On the thought-control question, the rise of independent thinking and the awareness of people's rights have undermined the dominant ideology. Value systems that differ from the official ideology have been taking shape in society and have sometimes obliged the government to make adjustments in its official verbiage. To be sure, the government's control of speech and its use of lies for the purpose of indoctrination continue, but the effectiveness of these methods has sharply declined. In particular, the information revolution ushered in by the Internet has given rise to a radical new variety in the ways in which Chinese people get information and express themselves. The regime's traditional ways of blocking information and controlling political discussion are now largely obsolete.

Of the four pillars of Mao-era totalitarian rule, the only one that is still basically standing is the political monopoly with its bag of tools for repressing alternate views. But even that pillar is less than it once was. Recent years have made it clear that although officials at all levels still cling to power, moral authority, in the popular view, lies increasingly with the people. Today, a victim of terror no longer faces the double threat of prison that confines the body and humiliation that assaults the spirit. Political persecution can still bring economic loss and loss of personal freedom, but it can no longer destroy a person's reputation or turn a person into a political leper. Indeed, today it can have the opposite effect—not merely failing to destroy one's dignity or spirit but actually helping a person to achieve spiritual wholeness, and even, in the view of others, to rise to the status of "conscience of the people" or "hero of truth," while the government's bullying comes to be viewed as "dirty work." Victims of persecution these days no longer must perform contrite self-denunciations, or beg the organization for forgiveness, or humiliate themselves in front of crowds. Today many are able to face down the regime's pressure. We have seen cases where, speaking from a defendant's dock in court, people deliver eloquent statements of self-defense that turn the tables, putting the regime and its courts on the moral defensive.

In parallel with these changes, a global trend toward freedom and democracy has been steadily gaining strength after the collapse of autocratic rule in the Soviet Union and Eastern Europe. Human rights diplomacy in the world community and pressure from international human rights organizations have made the cost of maintaining a dictatorial system and a politics of terror increasingly high even as the effectiveness of such repression continues to decline. The world situation obliges the Chinese regime, both at home and abroad, to put on hypocritical "shows" of human rights and democracy.

These trends in China and in the world are all fundamentally grounded in humankind's spiritual nature. The moral strength of nonviolence, which has been shown several places in the modern world, is grounded in the fact that human existence is not just physical but spiritual as well. The core of the human moral sense lies in recognition of the dignity of persons, and respect for this dignity is the natural source of humankind's sense of justice. When a political system or a state makes it possible for people to live in dignity, people naturally offer it their allegiance. As Thomas Aquinas put it, virtuous government is not just the maintenance of order, but, more importantly, the establishment of conditions for human dignity; if a state fails in the latter cause, it will arouse all kinds of resistance, and opposition from people's consciences will be in the lead among them.

The reason why liberal democracy is gradually replacing dictatorship in today's world, and why the end of the Cold War can be seen, as Francis Fukuyama has written, as the "end of history," is that liberal democracy acknowledges and respects human dignity while dictatorship negates it and defiles it. In transitions toward liberal democracy, the splendor and special strengths of nonviolent resistance are plain to observe: although people must still deal with tyranny and the suffering that it causes, they can respond to hate with love, to prejudice with tolerance, to arrogance with humility, to degradation with dignity, and to violence with reason. Through the power of sincerity and goodwill, victims can take a bold initiative: they can invite victimizers to come home to the rules of reason, peace, and compassion. This tactic can deliver everyone from the vicious cycle of forever replacing one ferocity with another.

Recognizing that there is no way, in the near term, to replace China's dictatorial political system with something better, I can see the following ways for Chinese society to continue its healthy bottom-up transformation:

1. Short of attempting to take over political power, the nonviolent rights-defense movement can work to expand civil society and thereby provide people with space within which they can live in dignity. The movement can help people to change the ways in which they see their place in society, i.e., no longer to accept living in ignorance and timidity, hardly better than slaves. Wherever the social control of the dictatorship is weak, the rights movement can use nonviolent resistance to shrink the space that the government controls and to increase the price that it must pay in order to maintain its domination within that space. Popular power can grow an inch every time official power is obliged to retreat an inch.

2. Without pursuing a grand program of total societal transformation, the rights-defense movement can concentrate on putting freedom into practice in daily life. By changing the ways in which people think and express themselves in their everyday dealings with authorities—especially through the growing numbers of rights-defense cases—the movement can foster ethics in society, bring people together, and help people figure out how to cope. The overarching authoritarian structure can remain unchanged while the rights movement operates inside its belly, inside countless small environments. For example, the reason why senior news reporters Lu Yuegang and Li Datong at *China Youth Daily* recently were able to defy the state's propaganda system had a lot to do with the health of the small environment at their own newspaper.

3. No matter how strong the freedom-denying power of the regime and its apparatus becomes, each individual person can still attempt to view him- or herself as a free person, i.e., to live an honest life in dignity. In any society governed by dictators, if people who pursue freedom state and practice this ideal pub-

licly, and if they can find ways to act within their immediate daily contexts without fear, then ordinary daily life can become a force that undermines the system of enslavement. If you yourself believe that you have a human conscience and are willing to follow it, then expose your conscience to the sunlight of public opinion and let it shine there for all people to see, especially for the dictators to see.

4.  While insisting on the basic principles of liberalism, we must also practice tolerance and support plurality of opinion. When people who engage in high-profile confrontation with the regime hear about people who are making different choices, perhaps pursuing matters in more low-key ways, the high-profile people should view the efforts of the low-key people not as errors but as contributions that are complementary to their own. People who are more confrontational are not necessarily great heroes who are therefore in a position to assign moral blame to others. This kind of aggressive moral blame is, to be sure, different from the regime's aggressive political blame, but it is still far from the kind of tolerance that liberalism calls for. The decision by one person to pay a heavy price for the ideals he or she has chosen to pursue is insufficient grounds to demand that any other person make a similar sacrifice.

5.  Regardless of whether a person is working inside or outside the system, or working to change things from the top down or from the bottom up, we should promote everyone's freedom of speech. Even words and actions that are couched in the styles of officialdom, so long as they do not harm the rights movement or free speech among the people, should be viewed as potentially positive contributions to our society's transition and should have our full respect. People who favor top-down change should maintain healthy respect for those who are exploring possibilities from the bottom up. The whole project of finding a way to a successful transition to democracy will be easier if the advocates of "top down" and "bottom up" approach each other as equals and with respect. All roads lead to Rome.

However, this sort of tolerance in no way implies tacit compromise with tyranny or an acceptance of complete relativism. The liberal movement should maintain a nonnegotiable position of opposing all of the government's techniques of forcible repression in whatever form, be it by intimidating people, buying them off, forcing them to express agreement, firing them, blacklisting them, or arresting them and charging them with crimes. None of this should be tolerated in the slightest.

6. We must face squarely, with no illusions, the fact that the dictatorial system will be with us for some time. We must do what we can to empower ordinary people rather than pinning hopes on the emergence of an enlightened ruler within the regime. In the push-and-pull between the ruling authority and civil society, official policies will change from time to time, but our own unchanging priority must always be to encourage and support the rights-defense movement and to protect the independence of civil society. Especially when sycophants are many and those who dare to speak against harsh government are few, we must commit ourselves to criticizing and opposing the dictatorial regime from our position outside of its system. When the official attitude is rigid, we should force it to soften; when it is soft, we should pursue the opportunity to expand civil society. While welcoming any enlightened decision that comes out of the system, we must maintain our "outside" position and make no change in our own standards.

In sum, China's road to a free society is going to depend on gradual improvements from the bottom up. It is hard to see any prospect of a top-down democratic transition of the kind Chiang Ching-kuo brought to Taiwan. Change from the bottom up will depend on the growing self-awareness among the people, on popular rights-defense movements, and on the autonomous, protracted, and ever-expanding pressures that this awareness and these movements place upon the regime. In a nutshell, rather than to seek radical change of this regime, flawed though its legitimacy is, and then to expect that the abrupt change will lead to a remolding of society, people who are pushing for a free and demo-

cratic China should concentrate on gradual change in society and ex-
pect that this will eventually force a change in regime.

Beijing, February 26, 2006

*Originally published in* Guancha *(Observe China), February 26, 2006*
*Translated by Perry Link*

# THE LAND MANIFESTOS OF CHINESE FARMERS

◆　◆　◆　◆　◆

### Farmers Declare They Are Taking Their Land Back

During the final month of 2007 in mainland China, there was a spate of public declarations in which farmers laid claim to their land.

On December 9 in Heilongjiang Province, 40,000 farmers from 72 villages, one of which was Dongnan'gang Village in Fujin township, declared before the whole country that they owned their land by right. A few days earlier, on November 28, villagers convened a democratic assembly to begin a reclaim of land that had been forcibly taken from them. The next day they surveyed the land, and the day after that prepared to re-allocate the land. On December 9, redistribution formally began.

On December 12, in adjacent areas in western Henan (the Sanmenxia Reservoir District) and eastern Shanxi (Dali County, Huayin City, and Tongguan County), approximately 70,000 farmers from 76 incorporated villages issued the following public declaration:

> We farmers from these four areas hereby jointly resolve to take back ownership of our land. It is land that has been ours to have and to hold down through the generations. We will confer permanent title to property based on an average amount of land per family member. We are putting an end to the illegal land seizures that officials at all levels have been carrying out for years.

On December 15 in Jiangsu Province, 250 farmer households from Shengzhuang Village in Yixing City claimed permanent ownership rights to the land on which they lived under the principle that "houses belong to those who dwell in them":

> Shengzhuang Village has a history that stretches back more than 1,500 years. To one generation of farmers after another, living under successive dynasties, it had always been perfectly clear what piece of arable land belonged to what family, and what parts of the bamboo-forested hillsides each had rights over . . .
>
> These lands belonged to our ancestors, and beginning now they will revert to us and to our children and our grandchildren. All the residential land of Shengzhuang Village shall once again be the permanent property of families in the village. The arable land and mountain forests shall forever be shared fairly among all the villagers, for us to occupy, till, and develop through the generations to come.

In the last few years "the land question" has become a hot topic in the recurrent debates over "reform." The question has pitted proponents of privatization against those who want to maintain the current system. Yet for all their intensity, these debates have been largely limited to the urban elite—intellectuals, businessmen, and officials. The voices of farmers themselves has not—until now—been heard. At last farmers are speaking for themselves, loud and clear, and a silent nation is hearing a cry from deep inside its heartland.

These farmers' declarations—at once realistic, reasonable, and grounded in history—represent a breakthrough against the unreasonable land system that has been in place in China since the Mao era. Chinese farmers are now making plain their determination that land ownership be privatized. Their manifestos, distilled from their bitter experience in the Communist era, go far beyond the institution of "land-use" rights that began thirty years ago at Xiaogang Village in Anhui Province. These new demands represent a self-awareness on the part of the farmers, a true awakening. They are saying, in effect:

this land under our feet does not belong to the state and does not belong to some "collective." It is land where we farmers have lived for generations; it is ours. And beginning today we farmers will no longer pursue our rights by kneeling to ask favors; beginning now we will stand up and declare what we are entitled to. *We alone are the masters of the land beneath our feet; it is entirely up to us to decide what to do with it.*

## At the Outset the Communist Party Stripped the Farmers Bare

In the cycles of order and disorder that extend through China's long history, "order" has meant suffering for Chinese farmers, and during "disorder" they have suffered as well. That much is "normal." But although earlier dynasties may also have been grasping and ruthless, in matters of robbing and exploiting farmers, and in using odious trickery to do it, none compares to what the Communist Party did. In 1947, at a crucial point in their struggle for power, when they wanted to win the broadest possible support among farmers, the Communists pushed a land reform under the slogan "Down with tyrants, distribute the land." They also published an "Outline of China's Land Law" that clearly promised that farmers would *own* land after it was redistributed to them. It recognized their right to manage their land as they saw fit and to buy it and sell it freely. Then, as soon as they gained power, the Communists reversed themselves by launching their socialist revolution and its comprehensive "nationalization." In urban areas, all private property in industry and commerce was seized by force; in the countryside, a rousing "collectivization" saw all land wrested from farmers. From the campaign for cooperatives in 1951 through the People's Communes of 1958, Mao Zedong first liquidated the landlords and rich farmers, then forced the ordinary farmers into communes. In the end not an inch of ground anywhere in the vastness of China belonged to any farmer or to anyone else. The Communist regime became the largest, indeed the only, landlord.

This comprehensive nationalization laid the economic foundation for Mao Zedong's totalitarian system. City-dwellers who had lost all private property were reduced to cogs in the machine of the regime's "work units," and farmers who had lost their land were reduced to virtual serfdom in the "communes." If the two must be compared, it was the farmers who suffered the grimmer fate. They were at the lowest level in the new system of nationwide bonded servitude. Denied the freedom to move, they were bound to land that was no longer theirs, had no social security, and had turned into mere feeding tubes to support Mao's industrialization in the cities. The cost of this industrialization project was that people all over China, urban and rural alike, were mobilized into a slave-wage system. Farmers, who were 90 percent of the population when the project began, paid the biggest price and reaped the smallest benefit. During the catastrophe of the insane Great Leap Forward, the poverty of farmers reached the point where they did not even have food to eat or clothes to wear. The ghosts of starvation victims haunted the land, and people were reduced even to cannibalism. Most of the tens of millions of unnatural deaths were of farmers.

### The "Responsibility System" Was Only Semi-Liberation

When Mao died and "reform" became possible, the deeply victimized farmers were the first to take action. Beginning in Anhui, and at huge political risk, they instituted a system in which people took responsibility for their own harvests. Today this is called "the revolution that liberated the serfs." But in truth it was only a half-baked liberation, because it never included the privatization of land. All any farmer ever got was a *right to use* land that remained "collective." They could not own land. Now, whenever farmland needs to be "developed" for urbanization or commercial purposes, it reverts to "state property." State ownership may seem an abstract concept, but in practice it means that state officials at the various levels are always free to decide what to do with land in the name of the state. In more than twenty years of urban modernization, and across a "great leap forward" in real estate values, officials wielding the power of the state and invoking "government ownership of land" have colluded with businessmen all across our country to carry out a kind of Chinese Enclosure Movement. The biggest beneficiaries of the resultant land deals, at all levels, have been the Communist regime and the power elite. The farmers—once again—have been sacrificed.

## Of Society's Weak Groups, Farmers Are the Weakest

The key point in all this is that, in authoritarian China, officials are big and strong while citizens are small and weak. Farmers are the weakest among the weak. Without a free press and an independent judiciary, they have no public voice, no right to organize farmers' associations, and no means of legal redress. "Petitioning" is their only recourse, but when officialdom guards its own interests and blocks petitioners, this, too, becomes an empty exercise. Petitioners endure great risks and hardships but end up with nothing. And this is why, when all recourse within the system—through public opinion, the courts, or administrative machinery—is stifled, people are naturally drawn to collective action *outside* the system. It is why the government reports so many "mass incidents" every year. As the proverb says, "it is the mandarins who force the people to revolt."

Most of the major clashes that have broken out in China in recent years have pitted commoners against officials. Most have occurred at the grassroots in the countryside, and most have been about land. Local officials, protecting the vested interests of the power elite, have been willing to use a range of savage means, drawing on government violence as well as on the violence of the criminal underworld, to repress the uprisings. Bloodshed has occurred. An especially severe clash took place, for example, on December 6, 2005, in Dongzhou Village in Guangdong, where authorities dispatched more than a thousand police to quell a disturbance. They used tear gas and machine-gun fire against a thousand or more marching villagers, of whom hundreds were arrested and at least three were killed.

## When Oppression Forces Revolt, Farmers Turn to Self-Liberation

Let us look more closely at exactly what China's farmers said about their land in the three cases noted above.

The 250 farmer families who issued the manifesto in Shengzhuang Village in Jiangsu claimed that a powerful clique of local officials and businessmen had seized their land in the name of "the public good" and of building "public infrastructure," but then in fact had used it to build guesthouses, restaurants, dance halls, and shopping districts—all for private commercial purposes. This led them to ask:

What is "public" about any of this? What does it have to do with the welfare of us farmers? Whose "state" is this, after all? Whose interests are these "public interests"? Whose interests are the "collective" ones? Every time a land seizure happens, all of us farmers oppose it. We all sign statements registering our opposition, but the village chiefs and Party committee arrogate to themselves the right to "represent" farmers and go ahead anyway . . . Every time they come to put us down, we see officials, police, and the underworld doing "collaborative law-enforcement." Their hired thugs are like the bandits of old, who built stockades around their mountain strongholds and knew how to beat, smash, and loot, but that's all. "We're here to bulldoze your land in the name of the government," they tell us. "You have to cooperate. To resist is to resist the government." They even tell us "it's against the law for you to go on living here."

The farmers in Fujin Township in Heilongjiang also saw through the corruption that was going on in the name of the "state" or "collective." They made the point clearly:

For a long time this term "collective ownership" gave farmers ownership of land in name but not in reality. Now officials in Fujin, in league with local magnates, and acting in the name of the state and the collective, are seizing and divvying up farmers' lands on a huge scale. They have become in fact the new "landlords," while the farmers, the ostensible landowners, have been turned into something like land-renting serfs. We are resolved to end this usurpation. By vesting land ownership in farmer families and individual farmers, we are making farmers the masters of the land in the true sense.

In their declaration, the 70,000 farmers of Sanmenxia Reservoir District said:

We in the countryside see quite clearly that, as things stand now, no governmental law or policy can ever control land use. But when rights to the land are restored to the farmers, those local bullies, blind with their greed, are going to find it much harder to act so high-handedly, because now they will be trying to steal the land not of some abstract "collective" but our land, our lifeblood, and they will have an all-out fight on their hands. Once this power of the farmers themselves is mobilized, the government can relax in its duties to protect the land.

And:

In recent years central government officials have thrown a few sops to farmers, but if they really want to make a difference, they must give us rights to own land and to start businesses. Only these two rights will get at the roots of the problems in the countryside. Nothing else will put farmers on an equal footing with city people and let them share in the fruits of modernization.

## A Greater Revolution

The "responsibility system" pioneered in 1978 in parts of Anhui, where farmers took it upon themselves to begin accounting for their harvests on a per-household basis, can be called the "first revolution" in the liberation of Chinese farmers as well as the first step in the whole of the post-Mao reforms. Now, almost thirty years later, we can say that these manifestos about land ownership by farmers in Jiangsu, Heilongjiang, and Shanxi stand out as a "second revolution" through which China's farmers are freeing themselves. The second revolution is more revolutionary than the first, and the authors of the manifestos know this. They are laying claim not only to land ownership but to their rights as citizens.

At home in Beijing, December 19, 2007

*Originally published in* Zhengming *(Cheng Ming Monthly), January 2008*
*Translated by A. E. Clark*

# XIDAN DEMOCRACY WALL AND
# CHINA'S ENLIGHTENMENT

◆　　◆　　◆　　◆　　◆

THE OFFICIAL COMMEMORATION of thirty years (1978–2008) of reform in China will soon be upon us, and it is bound to bulge with self-congratulation. The government will put on an ostentatious show that arrogates all achievements to itself and displays a glorious report card on reform for the whole world to see. All the positive changes will be described as having been initiated by official power and unfolding from the top down. In my view such a reading is not only unjust but also very far from actual history.

The thirty years of reform can be explained by two very different logics. According to one—the logic of the Party-state, which makes sense only at a superficial level—everything started with the 1978 Third Plenum of the Eleventh Central Committee of the Communist Party of China, where the Deng Xiaoping line of "reform and opening" was officially announced. Next, by this logic, reform policy was consolidated in the 1979 debate over Deng Xiaoping's slogan that "practice is the sole criterion for testing truth." What was actually happening at this level is this: the rulers of the Party-state were making moves to protect the vested interests of the regime and the power elite. They devised what would turn into "crippled" reforms that changed only the economy, not the political system; they made efficiency their priority and ignored social justice; they worshipped GDP growth as a be-all and end-all; they responded to the people's political demands with a massacre in 1989; and they used material interests to buy people off and to try to gain popular acceptance of their political system.

The other logic by which to understand the reform era is to see it unfolding at the popular level, beneath the surface and with a much deeper engagement with reality. Popular demands were that economic, political, and cultural reforms all proceed simultaneously. The earliest reforms, which were rural reforms in Anhui, grew out the struggle of China's very poorest farmers for the bare minimum of food and clothing that they needed to survive, and the move toward self-rule in villages by electing "village committees" grew out of the collapse of the People's Commune system. In the cities, the strong desire to seek new knowledge, to create new wealth, and to protect people's interests brought about an awareness of the market and of people's rights, and this stimulated popular demand for individual freedom and social justice.

In short, the decisions to begin economic reform and to allow more personal freedoms, as well as the calls for political reforms and the decision to begin actually making a few reforms, were not favors granted from the top but rather concessions that the top was forced to make because of pressure from below. It was precisely things like extreme poverty, a spiritual desert, and the incessant violence of "class struggle" that led people to perceive the bankruptcy of the Maoist system, and these perceptions led in turn to the "April Fifth Movement" in 1976, when people flocked to Tiananmen Square to commemorate Premier Zhou Enlai, as a way of demonstrating their dislike of radical Maoism. The same basic perceptions led to the initiatives of Anhui farmers in the late 1970s to de-collectivize agriculture by crediting individual households with the harvests they produced; and they led, too, to the "Democracy Wall Movement" of December 1978 to December 1979, when people in Beijing could post political opinions at Xidan Street in Beijing. This is where Wei Jingsheng posted his famous call for democracy as the "fifth modernization" [to be added to the "Four Modernizations" touted by the Party—Ed.]. It was precisely the huge human-rights disasters of the Mao era that led great numbers of aggrieved people to form a "petition and complaint movement" that brought pressure for "political rehabilitation" of people who had been wronged.

In the regime's version of its glorious accomplishments during thirty years of reform, the 1979 "great debate on the criterion for truth" is listed as the sole cause of the "liberation of thought" movement. I do not deny that this debate was important in the initial stages of the reforms, and I commend Hu Yaobang—chief of the Party's Propaganda Department at the time, later to become Party General Secretary—for promoting the debate. But to attribute the entire "liberation of thought" movement to this one causal factor is far from historical truth. Such attribution is merely officialdom's attempt to monopolize the discourse of reform and to suppress popular thinking.

In reality the transformation of the political thinking of the Chinese people began much earlier than 1978. The first inklings of "thought liberation" came in 1971 with the astonishing "Lin Biao Affair," when Mao Zedong's "closest comrade-in-arms," Marshal Lin Biao, suddenly attempted a coup against Mao, failed, tried to flee by air to the Soviet Union, was shot down, and died in the crash—or so the official story goes, unclear in its details even today. Later in the 1970s, underground literature about "educated youth" who had been sent to the countryside during the Mao era stimulated a great deal of self-enlightenment among young people. This was one of the subterranean causes of the April Fifth Movement in 1976. Then, after Mao died and the Cultural Revolution officially ended, it was at "Democracy Wall" that political modernization was first mentioned. The political reform of the 1980s was also driven by this popular self-enlightenment, and it was only after it gained some momentum that the "enlightened faction" within the Communist Party responded to it. These spontaneous popular forces for reform were rooted in the human longing for freedom and justice, not some slogan of the rulers, and once they got going they were hard to turn around. Ideas from below continually pushed the reforms, and popular demands continually challenged the logic of officialdom. The scope of the public sphere and the number of people who entered it grew ever larger.

I went to college during 1977–1982, which made me part of the first generation of students to go to college after the Cultural Revolution. Like others during the early years of reform, we were in a state of extreme spiritual hunger. Our thirst to absorb new ideas was so great that we devoured anything and everything, indiscriminately. As I remember, the cultural events that preoccupied us and changed our thinking had nothing to do with the "great debate on the criterion for truth." What mattered to us were all kinds of other things, which seemed to arrive in wave after wave. Perhaps most important were the popular songs of the Taiwan singer Teresa Teng and the poems in the unofficial literary magazine *Today*. Both of these things interested us far more than the "truth criterion," and also much more than the fashionable "scar literature" and "reform literature" that filled the mainstream magazines. The warm sounds of that so-called decadent music and those poetic "voices of rebellion" were exactly what we needed in order to melt the wintry ice of Mao-era "class nature" into a springtime of universal human nature and to convert the aesthetics of "revolution" into something more palatable.

In the 1970s, Teresa Teng's romantic songs took a generation of Chinese youth by storm, reawakening the soft centers of our beings. They dismantled the cast-iron framework of our "revolutionary wills" and caused these to collapse; they melted our cold, unfeeling hearts, which until then had been tempered by cruel "class struggle," and they revived sexual desires that we had long repressed into the darkest recesses of our beings. Long-suppressed human softness and tenderness were finally liberated. The government forbade the broadcast of this "decadent bourgeois music," and Li Guyi, the first mainland singer to imitate Teresa Teng's style, was subjected to a parade of official criticism sessions. Nevertheless, where privacy could be found, people huddled around "bricks"—our nickname for the little square Japanese-made radio-recorders on which popular songs could be heard. We listened and listened, until we could sing the songs ourselves, everywhere—in the halls, in the cafeterias, in bed. Anyone who owned a "brick" always had plenty of friends.

It was also in those years that our generation received "aesthetic baptisms" into worlds of foreign films, literature, music, and art. Cinema and television from Japan were the most popular. Films like Junya Satō's *The Proof of Man* and *Pursuit,* starring Ken Takakura, as well as Yōji Yamada's *The Yellow Handkerchief* were among our favorites, as were television series like "Sugata Sanshirō," "Astro Boy," "The Story of

Oshin," and others. Theme songs like "Morioka's Song" from *Pursuit* and "Straw Hat" from *The Proof of Man* were very popular for a while. Moreover, the works of famous Japanese directors like Akira Kurosawa, Kenji Mizoguchi, and Yasujirō Ozu had major influences on the Chinese avant-garde film directors of the 1980s.

In our political awakening, the "new-enlightenment" thinking that appeared on Democracy Wall was by far most important. Its spiritual breakthroughs left us with deep impressions—much deeper than anything that came out of the government think tanks or from establishment intellectuals. The aesthetics of the poems in *Today* were very different from what "scar literature" had to offer; the brilliance of Hu Ping's essay "On Freedom of Speech" went well beyond official "liberation of thought"; and the awakening to modern politics that appeared in Wei Jingsheng's "Democracy: The Fifth Modernization," in Ren Wanding's "A Chinese Declaration of Human Rights," and in Xu Wenli's "1980 Proposals for Political Reform" completely transcended the Communist Party's pedestrian notion of "correcting past mistakes."

As a thought experiment, try to imagine how things would have been different if "reform" thinking had sprung only from officially sponsored literature and art and there had been no unofficial counterparts. What if, in literature, we had had only flat, didactic "scar" stories like Liu Xinwu's "The Homeroom Teacher" and other works that appeared in *People's Literature,* but had no underground poems like Bei Dao's "The Answer" or Mang Ke's "The Sky," and no underground fiction like Wan Zhi's "A Night of Rain and Snow"? What if, in art, we had only the works in government-sponsored art exhibitions but not the rebellious spirit of the works in the "Stars Exhibition"? What if, in political philosophy, we had only "Practice Is the Sole Criterion for Testing Truth" as presented in the *Guangming Daily,* but lacked "Democracy: The Fifth Modernization," which was published in the unofficial magazine *Exploration,* and "On Freedom of Speech," which was published in *Fertile Ground,* another unofficial magazine? If there had been only officialdom's "liberation of thought" without the seminal initiatives of the "Democracy Wall Movement," China's intellectual spirit in the reform era would have been too etiolated to bear thinking about.

Friedrich Hayek, the famous philosopher of liberalism, wrote that "ideas change the world." Especially in times of great social transformation, new ideas that bring in new ways of looking at the world can play pioneering roles in the transformation of society. When yesterday's heresy becomes today's article of faith, the arrival of a new society cannot be far off. This has been true in the transition from traditional dictatorships to modern democracies, and true as well in the transition from modern totalitarianism to free societies. The European Enlightenment was the fount of social modernization in the West, similarly to the way in which the May Fourth Movement began the process of social modernization in China. In the transition from communist totalitarianism toward freedom and democracy, the former Soviet Union went through "intellectual thaw" under Khrushchev and "new thought" under Gorbachev; in China, the transition began after the death of Mao Zedong with the "liberation of thought" and the "new enlightenment."

The crucial significance of the ferment around Democracy Wall in bringing change to Chinese society appears on four levels:

1. Democracy Wall was the first site at which the sharp divide between popular and official expectations of reform were laid bare. Popular demands were for a thoroughgoing reform that would lead to a free and democratic China; the official plan was for a crippled reform that would graft economic growth onto dictatorial politics. This divide took shape during the Deng Xiaoping era, and it has lasted to the present day.

Deng Xiaoping's sordid schemes for reaching the pinnacle of power showed a talent for mind-boggling opportunism. Before he gained power, Deng wrote a letter to Hua Guofeng, chairman of the Party-state, avowing his loyalty, but then, as soon as power was in his hands, he turned around and purged Hua Guofeng. That's how he treated people "above" him; toward those "below," like the young people who wrote for Democracy Wall, he did this: he capitalized on their efforts in order to build his own popular support, and then, once that purpose had been served, mercilessly crushed them. It was precisely the fact that notions of reform on Democracy Wall transcended the crippled model that Deng Xiaoping had in mind that led Deng in 1979 to insist on maintaining the "Four Cardinal Principles"—the socialist road, the people's democratic dictatorship, leadership of the Communist Party, and Marxism-Leninism-Mao-Zedong-Thought. On this score not even the opposition of Hu Yaobang could soften Deng's iron fist. It was the leading edge of the Deng tyranny.

2. Democracy Wall revealed the limits of establishment intellectuals who "work within the system" and made clear the difference between what they do and what independent thinkers outside the system do. While Democracy Wall activists were publicly opposing the parts of the Deng reforms that protected dictators, and were calling for political democracy, basic human rights, and freedom of speech, the establishment intellectuals were casting themselves as the government's loyal opposition, criticizing government actions but remaining loyal to its avowed goals. They cheered Deng-style reform and went all out to praise the aspects of Mao Zedong Thought that claimed to "seek truth from facts." They sought to revive a notion of "Marxist humanism." They pushed for less "Party-nature" and more "people-nature" in the media but did not challenge the basic premise that media should be controlled. They were enthusiastic about their return to the political stage, and beat the drums for Party-approved reforms, but were generally cold to the suppression of Democracy Wall. They did nothing to speak up for Wei Jingsheng when he was hit with a heavy jail sentence. Even on less dangerous questions, like the suppression of *Today*, they hardly did better. Bei Dao and Mang Ke, two of *Today*'s stalwarts, issued a *cri de coeur* to the intellectual world but received only one response—a letter from the senior writer Xiao Jun, and that letter was muddled.

3. Perhaps most significant of all, the language of the Democracy Wall movement broke free of Maoist language and the "revolutionary" mode of thought that went with it. Democracy Wall laid a foundation for language—and hence a system of values—that was independent of official ideology. In literature, the poems and stories in *Today* represented the first breakthrough against the iron hegemony of Maoist language that dated from the Yan'an Rectification Campaign of 1942 to 1944. In political essays, although we should admit that Wei Jingsheng and some others still did not succeed in purging every trace of Mao-style usage from their writing, someone like Hu Ping, in his essay "On Freedom of

Speech," does manage to pull totally free of Maoist cant. In retrospect, what really seems surprising, given that the whole society at the time was still immersed in Mao-language and Mao-concepts, and given that the establishment intellectuals were still using Maoist language to talk about the reforms, is not just that Democracy Wall made political breakthroughs but that it could make them in a totally new idiom. *That* is impressive.

4. Democracy Wall marked a transition in the way people have resisted the regime. During the Mao years solitary heroism was the only mode of resistance, but with the Wall, group solidarity began. We can say, therefore, that the contributions of Democracy Wall to China's progress were not just in supplying ideas but in establishing a new ethical standard. When Deng Xiaoping shifted from exploiting Democracy Wall to suppressing it, bringing down on it all of the brute power of Party dictatorship, the Democracy Wall group did not respond with bursts of tears and contrite self-criticisms as people in earlier times were forced to do. Instead they stood together as courageous people unafraid of despotism. Their moral courage was different from that of individual martyrs like Lin Zhao during the Anti-Rightist Campaign and Yu Luoke during the Cultural Revolution, because they did not stand in glorious isolation but stood together as a community whose members encouraged one another, even in the face of prison. Thirty years ago, the magnificent performance of Wei Jingsheng and others in the Communists' courts and prisons drew a line in the sand for a whole generation's courage and perseverance in resisting tyranny. The predominant social pattern in China today, captured in the watchword "morality is with the people, power with the government," had its earliest origins in the Democracy Wall movement.

Let us think back to the eve of National Day, October 1, 1979, when Bei Dao, Mang Ke, Huang Rui, and a few dozen others in Beijing took to the streets to protest the government closure of the art exhibit of the Stars group. This band of "unofficial" artists, who had not been to university, paraded through the streets of Beijing in the brisk autumn wind, past rows of military police, holding up banners that read "We want freedom of speech!" and "We want artistic freedom!" It was the first demonstration for freedom of speech in the history of the People's Republic of China. The sight of disabled painter Ma Dasheng walking along on crutches at the head of the procession has, in popular memory, become one of the most symbolically meaningful images of that era.

Thirty years have passed between the fight for "freedom of speech" at Democracy Wall and the "rights-defense movement" that is popping up all around the country today. Rights advocacy by unofficial thinkers thirty years ago has now permeated to all levels of society, and it is this spread of rights consciousness that stands as Democracy Wall's greatest achievement. Without the protection of basic human and political rights, an individual person has no way to counter arbitrary force from the agents of a powerful government; no way to pursue personal happiness within a fair social system; no way to publicly express religious faith, political opinion, or even pastimes that are "unapproved"; no way to rely on legal guarantees of personal property; and hardly any hope, as the government denies rights and robs benefits, of ever getting any justice, whether from government, from courts, or from the media.

Whatever the rights issue might be—security of property, opportunity for self-development, the struggle for human rights or self-rule, a more equitable distribution of society's wealth, or long-term peace in society—it will rest ultimately on questions of freedom of speech and political freedom. And it will be better to fight for basic human rights from the bottom up than to beg the authorities on high for the favor of a few bread crumbs.

It is true that a variety of currents of thought have developed in society since the Tiananmen Massacre of 1989. Both the "old left" and the "new left" have again unfurled the banners of Mao Zedong, while "old" and "new" Confucianists are again hawking slogans about "Kingly Government." All these groups have taken note of the fashionable ultranationalism in society, and have draped themselves one way or another in the national flag. Still, I firmly believe that the concepts of freedom of the Democracy Wall generation, and its artistic values as well, will continue to be the core values leading to China's political and social transition.

In the great enterprise of creating a free China of the future, the pioneering efforts of the Democracy Wall generation have already earned a sure place in history. They have lasted thirty years and are still going strong today.

At home in Beijing, June 15, 2008

*Originally published in* Zhengming *(Cheng Ming Monthly), July 2008*
*Translated by Michael S. Duke*

# THE SPIRITUAL LANDSCAPE OF THE URBAN YOUNG
## IN POST-TOTALITARIAN CHINA

◆　◆　◆　◆　◆

CHINA'S POST-TOTALITARIAN ERA has two distinguishing characteristics. First, the rulers still want desperately to hold on to their dictatorial system in the midst of a crisis of legitimacy. Second, society no longer approves of such a system of dictatorship. A spontaneously growing civil society is gradually coming into being, and, although it does not yet have the strength to change the existing system, the increasing pluralism of its economy and its values, like water dripping on stone, is gradually eroding our rigid political monism.

In spiritual life, post-totalitarian China has entered an Age of Cynicism in which people no longer believe in anything and in which their words do not match their actions, as they say one thing and mean another. Even high officials and other Communist Party members no longer believe Party verbiage. Fidelity to cherished beliefs has been replaced by loyalty to anything that brings material benefit. Cursing the Party in private, complaining about it, and ridiculing its claims to be "great, glorious, and correct" have already become our people's chief after-dinner entertainment. In public contexts, though, people's vested interests—the enticement of joining in the spoils—still lead the great majority to sing the Party's praises in a *People's Daily* type of language. This public pandering is uttered as eloquently as are imprecations in private from the very same people. Both postures have become second nature to people.

The split personalities of people who work "within the system," especially among the rising middle-aged elite, can be seen in the widespread "covert operator phenomenon." In public, these people stick strictly to the book and never pass up an opportunity to advance their careers. But in private their language is completely different. They say things like, "I'm in the government and you're on the outside, but our inner thoughts are really the same; it's just that our methods are different—you're outside shouting in protest and we're inside dismantling the system . . ." They give you some so-called internal information or analyses of political trends, or they tell you the special characteristics of all the top decision-makers and tell you which has the best chance of becoming the mainland's version of Chiang Ching-kuo, who led Taiwan's transition to democracy in the 1980s. They may even confide to you some astonishing strategy for achieving peaceful evolution of the system—and so on and on. They're sure that the greatest impetus toward peaceful evolution comes from the enlightened faction within the system, people who "live in the camp of Cao Cao but work for a victory of Han [as did a legendary hero in the classic novel *Romance of the Three Kingdoms*—Ed.]." They also believe that the higher their official positions, the better "cover" they will have, the deeper they can sink into the system, and the better the possibilities will be for "inside" and "outside" forces to unite for success. On one point they are most unanimous: that there are many people with good ideas inside the system and that their work for political reform is much more significant than what "outside" people can achieve.

Every time I talk with the "inside the system" people I come away feeling that each aspires to the great role of a Gorbachev, has the mettle to suffer in silence for the common good, and commands much political wisdom. Perhaps my mind is too contaminated by all those revolutionary films I watched when I was young, but I still tend to see these people as brilliant underground operatives.

The phenomenon is not limited to officialdom; it is found in the worlds of media, education, culture, and the economy as well. A number of acquaintances of mine from the days of the 1989 protests went into business and got rich after the massacre; now, after the passage of a decent interval, they have been inviting me to join them at sumptuous banquets. At these occasions they speak expansively about the great affairs of the world and swear that they by no means went into business just to get rich. They wanted to make a difference in the world. They enumerate the ways in which their moneymaking is good for Chinese society: (1) it contributes directly to the processes of marketization and privatization, which are the most basic economic building blocks for the political democratization to come; (2) it allows them to help friends who are in dire need, and at the same time to provide economic resources that people outside the system can use to return to the political stage (they are most fond of saying that a revolution needs money, and they are now making as much money as possible for that reason); (3) above all, they hold that a revolution done by rich people inevitably will be the least costly of revolutions, because the market has taught such people—themselves—how to make good cost–benefit calculations. The new revolution will not, like Mao's, incur huge costs while bringing few benefits. With wealthy people in charge, they argue, the chances of violent revolution are minimized and the chances for gradual, peaceful evolution are greatest.

For these reasons they are not entirely opposed to the vacuous watchwords of recent leaders, such as Jiang Zemin's "Three Represents" (that the Communist Party represents advanced productivity, advanced culture, and the people's interests) or Hu Jintao's "New Three Principles of the People" (that the people enjoy their rights, the Party seeks the people's benefit, and the Party's concern is for the people). These nostrums, in their view, are at least better than Mao Zedong's violent revolutionism or Deng Xiaoping's "Four Cardinal Principles" of insisting on the socialist road, the people's democratic dictatorship, the leadership of the Communist Party, and Marxism-Leninism-Mao-Zedong-Thought. Some of these nouveaux riches even believe that these theories represent the first step in a shift in Communist Party ideology away from hostility and toward the concept of human nature (as opposed to class nature)—as if wrapping the hard Party line with a soft layer of popular culture were better, all things considered, than glinting, naked slogans in hard, cold steel.

The saddest thing about the general erosion of our younger generation is that this kind of cynicism has taken hold as their life philosophy.

Many people were expelled from the Communist Party in the purge that followed the Tiananmen Massacre. Many others withdrew voluntarily. So for a few years the number of people joining the Party declined steeply. But, after ten years of co-optation and forcible political amnesia, the number of young people seeking to enter the Party has been rising again. In order to advertise how attractive the Party is to the young, the regime in recent years has used the July 1 anniversary of the Party's founding to present a barrage of propaganda on the great increase in Party-membership applications from young people. They particularly emphasize the increasing number of university students applying for membership. A report on China Central Television claims that as many as 60 percent of university students now apply. The statistic tallies with another recent media report that 65 percent of Chinese youth support the Communist Party. Between the lines, this report reflects the actual reasons why young people join and support the Party: there has been a radical shift from idealism to materialism. The report says nothing about the principles of the Communist Party, high-minded Communist ideals, or the Party's fighting spirit. It skirts all that to emphasize the Party's "glorious achievements"—from Mao Zedong's declaration that the Chinese people have "stood up," to Deng Xiaoping's that they have "riched-up," right until now, when Jiang Zemin's "Three Represents" and Hu Jintao's "New Three Principles of the People" have captured it all. All this propaganda is aimed at telling people that the Communist Party, from the beginning of "reform and opening," has accomplished the spectacular political achievements of increasing the nation's strength, raising the nation's prestige, and enriching the nation's people, and that that is why the Party holds such great attraction to the nation's youth.

One can be skeptical of these government statistics, yet anyone familiar with today's urban young people will probably not have much doubt about them. The post-Tiananmen generation, raised with prospects of moderately good living conditions inside a culture of pragmatism, is not very interested in things like deep thought, noble character, incorruptible and well-ordered government, humane values, or transcendent moral concerns. Their approach to life is practical and opportunistic. Their main goals are to become an official, get rich, or go abroad. Their primary interests and pleasures are to follow trends in fashion, ape the "coolness" of celebrities, and maintain a high level of consumption. They are hooked on Internet gaming and one-night stands. All this happens because, even before the young set out on their own in life, their environment—in the family as well as in the society at large—has already imbued them with attitudes of entitlement and privilege, and a single-minded pursuit of self-interest.

Unrelenting inculcation of Chinese Communist Party ideology has created ruptures in history and produced generations of people whose memories are blank. The people of mainland China have suffered some unimaginable catastrophes after the Communist accession to power, but the post-Tiananmen generation has no deep impressions of them and lacks firsthand experience of police-state oppression. Their personal experience shows them only the truth of slogans like "Seek money" and "Power brings riches." They see "the end justifies the means" in every-thing around them. "Success," in their eyes, is to get rich overnight or be a celebrity in film or popular music. They have no patience at all for people who talk about suffering in history or any evils in today's soci-ety. A vicious Anti-Rightist Campaign? A huge Great Leap famine? A devastating Cultural Revolution? A Tiananmen massacre? All of this criticizing of the government and exposing of the society's "dark side" is, in their view, completely unnecessary. They prefer to use their own indulgent lifestyles plus the stories that officialdom feeds to them as proof that China has made tremendous progress.

China's "one child" population policy has contributed to the prob-lem. Most of today's urban young have no siblings and grew up at the centers of their families, as "little emperors," in the popular phrase. They have gotten used to seeing their desires placed at the center of everything and have had no worries about material life. They cannot comprehend the hardships that their parents' generation endured or that the lower strata of society still endure today. They develop a "me first" worldview and lack feelings of concern for others. When they pass the entrance exams to make it into university, they become even more the darlings of their families and the pride of their communities. Their families pamper them into absolute egotism, then society channels them into invidious competition for wealth, status, and the pleasures of con-spicuous consumption.

In similar fashion, the great majority of rural children who score high enough to get into college turn out not to be very concerned with help-ing farmers escape prejudice and poverty. They aim instead to succeed as urbanites, join the elite, and completely escape the fate of farming generation after generation. That they think this way is quite under-standable, of course.

In recent years, nationalism in mainland China has become even more virulent in parts of the population than it is within the re-gime. Especially in its anti-American, anti-Japanese, and anti-Taiwan-independence versions, nationalism has become the greatest of social passions among some of the young. It is a way not only to express con-cern for China but to vent hatred upon other countries: the American "spy-plane incident," Japanese "buying sex in Zhuhai," a Japanese student at Northwest University "humiliating China," Japanese prime minister Koizumi visiting the Yasukuni Shrine, the Chinese businesswoman Zhao Yan being beaten by American police, the China-Japan Asia Cup final . . . all these incidents, blown way out of proportion, have served to stimulate the collective indignation of "patriotic" Chinese youth. Na-tionalist invective on the Internet has grown increasingly violent, even thuggish. Murderous curses spring up everywhere, peppered by gran-diloquent posturing about "sacrificing one's life for the nation."

On the other hand, no matter how "patriotic" these "angry youth" get, they do not let their patriotism interfere with their self-interest. Not only are they universally silent about government violence, they avoid mention of violence in society as well. Numbed social sympathies and atrophied senses of justice have already become epidemic social diseases in China: no one cares for an old man who falls down sick in the street; no one tries to rescue a peasant girl who slips and falls into a river; a hooligan beats and rapes a woman on a bus while none of the many strong young men on the bus lifts a finger to help her; another hooligan parades two young women down a street "as an example to the masses" while everyone stands around enjoying the spectacle and no one makes a move to help . . . Chilling reports like these appear regu-larly in the media, even on state television.

So these are the two sides of the "patriotism" of China's "angry youth": vehement, heroic talk against foreigners, and cowardly inaction against the ills of their own society.

The "patriotic" young woman who challenged President Clinton with a fairly unfriendly question when he visited Peking University in 1998 is today married to an American. This dramatic piece of news stirred up hot commentary among "patriotic youth" when it came out.

Sadly, however, the gaping disconnect between the woman's language and her actions did not lead these people into the least bit of psychological analysis or self-interrogation. They just cursed her, unreflectively, then just as naturally went off to study in America. When these students are cursing America, they are filled with righteous indignation; when sitting on a plane headed for Boston, their hearts are even more wild with joy.

A few days ago, I read an Internet post by someone who had signed on as "leonphoenix." It read: "I like American commercial products and American blockbuster movies. I like American freedom. I envy American wealth and power, but usually I still shout, with everyone else, 'Down with America!!!' This is an unavoidable reaction; it is the instinctive feeling of an underdog." Protecting himself with a pseudonym, leonphoenix exposed the truth about this cynical "patriotism."

We can see here why "liberal" professors often complain that official brainwashing during the 1990s has had its greatest effect among university students.

The educated young have the same cynical attitude when they apply to join the Communist Party. The number of applicants who are university students has gone up, but the ones who genuinely believe in communism are as rare as phoenix feathers and unicorn horns—just as rare as the students who say "no" to the barbarism of the state system or to the violence that occurs around them. I do not know whether the Peking University student who married the American was a Party member. If she was not, then her behavior represents the practical survival mentality of most Chinese youth. If she was, then what she said in school and what she chose after graduating form a perfect example of the cynical opportunism among Chinese youth today: here we have "the rationality of economic man" run amok. Maximization of personal profit becomes the core value. If we wanted to put it nicely, we could call this a reawakening of the autonomy of the individual. Put more bluntly, it is sheer pursuit of personal gain.

It is one thing to seek entry to the Communist Party without a belief in communism, and to denounce America while one is addicted to American fads; most bizarre, though, is that these young people seem splendidly unaware of these self-contradictions and free of the slightest moral concern about them. On the contrary, they feel quite satisfied with themselves: if they get what they want to get, then the choices they made were right.

Any Chinese student who wants to have an effect in the world wants to join the Party. This is not idealism, just the need for a tool. In China under the Communist Party, no matter what your job is after graduation, you will do better as a Party member. Moreover, surveys of the aspirations of university students in recent years have shown that the number one choice in occupations now is an official post in the Party-state. In their talk about joining the Party, students speak entirely without officialese. Their talk is purely pragmatic, and quite eloquent.

A third-year university student became flushed with anger as he debated these things with me. "In China," he said, "you have to join the Party if you want to get anything done. It's the only way to advance or get power, and without power you're nowhere. What's wrong with joining the Party? What's wrong with being an official and getting rich? You and your family get a decent living, and you can also do more for society than others can."

The Chinese Communist Party's own mode of survival resembles that of these students. On the surface, the Party's approach, with all of its ideological preaching, might seem quite different. But anyone familiar with the Chinese Communist Party's history of seizing power, wielding power, and maintaining power will easily see the parallels. The key element is opportunism that puts self-interest above all and permits any means, however unscrupulous, in the pursuit of goals. Devious survival techniques captured in traditional clichés like "Hide one's strengths and bide one's time," "Choose humiliation over defeat," "Whoever feeds me milk is my mother," and "You can't be a great man if you're not devious" have been watchwords for the interpersonal relations of Party leaders as well as for their relations, collectively, with the world. In the post-Mao era, Deng Xiaoping's pronouncement that "black or white, a cat that catches mice is a good cat" is said to have brought a "decline of communist ideals." In fact, however, Mao Zedong's own survival strategies always had to do with power. When did Mao ever hold on to some ideal or maintain some moral bottom line? His high-sounding rhetoric about liberation of the whole world never kept him from persecuting or murdering people, even to the point of letting it be known he would have no regrets sacrificing one-third of humanity to see the globe turn red.

In short, all these groups—college students and young intellectuals who want to join the Party, officials who are "working within the system," and my acquaintances who have gone into business to get rich— are positioned similarly. Almost none of them support the current political system in any genuine moral sense, and yet the practical roles that they play all help the system to maintain its stability.

That people can live at ease with their split personalities, and be untroubled by them, is a good illustration of the split consciousness that permeates the whole of society. Street gossip, sarcastic political ditties, and dirty jokes have all burgeoned in China since the 1989 massacre, and all these things function in two different ways: on the one hand they express dissatisfaction and attack the regime, on the other hand they help people to accept current realities by blowing off steam and relaxing their nerves.

China has entered an "Age of Sarcasm." Anywhere outside of state-sponsored parties, entertainment shows, or the comedies and skits on television, China's rulers and official corruption have become the main material for the sarcastic humor that courses through society. Virtually anyone can tell a political joke laced with pornographic innuendo, and almost every town and village has its own rich stock of satirical political ditties. Private dinner gatherings become informal stage shows for venting grievances and telling political jokes; the better jokes and ditties, told and retold, spread far and wide.

This material is the authentic public discourse of mainland China, and it forms a sharp contrast with what appears in the state-controlled media. To listen only to the public media, you could think you are living in paradise; if you listen only to the private exchanges, you will conclude that you are living in hell. One shows only sweetness and light, the other only a sunless darkness.

For people in the lower strata of society, the bitter complaint about hardship and injustice represents their true inner feelings. But for those who benefit from the system—the power-holders, their associated elites, and the urban middle class—the sarcasm of jokes and ditties has become just a way of amusing themselves over cards or meals. The complaint has long since lost the sharpness of daggers or spear points, and hasn't any genuine moral force, either. The mocking ends when a gathering ends, and it has absolutely no influence on the other stage shows that these people perform in the public arena. The popular entertainment can even have a druglike narcotic effect. Amid the revelry of eating, drinking, slapping their poker cards onto a table, or shuffling mahjong tiles—"consuming" everything in sight—the revelers consume good jokes about hardship, corruption, and injustice. When the laughter ends, everything reverts to standard operating procedures for these people: when they need to lie, they lie; when they need to be ruthless, they are ruthless; when they need to grab personal gain, no scruple stops them.

After years of spanning such huge discrepancies, no feelings of awkwardness get in the way. And so it is that the Communist regime, while incessantly reviled in private, still sails along, fully "stable"; and so it is that high officials, the butts of derision all across the country in private, continue to parade in grandeur, on and on.

The country lives with two black curtains. Government prohibitions, published and unpublished, produce an official black curtain behind which members of the power elite jockey with one another to divide up assets that properly belong to all of the Chinese people. Meanwhile citizens have built their own, unofficial black curtain, behind which they vent grievances they are not allowed to express in public, and seek some diversion as well. But everyone, on both sides of both black curtains, is obliged to live within a single set of rules—the unwritten rules of the Party-state.

We are left with the paradoxical but undeniable conclusion that the spiritual landscape of post-totalitarian China is split and unified at the same time. The splits between "inside the system" and "outside the system," between official and popular language, between public postures and private commentary, between dreadful realities and comic performances—all these should be mind-boggling. Yet, miraculously, our "cynical survival mode" unifies all of them: bitter reality becomes popular comic skits; venting complaint turns into self-anesthetization; ridiculing the power elite degenerates into mere popular amusement. Other than pleasure-seeking and consumerism, it seems that the only fruit of our social development is a cancerous overgrowth of "the rational economic man": maximize personal gain, and that's all.

At home in Beijing, September 15, 2004

*Originally published in* Kaifang *(Open Magazine), October 2004*
*Translated by Michael S. Duke*

# WHAT ONE CAN BEAR

*For my suffering wife*

You said to me
"I can bear anything"
with stubborn eyes you faced the sun
until blindness became a ball of flame
and the flame turned the sea to salt

Beloved
let me ask you through the dark
before you go to your grave, remember
to write me a letter with your ashes, remember
to leave me your address in the netherworld

Your bone-shards will lacerate the page
so you cannot complete a single word
the shattered brushstrokes will pierce your heart
and the scorching heat of your insomnia
will surprise you

A stone that has borne the weight of the world
is hard enough to break my skull
the white lozenges formed from my brains
will poison our love

and our poisoned love
will poison our selves

In the labor camp, December 28, 1996, my birthday

*Translated by Isaac P. Hsieh*

# A KNIFE SLID INTO THE WORLD

*For my Xia*

You're a knife
a little one that could never
injure anyone at all
slid into the world
leaving no bloodstain, not cutting
just dizzying
just the true form exposed
just a beam of cold light lingering on the rot
you insert yourself into the noisy city or a party
but what's inside you is far away
the knifetip's shine doesn't dazzle
but still you bring about
the feeling of watching ants from a seat in the clouds
a hat lost in a deep ravine

A knife
your only gift
is nourishing wounds in dark places
stretching out your limbs between the pages of books
slim and bright

A knife
but you've never had a sheath

you're confident that your existence
is a danger
even though you smile every day
you have the power to mortify

Like an observer placed outside the world
detached and leisurely
astonishingly sharp
astonishingly perfect
all on the spine side of the blade

In the labor camp, March 31, 1997

*Translated by Nick Admussen*

# BELLICOSE AND THUGGISH

The Roots of Chinese "Patriotism" at the Dawn of
the Twenty-First Century

◆　◆　◆　◆　◆

DURING THE LAST CENTURY of China's history the nation has fallen
victim to cycles of self-abasement and self-aggrandizement, and this is
because we have never been able to escape the clutches of the demon of
nationalism.

Some say that a century and a half ago the Opium War plunged
China into "the greatest transformation in a thousand years." If so,
then today, after traversing a tortuous, painful, and traumatic path, and
after missing plenty of opportunities to transform ourselves, we now
perhaps should say that China has reached "the *most* favorable situa-
tion in a thousand years." It is most favorable because never before has
it been so clear where we ought be headed.

Over the hundred years before the Communists seized power in
1949, China's internal and external environments never presented us
with a clear direction. At the beginning of those hundred years, we
suffered repeated humiliations by the gunboat diplomacy of the Great
Powers. Such events, painful as they were, did let us see that the West
was advanced in technical matters, and this led our forebears to pursue
"foreign learning" in the hope that "technology will save the nation."
But then China's defeat in the First Sino-Japanese War (1894–95) showed
that the ships of our new Beiyang navy, even though they had advanced
armor and weapons, were badly organized and by themselves could not
"save the nation." This led us to look for defects in China's political sys-
tem and to turn toward "establishing a constitution to save the nation."

Finally, the chaos after the Republican Revolution of 1911 and Yuan Shikai's attempt to reinstate the Confucian imperial system, with himself as emperor, caused people to look beyond both "technology" and the "political system" to deeper issues in Chinese culture as the root cause of China's problems. Soon the "cannibalistic" teachings of Confucius, embodied in the ruling imperial system, came to be seen as the roots of China's ruin. The "new culture movement" of the late 1910s and early 1920s called for "Science and Democracy" and "Down with Confucius and Sons." Now it was culture that would "save the nation."

From "our technology is not as good as other people's" to "our political system is not as good as other people's" and on to "our culture is not as good as other people's," Chinese reflections on our own defects probed ever deeper. But the primary mindset that guided the probing was neither "liberation of humanity" or even "enriching the people," but rather a sense of shame at China's loss of sovereignty and other national humiliations. All the reform efforts sprang from this kind of relatively narrow nationalism; the goals of enriching the state and of strengthening the military took precedence over ideas that could lead to human freedom. This was the main thrust of the great May Fourth Movement as most intellectuals experienced it. The great majority did not see the movement as going much beyond slogans like "Boycott Japanese goods," "Refuse to sign the Treaty of Versailles," and "Down with traitors who sell out the nation." (See Deng Chaolin, *Memoirs,* Dongfang Publishers, 2004, internally restricted edition, pp. 161–168). It was right when this desperate quest to learn from the West in order to build military strength and save the nation had suffered one setback after another that Soviet Russia came on the scene. Its October Revolution placed before China a radically different model of modernization.

In China's communist era, despite all of the rhetoric about internationalism and "liberation of mankind" during the Mao years, the regime, especially in its claims to legitimacy, has consistently stressed nationalism. Nationalism has taken different forms at different stages—an arrogant, bellicose style under Mao; a pragmatic, defensive style under Deng Xiaoping; and a resurgence of the arrogant, bellicose style under Jiang Zemin—but the underlying passions that shape the policies have always been caught up in a vicious cycle between self-abasement and self-aggrandizement.

## I. The Bellicose Nationalism of the Mao Zedong Era

The truculent and bloodthirsty forms of ultra-nationalist sentiment that some mainlanders displayed after 9/11 sprang from roots that lay deep within the shrill warmongering of Mao Zedong. I recently read an Internet post that could well have been a *People's Daily* editorial in the 1950s: "Bury the Wolf-hearted American Imperialist Ambition for World Hegemony." The author calls the United States "politically, militarily and economically the most completely thuggish rogue nation in the world." It dubs the U.S., Great Britain, and Japan "the true axis of evil" and calls on "the people of the entire world to unite, cast off their illusions and resolutely struggle to bury the wolf-hearted American imperialist ambition for world hegemony and to prevent it from visiting an enormous catastrophe upon the entire world." Toward this end, the author concluded, China's priority should be to unite with the Islamic world and Russia to launch an attack on American hegemony.

Turning to the American-led war on terror, the author produced an incomparably absurd—yet frightening—conclusion: "If Islam loses, China and Russia will be in danger. If China loses, Russia will lose for sure—and vice versa." This is why, in his view, China and Russia should join in supporting Islamist hatred of the U.S. and spare no means to attack America, and why the most effective tools for doing so are "without doubt" terrorist attacks in the style of Osama Bin Laden. China's primary allies from a strategic point of view are not the traditional communist-bloc nations (North Korea, Cuba, and Vietnam), but the Islamic enemies of the United States (Iraq, Iran, and the Palestinians). Islamic fundamentalists and their doctrine of terrorism are not the enemies of world civilization; they are the main allies whom China must unite with in order to defeat the U.S.; they are China's best national security shield. Jiang Zemin's state visit to Iran and Syria after 9/11 was therefore a correct foreign policy move.

Most of the posted comments following this article matched it in truculence: "We must turn the Taiwan Strait into a fiery and bloody grave of the Taiwan independence forces"; "Burn the American aircraft carriers to ashes"; and so on. These comments are typical of today's "bellicose nationalism."

The nostalgia for Mao Zedong that we see in China today is in part a longing of the poor and downtrodden—the losers in the economic boom—for the egalitarianism and job security of the Mao era. But it is more than that. For the "patriots" in today's rabid nationalism, it is nostalgia for a time when China dared to say "no" to both of the world's superpowers, the U.S. and the Soviet Union. I almost think we are back in the murderous Mao era when I hear so many "quotations from Chairman Mao"—things like "paper tiger," "the East Wind prevails over the West Wind," and so on. In particular, today's bellicose patriotism draws upon the Mao-era mentality of "China at the center of the world."

The origins of that idea, of course, preceded Mao. China's emperors of old had no concept of sovereignty over a "nation" or a "state." They thought in terms of All Under Heaven and embraced the very self-regarding notion that they were at the center and rightly should look down on everybody else. In the long history of imperial China until the latter half of the nineteenth century, no challenges from outside came along to force much of a change in this outlook. China was sui generis. Even foreign invaders like the Mongols in the Yuan period (1271–1368) and the Manchus in the Qing (1644–1911) ended up being Sinicized. We Chinese had little reason to look beyond our borders.

Even when we did peer outside, we never had the idea of a "nation-state" with clearly marked borders, but only the idea of All Under Heaven, with ourselves at the center. Imperial rulers took themselves to be masters of this borderless expanse. They governed using "ritual and propriety," and unsubmissive peoples at the fringes of civilization were "barbarians." The rulers saw themselves as occupying a central court to which distant peoples, their "tributary subjects," came to pay homage. The role of the central authority was to "grant favor." The various small "barbarian" groups stood to the great civilized Han as inferior to superior, as vassal to lord, as margin to center. There was no idea of equal relations between states.

Even when the Western powers used modern weaponry to force China's doors open, the Sinocentric worldview of our forefathers did not change much. The nobility and the gentry class in late Qing times rarely spoke of Westerners without using pejorative terms; they seem truly to have believed that these "ocean people" from across the seas were "half human and half beast," a "hybrid of human and fish," or "bastards of bug and man." Protecting the vanity of the Great Celestial Empire, conservative officials and benighted gentry concocted stories and spread rumors to inflame the xenophobic passions of commoners. Christian missionaries, for example, were said to eat babies, cut out people's hearts and gouge out their eyes, drug and poison people, cause hallucinations, desecrate ancestors' graves, seduce and rape women, abduct children, stockpile weapons, and teach banditry. The major cases of grievance that Western missionaries brought against China because of this nonsense had a lot to do with why the West forced the humiliating "unequal treaties" upon China.

China's defeat in the 1894–95 war with Japan, a country once thought to be "as small as a pebble," finally forced Chinese to start reining in the arrogant notion that the Son of Heaven rules all. But the Qing imperial court still manipulated the violence of the Boxers—the "Righteous and Harmonious Fists"—to vent its hatred of foreign countries and to protect its vain claim of China's centrality. The term "foreign devils" survives in use in China even today.

A century of humiliating defeats and of falling behind did little to erase China's underlying arrogance and self-centeredness. All it did, really, was to flip the self-obsession to the other extreme, the extreme of self-abasement. Then, when China did begin to grow strong again, the self-centeredness flipped back toward narcissism and arrogance, only now it had more steam.

Before they gained power, the Chinese Communists always stressed that the first goal of the Chinese Revolution was "anti-imperialism" and the second was "anti-feudalism." After gaining power they continued in this vein, calling for the elimination of "the three big mountains that weigh on the people's necks"—the first of which was "imperialism." On August 18, 1949, Mao Zedong published a report, called "Farewell, Leighton Stuart," on the departure from China of the U.S. ambassador, Leighton Stuart. The report became famous as an anti-American proclamation and as China's farewell to semicolonial rule. A few weeks later, when Mao declared in another famous speech that "the Chinese people have stood up," Chinese nationalism took a turn from cowardice and self-abasement back toward ill-informed arrogance.

Mao pursued a two-pronged foreign policy whose prongs were contradictory but worked well in tandem. On the one hand, to guard against military reinvasion by imperialists and "peaceful evolution" under capitalist influences, Mao closed China's doors and sealed the country off, keeping the Chinese people ignorant of the outside. On the other hand, he touted "internationalism" and the "liberation of all mankind" in an attempt to play the role of leader of the whole world and to return China to its position at the center. The result, for the rest of the Mao era, was that China's traditional mentality about its place in the world came roaring back and bellicose patriotism ran rampant.

The bellicose patriotism of the Mao era had four main historical conditions:

First, the victory in 1949 of the Soviet-backed Chinese Communists in their Civil War with the American-backed Chinese Nationalists (Guomindang) led China into a one-sided foreign policy and cut it off from much of the world.

Second, in the Cold War confrontation between the two major systems existing in the world, China stood with the Soviet Union and against the United States. It fought the U.S. to a stalemate in Korea (which the Chinese people were told was a "great victory" over U.S. imperialism), and when the French were defeated in Vietnam the reports of victory over Western imperialism were again flamboyantly exaggerated. The hype contributed to mindless self-confidence and a militarization of the economy, and fed into the disastrous Great Leap Forward.

Third, communism that liberates all humanity and internationalism that supports the Third World became ideological cover for an ambition that China return to the center of the world.

Fourth, a warmongering attitude prepared the nation to be ready at all times for the outbreak of World War Three.

Mao Zedong's unbridled ambition and unrealistic imagination took full advantage of these four conditions. Mao had a superstitious belief in the power of the subjective will as well as in the barrel of the gun, and, once he was in power, was obsessed by the illusion that he could become the leader of world revolution. The economic program of the Mao era has sometimes been described as a planned economy, and sometimes as an attempt to overtake the major Western economies, but in fact it is probably most accurately viewed as dedicated to preparing for war. From the Korean War in the early 1950s onward, Mao was making the preparations. His 1950s and 1960s policies of stressing heavy industry, taking steel as "the key link," encouraging population growth, moving war-related industries to a "third front" in the hinterland, and pursuing nuclear weaponry were all economic policies that were aimed at military goals.

In the 1950s, when China's economy was weak, and in complete disregard for questions of life and death among the Chinese people, Mao poured resources into supporting the Communist bloc in its Cold War with the U.S. In the 1960s, having decided to compete with the Soviet Union for the position of hegemon in the international communist movement, Mao unveiled slogans about opposing "revisionism" and whipped up fears that war was "inevitable"—when in fact it was not—and in so doing pitted China against both of the world's superpowers. It was then, too, that Mao came out with his "Third World" theory whereby Maoist revolution would be exported to underdeveloped nations. The idea was that there could be a replay of how China's own revolution happened. Guerilla war, with "the countryside surrounding the cities," would be played out on the world stage as Third World countries surrounded the capitalist First World, and the entire globe would be "liberated."

At bottom, all of the aggressive, expansionist, and bellicose rhetoric, and the fanciful talk of leaping straight to greatness, depended on the complete rebirth of a self-centered mentality of Chinese world domination. It depended, too, on Mao Zedong's inflated ambition to be emperor and savior of All Under Heaven. For example, in order to enlist the Soviet Union's aid in developing nuclear weapons to make China into a military superpower, Mao Zedong completely disregarded the death by starvation of approximately forty million Chinese people and continued to export rice to the Soviet Union. On August 19, 1958, Mao proudly told a group of provincial-level leaders that "some day we will draw up a plan for world unification and set up a Committee to Manage the World."

Mao used his absolute power to implement his personal will, and he incited the Chinese people to hold others in contempt. Mao's authority at the time truly was as the popular saying has it: "Every word is worth ten thousand words from others." The Chinese people really did believe him when he said that all reactionaries—including American imperialists and Soviet revisionists—are "paper tigers." They also genuinely believed that "the East Wind will prevail over the West Wind" and that the Chinese people are destined to liberate all of humanity. Behind all the high-sounding rhetoric, though, lay more primitive, less civilized undergirding: the All-Under-Heaven mentality; ambitions of hegemony; educating people in hatred; a philosophy of "struggle"; and the worship of violence (including superstitious belief in "the barrel of the gun"). These ideas were not only Mao Zedong's; they came to pervade all of the Chinese people and were embraced especially by the young, in whom they reached a crest during the Cultural Revolution.

These young, the post-1949 generation of Chinese "raised under the red flag," had been indoctrinated, from childhood on, in the ideas of revenge for historical grievances, worship of violence, "class struggle," and world revolution. Every word from Mao Zedong, however trivial, was sacrosanct. Mao infused them with passion for violent revolution, then offered them the Cultural Revolution as a stage upon which to practice it. During the Cultural Revolution, swarms of rebellious Red Guards attacked foreign embassies in China, smashing and burning; some specialized in disrupting international rail service; others, in their fanaticism, sought more than violent revolution inside China and set out to "liberate all humanity" by stealing across borders into Vietnam, Thailand, Burma, and elsewhere, throwing themselves into Maoist guerrilla warfare. Some set up their own "educated youth brigades."

On September 1, 1966, Red Guards at the secondary school attached to Tsinghua University published a statement called "Smash the Old World, Create a New One." It announced to the whole world, in grandiloquent terms, that "we Red Guards will be the executioners of imperialism, especially American imperialism; we are personally digging the graves of the old world." In 1967 a long narrative poem, the collective work of a group of Red Guards (one of whom was Guo Lusheng, who later, under the name "Index Finger," became a founder of the modernist underground "misty poetry"), was infectiously popular for a time. It was called "Dedicated to the Brave Warriors of World War Three," and it brought the vaulting heroism and deranged visions of liberating the whole world to a new height of absurdity. It tells of Red Guard soldiers who throw themselves into World War Three, hurtle through Europe and eventually help to subdue the world's two superpowers. Having occupied Moscow and watered their horses in the Don River, they plant the five-star red flag of China atop the Kremlin—similarly to the way the communist armies had hoisted a red flag over Nanjing after capturing the enemy capital in China's civil war. Then the heroes head off to smoke the tobacco of South America, to drink from the clear waters of Africa, and finally to land in North America, where they capture Washington, D.C., and—as at the Kremlin—install China's five-star flag atop the White House.

A television series about drug trafficking, called *Black Ice,* has recently drawn a lot of attention. There is fitting irony in the fact that the kingpin drug dealer in this series is an aging Red Guard who, in his youth, had gone to Burma to throw himself into world revolution. Now he is middle-aged, but he still dresses in military khaki, wears a Mao Zedong badge and—like most of the old Red Guards who refuse to reflect on what they did—feels strongly nostalgic about his years of rebellion. He is vicious, merciless, and has a mind full of dark plots about achieving power and ruling the world. He makes and sells drugs not primarily for the money but to fulfill his youthful drive for power. His rebellions in the Mao era failed to get him power, but now, adapting to the times, he uses the moneymaking methods of Deng Xiaoping and Jiang Zemin to pursue the same goals. He embodies in one person the difference between two eras: yesterday's Red Guard is today's big drug dealer, and yesterday's transnational revolution is today's transnational crime. But certain things are the same: the lust for power, the ambition to rule the world, and no scruples about means in reaching one's goals.

## II. The Cynical Patriotism of the Deng Xiaoping Era: "Hiding Strength and Biding Time"

During the Deng years, pragmatism replaced Utopian illusions, economic development replaced class struggle, military downsizing replaced military expansion, civilian spending replaced military spending, and a "defensive patriotism" replaced aggressive patriotism. In foreign relations, Deng abandoned the three pillars of Mao's foreign policy—drawing lines based on ideology, leadership of the Third World, and preparation for World War Three—and replaced these with policies that put practical national interests first, built better relations with the developed countries, cut the armed forces by one million, and did what it could to preserve a peaceful international environment.

The Chinese people in the 1980s were seeking desperately to escape the poverty and strife of the Mao era. When the door to the outside world suddenly opened to us, political reform became a hot topic. The outside world's wealth and colorful variety made us all the more aware of our own backwardness and poverty. Countervailing feelings welled in us simultaneously: a feeling of national shame along with a strong desire to catch up; envy of the wealthy West along with pride in our ancient culture. Even as the government increasingly stressed patriotism in its new ideology, and even though the prediction that "the twenty-first century will be the Chinese century" had already begun to appear in the debate over a "clash of civilizations" between East and West, these trends were held in check by a preference for the open-minded thinking that continued to arrive from the West and that took increased freedom as its main goal. Our sense of backwardness and inferiority at the time did give rise to emotions, but the emotions were mostly yearnings for the things the West had and a desire to learn from the West—not, primarily, hatred of the outside world or expansionism.

After the Tiananmen massacre in 1989, world opinion condemned the brutal killings and Western governments imposed sanctions on the Chinese Communist regime, whose standing in the eyes of Western governments fell to a low point. Then, in an effort to stabilize its rule and to divert attention from its unpopularity, the leaders of the regime reverted to Mao Zedong's policy of looking for external enemies. They charged that the 1989 pro-democracy movement had been orchestrated by "anti-China" forces overseas; they even said it had been a remote-controlled plot to overthrow the Chinese government and that it was the latest proof that the desire to destroy China among Western capitalists, especially American hegemonists, had never died out. Accordingly China's core ideological mission had to be, they said, to oppose liberalization and "peaceful evolution" of China in a Westward direction. This was their new domestic policy.

In foreign policy, they turned toward a low-key posture that was captured in Deng Xiaoping's phrase "concealing our strength and biding our time, and never taking the lead." They did this because the great massacre in Beijing had plunged China back into diplomatic pariahhood, and the 1989 collapse of the Soviet empire in Eastern Europe had only worsened the international reputation of Communist rule. But on the other hand, China's economic growth could not do without the markets, capital, and technology of the developed nations. To lie low and get what one needed was only prudent.

But for a dictatorship like this one to promise "never to take the lead" is little but a nasty lie. Properly understood, the phrase has no moral content at all; it is an utterly practical device, aimed only at maximizing self-interest in the long run. The ultimate goal of the "biding time" policy is the same as that of earlier policies: to restore China to the center of the world and other peoples to tribute-bearing status. The policy rests on a faith in ebb and flow in world power; one place gets its turn, then another. When the regime is temporarily weak, it "endures humiliation and suffers in silence"—but simultaneously plans a return and sketches blueprints for revenge. Once back, it will "wipe out humiliation through acts of revenge," as the heroes of Chinese opera do, and stand as master of a powerful China at the center of the world stage.

The deceitful strategy of "concealing strength and biding time" is attributed to Deng Xiaoping, but in a larger sense it rests in the thinking of Mao Zedong.

In the era of "reform and opening," the first big outburst of Chinese nationalism came in 1993 when Beijing lost its bid to host the 2000 Olympic games. It was a devastating blow to the regime's sports diplomacy, but in another sense it helped the regime. It helped because the decision deeply wounded China's national pride, and to China's rulers, who were still in dire need of some way to recoup legitimacy after the Tiananmen massacre, that injury to national pride came as a wonderful opportunity. They seized it. If the Chinese people had not believed that the 1989 movement was instigated by "anti-China" forces in the West, now they might; if they did not believe that the massacre was "necessary" in order to protect national interests, now they might. The evidence that anti-China forces in the West had ruined Beijing's Olympics bid now lay right before their eyes. No room for doubt. Here was fresh evidence that the century of China's humiliation by foreigners, and their anti-China subversion, was still going strong.

This is how the first major wave of radical ultra-nationalism in the reform era got under way. It was a complaining, compulsive sort of nationalism, rather like that of a jilted lover. As in the Mao era, now it became acceptable, once again, to distort history, even to fabricate it, so long as the goal was to recount the dastardly crimes that Westerners had committed in China in the last century or more, and to show how they had humiliated the Chinese race.

But this jilted-lover variety of nationalist passion, in which complaint and accusation were the main components, carried within it the seeds of the Mao-style "bellicose and thuggish" nationalism that was about to make a return in the first years of the twenty-first century. The effort to popularize the Maoist reprise began with the release in 1996 of the book *China Can Say "No,"* which really had everything: ambition for Great China, ultra-nationalist hatred, Mao-style romantic-but-bloodthirsty lyricism, and garden-variety street obscenities. The book recounts a vast spate of crimes against China committed by American hegemonists, tells its readers that Americans—and Chinese people who like America—are nothing but "vulgar trash" fit only to shut up and "not even fart," and so on. Its apparent aim is to whip up hatred and bellicose nationalism. "If conciliation fails," the book's authors write, "we call upon the Chinese people to remember how to hate [and] to seek revenge!" Let a "virtual wailing wall be built" in the Taiwan Straits. "We solemnly recommend that authorities in Washington D.C. build a wall much higher and wider than the Vietnam War Memorial to accommodate the names of soldiers who will die in the future." The wall can serve as well as a "tombstone of the American spirit." Meanwhile the "finest paragons" of the Chinese nation are "destined to rise" from the glorious battlefield, fulfilling their mission that China "lead the twenty-first century" while American hegemony and its running dogs are "done for!"

In sum, we can see how the low-key formula of "concealing strength and biding time" was the incubator for high-flown rhetoric about the resurgence of Great China, and how the jilted-lover variety of nationalist passion incubated the passions of bloodthirsty revenge.

## III. Background to the Rise of Thuggish
## and Bellicose Patriotism

To whip up bellicose, expansionist patriotism in times of war might be easy. To do it in times of peace is not easy, but the following conditions help:

(1) A history of feelings of disdain for the world and a powerful feeling of vanity that the Son of Heaven once ruled All Under Heaven;

(2) A long history of having suffered humiliation at the hands of foreigners and the buildup of popular sentiment for revenge and settling scores;

(3) Pressure on people's livelihood because of an extremely large population and natural resources that are insufficient to support it;

(4) Rising diplomatic and military power in the present day;

(5) A solid record over an extended time of education-for-hatred in school curricula and the misleading of public opinion in controlled media;

(6) A national psychology that regularly alternates between extreme self-abasement and extreme self-aggrandizement; and

(7) A dictatorial regime that can manipulate the aggregate power of the preceding six conditions.

Condition number 7 is the most important one; it integrates all the others, ferments them into a brew and congeals them into a unity. This is because a dictatorial system has monopoly power over the most important of society's resources; it can use one-sided indoctrination in the controlled media to stir up patriotic sentiment; it can focus education on a certain kind of patriotism; it can build up the military without asking the opinions of the citizenry; and so on. Condition 7 is especially crucial in a large, poor, and technically backward nation. In a liberal society, even if a country is large and poor, conditions 1–6 by themselves will likely not be able to bring about a unified national psychology. If peaceful tolerance is the norm and ideas rise and fall in the give-and-take of open debate, bellicose nationalism will dissipate and eventually disappear.

The Seventeenth Congress of the Chinese Communist Party in 1997 marked China's transition from the Deng Xiaoping era to the Jiang Zemin era. All seven of the above conditions were in place in China at the time, which meant that Jiang Zemin, who was not content with Deng's recumbent foreign policy of "not taking the lead," could now come out with his more bellicose "Great Power diplomacy." Chinese nationalism, no longer content to "conceal strength and bide time," was looking forward to world hegemony after a possible "fight to the finish" with the U.S.

Meanwhile many Chinese people in recent years—whether influenced by Deng-style pragmatism, by the extreme relativism of postmodernism, or by Li Zongwu's "Thick Black Theory" [a kind of amoral Machiavellianism that Li advanced in the early twentieth century, and whose popularity surged at century's end—Ed.]—have developed a second nature that is wonderfully free of principle and ready to pursue any opportunity. No scruples are needed—arrogance toward the weak is exceeded only by fawning toward the mighty. This kind of utterly unprincipled cynicism guides the foreign policy of the Chinese Communist Party as much as it pervades the official nationalism that the Party sponsors. The proud banner of a Chinese "economic miracle" and the expansion of the regime's diplomatic and military power have revived the primitive version of Mao-era "patriotism." Under the guise of restoring national honor and national "essence," thuggish language that unabashedly celebrates violence, race hatred, and warmongering passion now haunts the Chinese Internet. It appears as commentary on particular incidents. But what is at stake, in the background, is a major new turn in the abnormal nationalism that has beset China over the past one hundred years. This is a turn from the defensive nationalism that arises from mixed feelings of inferiority, envy, complaint, and blame to an aggressive "patriotism" that is based on blind self-confidence, empty boasts, and pent-up hatred.

The major cause of the new turn is a reversion to the China-is-center mentality. As China endured a century of foreign humiliation, deep-seated arrogance became the key element in its nationalism. The on-again, off-again feelings of inferiority that have appeared are alternate psychological expressions of this same underlying arrogance.

As our country entered the twenty-first century, there were five main factors that led many Chinese people to move in the direction of bellicose patriotism.

First, some important events took place right before the new century began. The return of Hong Kong from Britain to China in 1997 had great symbolic power for the rebuilding Chinese national confidence. It seemed the righting of historical wrongs had been achieved. Then in 1999, when NATO missiles accidentally struck the Chinese embassy in Belgrade, Yugoslavia, that event stimulated the greatest anti-American, anti-Western upsurge since the beginning of the reform era and was a shot in the arm for the passions of China's bellicose patriotism. It was at this juncture that the low-key foreign policy profile of "concealing strength and biding time" began to give way to "great power diplomacy" and to the prospect of "the rise of a great nation."

Second, some happy successes arrived together in 2001—some soccer wins, admission to the World Trade Organization, and above all winning the 2008 Olympics bid. The Chinese people suddenly had the feeling that a whole new century lay before them, awaiting their imprint. The prediction that "the twenty-first century will be the Chinese century" seemed ready to come true, and people were bursting with pride. The Olympics bid, to be sure, did have down sides: It would not bring the Chinese people much wealth and power in a material sense, and would give the corrupt power elite some great opportunities for profiteering; moreover it would provide a politically correct pretext for the government to put "stability above all," to stress economics over social justice, and to spend extravagantly, in essence wasting the people's wealth while trampling their human rights. But it would also give the government an opportunity to stage a spectacular show about national revival and new wealth and power. When three generations of Chinese Communist Party leaders joined the huge celebration of the successful bid in Beijing, appearing together at Tiananmen Square, over a million residents of the city took to the streets and the revelry lasted all night. This happened not only in Beijing but in other major cities. The world could see a resurgent China filled with self-confidence.

Third, expressions of admiration from the West began playing an important role. China's state-run media not only tooted China's own horn but also took advantage of admiring international comments on China's rise to Great Power status. In this effort the English scholar Joseph Needham's *Science and Civilization in China* became important, as did Napoleon's prediction that China was a sleeping giant that "when it awakes, will shake the world." All kinds of favorable comments on the Chinese economy from Western governments and international organizations like the World Bank and the International Monetary Fund became psychological resources for the building of national pride. The constant refrain of these voices, as reported in China's state media, was that the Chinese economy "is the best of all"; that "a very powerful China is on the rise"; and that "by 2015 or 2020 China's economy will surpass Japan's." Even negative comments from the West about "the China threat" were turned around to be evidence of China's new strength. Headlining these stories with words like "astounding," "unimaginable," and "miraculous," the Chinese media led the Chinese people into an extremely dangerous illusion—that the former "sick man of East Asia" is turning into the "mighty giant of the East" and that China has already risen to be the one "great power" in the world that can resist the United States.

Fourth, some important trends in international relations in the early 2000s seemed *un*favorable to China. Russia, at the time, was turning toward the West; relations between the U.S. and India were improving; the U.S. was making inroads into Central and West Asia; China was embroiled in spats with neighboring countries over maritime rights; the issue of North Korean refugees to China was causing diplomatic squabbles; and, most importantly, the Koizumi government in Japan was refurbishing its military and appearing more hostile toward China. All of these trends made the Chinese leaders feel more and more that they were surrounded by an unfriendly world, and xenophobic sentiment became a natural response. Because of the way events were reported in the Party-controlled press, that response tended to harden into hatreds and thirst for battle.

Of all such issues, the rivalry with the U.S. was most important. After the end of the Cold War, the Chinese Communist regime stood as the world's exemplar of dictatorial government, while liberal America stood as the world's only superpower. It seemed that a final struggle between the rival political systems would open up between China and the United States. The government of George W. Bush, when it first came to power, seemed to take China as the biggest potential adversary of the U.S. and pursued an overall strategy of containing the Chinese Communist regime. Bush was the American president most friendly toward Taiwan in all the thirty years since the U.S. and China resumed diplomatic relations. He approved an increase in military sales to Taiwan and took every public opportunity to emphasize America's commitment to Taiwan. Ignoring past taboos, he stated plainly that America would protect Taiwan if it came under military attack. Even on a visit to China, in a speech at Tsinghua University, Bush gave no face at all to the Chinese Communists in saying, again, that the United States would abide by its commitments to Taiwan under the "Taiwan Relations Act." Setting aside warnings from the Chinese government, the U.S. strengthened its relations with the Taiwan military and, in a move unprecedented in thirty years, invited the Taiwan Minister of Defense Tang Yaoming to visit the U.S.

It was in this tense atmosphere of China–U.S. relations that, on April 1, 2001, a midair collision occurred between a U.S. EP-3E surveillance plane and a Chinese J-811 fighter plane off Hainan Island in southern China. The resultant media hoopla stimulated a vast new outpouring of hatred toward the United States.

The 9/11 attacks that arrived a few months later led to a temporary relaxation between the governments of China and the U.S. The two sides cooperated, in a limited way, on "counterterrorism," but the U.S. did not—at least not right away—retreat from its policies on human rights, freedom of religion, nuclear proliferation, and the Taiwan question. Among supernationalists in the Chinese populace, however, the success of Osama Bin Laden's surprise attack provided an opportunity to vent invective toward the U.S. and stood, moreover, as a model of what could be achieved if scruples were set aside. A book called *Unrestricted Warfare* by two senior colonels, Qiao Liang and Wang Xiangsui, first published in 1999, found a new burst of popularity. For some Chinese, 9/11 showed American vulnerability, and it bolstered their confidence that China would be able to subdue the world's most powerful nation.

Fifth, a new, more vigorous challenge was appearing from Taiwan. Chen Shuibian and his Democratic Progressive Party (DPP) won the 2000 presidential elections in Taiwan, and in 2001 the DPP won again in the elections to Taiwan's Legislative Yuan. These elections not only demonstrated that democracy in Taiwan had matured to a stage where political parties could hand power back and forth in a peaceful manner; it also marked the rise of genuinely indigenous political forces in Taiwan. After the DPP took power, its series of moves toward "de-Sinification" and "rectifying Taiwan's name" (i.e., replacing "China" with "Taiwan" in the country's name) caused Taiwan and the mainland to drift further apart. Hatred for Chen Shuibian and his DPP deepened among parts of the Chinese populace, and there was stronger popular support for a military solution to the Taiwan question. Bellicose Chinese nationalism reared its head in a torrent of battle cries on the Internet: "Better to pound Taiwan into a barren island than to allow it to secede from the fatherland!"; "We're ready to tear Taiwan down and build it up again, but not to let it go independent"; and so on.

Together these five factors intensified feelings of bravado—still grounded in inner insecurity—among many parts of the Chinese populace. This duality of insecurity-plus-bravado has operated from the beginning of the Communist years in China, and it finds expression in a variety of face-saving tactics.

When a people like ours, who struggle with feelings of inferiority, have to face the facts of inadequate national strength, or of less than full respect from others, one way we try to feel better is to grab onto any piece of historical material that can make us proud. It is even all right to exaggerate a success wildly, so long as it contributes to an image of "number one" for the group. If it is hard to deny that we are inferior to others materially, we can claim, as Mao did, that we are superior spiritually. If we are not as good as others now, we can build a myth that we are bound to be the most powerful nation some day, because we certainly were in the past.

China's ruling group capitalizes on this psychology. In the state media, China's military, economic, scientific, and even athletic successes since 1949 are all spun as signs that China is on its way to world domination. Fighting the U.S. to a standstill in Korea in the early 1950s was spun as a one-sided victory of China's "volunteer army." When America sank deeper and deeper into the quagmire of its war in Vietnam, and eventually had to withdraw, this, too, became a great "victory" for China in 1975; there were never any clear winners in China's border skirmishes with India in 1962, the Soviet Union in 1969, and Vietnam in 1979 (and in each case there were heavy casualties among Chinese soldiers), but each time the Chinese Communists told the Chinese people that they had achieved great victories.

The achievements of Chinese people living in the West are reported and exaggerated on a similar principle. The people who are praised might be foreign citizens, but if they are ethnically Chinese, their accomplishments are touted as proof of the power of the nation and the superiority of the race. This happened when C. N. Yang and T. D. Lee won the Nobel Prize in Physics in 1957, and even when the Taiwanese scientist Yuan-Tseh Lee won the Nobel Prize in Chemistry in 1986. All such examples are trumpeted as the pride of the Chinese race.

Worse still, facts themselves cannot stand in the way when claims of national pride are at stake. Utterly phony "news stories" will do. One of the more famous examples is a report that the United States Military Academy at West Point erected a large photograph of China's heroic superpatriot Lei Feng (whom Mao had promoted as a model) and that American cadets were "learning from" him. Another said that U.S. soldiers fighting in the Pacific War all carried a copy of Sunzi's *Art of War* (sixth to fifth centuries BCE), which is why the Pacific War was won on tactics rooted in ancient Chinese wisdom. Yet another report tells how a Chinese woman named Wu Yang went to Oxford University, became the top student, and, amazingly, received a doctorate in only her second year; then she received a scholarship of 60,000 British pounds, which was the first time such a thing had occurred in Oxford's 800-year history.

A group of elite young economists (Yang Fan and others) have announced: "For more than a thousand years China was always the world's superpower; China's defeats have come only in the last 150 years." Or, as Lin Yifu, the economist who became famous for defecting from Taiwan to China in 1979, put it: "In the two thousand years before the Industrial Revolution, Chinese culture and civilization were indeed the most advanced in the world, and the most deserving to be called the world's highest achievements . . . people from all over the world made pilgrimages to the Central Empire."

## IV. Blaming and Complaining Turns into
## Patriotism-as-Violence

Excessive self-confidence and passions of blind hatred have led many mainland "patriots" to reject universal values. Cursing and shouts of "kill!" drown such values out.

Talk of armed attack on Taiwan and declaration of war on the U.S. has become fashionable in government think tanks, among intellectual elites, and in parts of the population as well. In the writings of the elites, this bellicose patriotism is presented as two major principles: first, "a great rejection" of Western hegemony, and second, preparation for "a great attack."

The "great rejection" idea is upside-down theory in the sense that it begins with a neat formula and then fills in facts to suit it. It says: in politics, reject Western "political hegemony" and oppose "peaceful evolution" in a pro-West direction. In military affairs, prepare for confrontation with American "military hegemony," and call for a multipolar international order. In economics, prevent "capital hegemony" from controlling China, and retain our people's economy as the indisputable top priority. In the cultural realm, prevent "Western discursive hegemony," which is also "cultural colonialism," and advocate the indigenization of scholarship.

Some of these thinkers have gone further and advanced the idea of "system hegemony" in the international order. This idea is that both the rule-making and decisions about rule-following in today's world are monopolized by the strong while the weak have no right to doubt them. In world trade, for example, the developed countries make the rules and the end result of the global circulation of capital is that the profits go mainly to the developed countries. The pattern extends to international organizations and even to the rules and standards used for international awards and prizes. They are all governed by "Western" values. Thus we have, in politics, the United Nations; in economics, the World Trade Organization; in military matters, NATO; in culture, the Nobel Prizes, Europe's three major film prizes, and the American Academy Awards; in sports, the Jesse Owens Prize; in music, the Grammy awards; in art, the Venice Biennale; and so on. Western rules and standards are everywhere. In the view of the hegemony theorists, the "system hegemony" of the West is unfair. It did not come about because Western culture and Western systems are superior to others or because they are intrinsically more "universal." It came about because the West has been economically, technologically, and militarily more powerful. Material differences, not value differences, put it where it is.

In the reform era, as Deng Xiaoping's emphasis on economic growth gradually replaced Mao Zedong's policies of "taking class struggle as the key link," and as people began to enjoy more decent standards of living, the Mao-era "enemy mentality" gradually dissipated in Chinese society. But the one-party dictatorship, with its paranoia about maintaining power, still needed an "enemy mentality" for use in maintaining control and still relied on its revolutionary faith that "political power grows from the barrel of a gun." The main difference is that the "enemy mentality" now has an exclusively overseas target, whereas under Mao the enemies were both domestic and foreign. (Today, only "a tiny minority" of people in China—who happen to be the country's best political thinkers—are called "agents of anti-China forces.") In the years since Mao, public hatred has shifted from class-based hatred to nation-based hatred, and Mao's maxim that "political power grows from the barrel of a gun" has gained the corollary of "national unity and dignity grow from the barrel of a gun." The xenophobic psychology, enemy mentality, and gun-worship of the Mao years have all found new life under the guise of "patriotism." Internally, this tool of "patriotism" has been useful to the Communist Party as a new ideology with which to control the nation after the total collapse of any belief in communism; externally, it has been useful in issuing military threats against Taiwan and the U.S. In the minds of the "bellicose patriots," the only language that American "hegemonists" and Taiwan-independence "elements" understand is the sound of ballistic missiles exploding. But it would be a mistake to take this hyperbolic language as empty talk. Someday it could well be a basis for action. Thuggery in language and thuggery in life are related.

The worship of violence marks a reversion to barbarism for human civilization. This reversion happens most easily inside autocratic political systems, and the extent of the return to caveman impulses is in direct proportion to the barbarity of the autocracy within which it takes place: the more barbaric the dictatorship, the more devoutly its people will worship violence. In recent world history, the worship of violence has always found convenient pretexts: for colonialism, the expansion of Western "civilization" was the rationale; during the Second World War, the efficiency of Fascism was the rationale; during the Cold War, it was the Communist ideal of one-world harmony; and now, for China, it is ultra-nationalism. In our new century, when freedom, democracy, and peaceful development have become the main tendency throughout the world, "ultra-nationalism" stands naked as nothing but a euphemism for the worship of violence in service of autocratic goals—be they the terrorism and holy war of Islamic fundamentalists or the refusal of dictatorial systems to accept political democracy.

China's Communist rulers, who can see the world's drift toward freedom and democracy as clearly as anyone, and who know that they are actually much weaker in the world than they would like to be, have no choice but to recognize the world's present course as one of "peace and development." On the other hand, as long as the Party refuses to accept political democratization, it will never be able to let go of its primitive barrel-of-the-gun mentality. Moreover, the people of mainland China, inured for decades to the ways of Communist dictatorship and with centuries of imperial experience lying behind that, carry within them habits of violence-worship whose poison will not be easy to eradicate. Every day the dictatorship continues is a day that this poison cannot be purged, and a day that "patriotism" continues to serve as an acceptable reason to tolerate bloodthirsty language that could, some day, turn into barbaric action. When a population gives its majority support to narrow nationalism in preference to the universal values of human freedom and dignity, it turns "patriotism" into an argument for despotic government, military adventurism, and thuggery.

In its actual power today, the Chinese regime is still far behind the U.S., and there is no chance of its becoming a world hegemon any time soon. The real costs at stake are domestic, in the national psychology of the Chinese people, who are being misled by a dictatorial system, for purposes of its own power, to embrace a thuggish version of nationalism and a pipe dream of world domination. All of this is profoundly corrosive of the universal values of human dignity and freedom. The mentality of world domination, to say nothing of the thuggish outlook, has not served the Chinese people well, either now or in earlier centuries. What these ideas have actually brought to the common people of China, past and present, has not been peace, success, honor, health, or a vigorous society, but bloodshed, defeat, ruin, humiliation, dismal lives, and societal collapse.

At home in Beijing, July 10, 2002

*Original text available at* http://zyzg.us/thread-148537-1-1.html
*Translated by Michael S. Duke and Josephine Chiu-Duke*

# STATE OWNERSHIP OF LAND IS THE AUTHORITIES' MAGIC WAND FOR FORCED EVICTION

◆　◆　◆　◆　◆

CHINA'S 2007 "PROPERTY LAW" may have brought some order to the question of land seizures by providing evicted people with compensation and guaranteeing their living standards. Yet one of the core purposes of the law is to preserve the principle of "public" ownership of land, and this is the provision that allows the government, using the powers and procedures of the law, to expropriate not only land and work units that have been communal property but also private residences and other real estate, provided only that such action is deemed to be in the "public interest."

The equal protection of public and private property in the Property Law has won general approval, but the rules about land ownership rights have been widely criticized. As conflicts between the government and the people over forced evictions and the commandeering of land have increased in frequency and intensity, many experts have called upon the government to reform the land ownership system as quickly as possible. The noted economist Mao Yushi, for one, has said the Property Law cannot resolve China's unending problems of illegal evictions. Only the privatization of land can do that.

In the past few years, forced evictions in the name of "public interest" have increasingly given rise to conflicts between the government and the people, and have caused people to resort to ever more virulent modes of resistance. Injuries and deaths in the wake of forced evictions are now common, and the suicides that occur are hardly random. The case of Zhu Zhengliang, who traveled with his wife from rural Anhui Province to Beijing in September, 2003, to protest their forced eviction, and who eventually attempted to immolate himself in Tiananmen Square (and was, thankfully, rescued and treated) is an extreme example of how evictions followed by the failure of all remedy can lead to despair. For the same kinds of reasons, in March 2007 the famous "nail house" stood in perverse isolation in Chongqing: Yang Wu and his wife, Wu Ping, became briefly famous at the time for refusing to sell their family home to make way for a shopping mall. They held out against the developer despite being left stranded in the middle of the excavation—like a nail sticking out of a board that cannot be removed or pounded flat.

It is a common pattern that the Communist government and its agencies draw up development plans in secret and then enter into commercial arrangements that properly should be no business of a government. Officials serve as the backers, protectors, and interested partners of developers. They look the other way when developers use criminal tactics of terror, intimidation, and violence to evict people from their homes and land. The tactics range from cutting off water and power to using police to detain people or even hiring thugs to beat homeowners, to set fire to their property, or to kidnap them in the middle of the night. When victims of such abuse take their complaints to government departments—whose job is supposed to be to protect such victims and to deal with the perpetrators—the victims find themselves wandering from the Eviction Office to the Petitions Office, and from there to the Public Security Bureau, to the Discipline and Inspection Commission, and finally to the courts. These agencies almost always side with the developers, law or no law. The Eviction Office sanctions the evictions, the Petitions Office forwards no petitions, the Public Security Bureau looks but does not see, the Discipline and Inspection Commission knows without needing to inquire, and the courts either refuse to accept suits or decide against plaintiffs. In short, lacking basic human rights, and with impediments stacked all along the way, evicted people who face greater losses day by day also face huge barriers to any administrative justice or legal protection. The result is that taking to the streets becomes a standard way of seeking protection of rights. Self-immolation, the most extreme of protests, is a last resort of the powerless.

*China Economic Times* reports an incident in which a family living in a house near Changchun Bridge in Beijing's Haidian District—a house that was slated for demolition—was sleeping in bed one night when five or six thugs carrying halogen flashlights and long wooden staves suddenly barged in. They tied up the entire family, blindfolded them, stuffed their mouths, and threw them outside as though they were garbage. Later, under cover of night, the family members heard a great crashing and rumbling sound, which lasted for less than forty minutes. Their house had been flattened by a steam shovel. To this day the criminals have evaded the law.

Zheng Enchong, a lawyer in Shanghai who helped more than a hundred evictees bring lawsuits against this kind of abuse, adduced evidence that exposed the illegal power-grabs and profit-nabs of government officials and certain meteoric millionaires, such as Zhou Zhengyi [the Shanghai property developer who at one point was rated the eleventh wealthiest person in China but in 2007 ran afoul the local power elite and was sentenced to sixteen years in prison on charges of bribery, embezzlement, and tax fraud.—Trans.]. Zheng's effrontery made him a thorn in the side of Shanghai's rich and powerful, and he began to receive a stream of threats, harassment, and surveillance. Then the authorities revoked his license to practice law. It was Zheng Enchong who had exposed Zhou Zhengyi's wrongdoing, so when Zhou was called to accounts, one would think that Zheng should get some credit. Instead he got a three-year prison term on the specious charge of leaking secrets.

When people struggle to protect their interests against the powerful government-business combines that expropriate land and evict people, they suffer misery, helplessness, and despair. Suicides lay bare the cold-bloodedness of officialdom and the avarice of capital for all to see. How is this cold-bloodedness and avarice able to have its way, without impediment? Why has forced relocation been so savage, and compensation so meager? Why do legal appeals go unheard and get nowhere? The most important factor—by far—is the enormous asymmetry between the government's power and the rights of ordinary people. Where citizens should have rights to private property, fair exchange, and legal recourse—to say nothing of rights to a fair trial and to personal safety—there is only a yawning gap. The plethora of tragedies that evictions cause—extending even to suicide—reveal not only the harm that monopoly of political power can produce but also the desperation in the resistance that people are prepared to offer.

China's reform began in rural areas in the 1970s when the "responsibility system" allowed "land-use rights" to farmers and allowed households to keep or to market their own harvests. This had not been possible under the "People's Communes" system that had gone before, and this devolution of power became an important motive force in economic reform. Among farmers there arose a craze for owning one's own home, and the craze spread to cities when "land-use rights" similarly became available there. Housing then became a commodity, and a market in land-use rights appeared in a number of guises. We should not doubt that the whole process was genuine marketization and privatization even though it sprang from offices of the Communist Party. Still, because the crucial item of land ownership remained a government monopoly, we can only call it a "half-baked privatization": the power to decide what property would be withheld and what would be parceled out remained exclusively in official hands, and huge profits, easy to scoop up, rested in the balance. These opportunities became the private preserve of the power elite, into whose pockets nearly all revenue from the sale land-use rights began to fall. The housing business became a disaster zone of corruption.

Today all land in China, rural and urban, remains legally "state-owned." The government can sell land-use rights to people, but what the people get are effectively leases. Under the rural "responsibility system," farmers can have what they harvest from their labor on the land, but could never realize a gain by selling it. This is why, in the face of the large-scale eviction that has been going on in cities, ordinary people feel that they have no way of resisting what the powerful combines demand, and no way to get fair compensation for their losses.

Before 1949, China had a group of people—landlords—who owned land and took profits from it, and another portion of the populace, but only a part, who rented land as tenants. After 1949, a thorough nationalization of property eliminated the landlords and set up a system of "equal rights to land" and "power of ownership." The owner of the land became the Communist regime acting in the name of the nation. Now it was, in effect, the sole landlord in China. Rural people in the Mao era, while farming "state land," were something like serfs. In the post-Mao period people became, at best, more like tenants. They have rights to use the land they rent. But a tenant can live on a certain piece of land only as long as the landlord is willing. When the landlord is no longer willing, he can evict a tenant, and that's that. From this perspective, the system of the Communist regime's expropriation of private property rights by force has been far more savage than anything that happened under any regime before 1949. Three points are worth examining in more detail:

1. *The phrase "state land" seeks to confer "legality" on forced evictions.* The term *state land* echoes a phrase that was in use in China in the early part of the first millennium BCE: "Of all under Heaven, there is none that is not state land." In that era private land ownership was not legally recognized, and rulers claimed to own all land as proxies of their states. Today China's entire regulatory framework regarding land, beginning with the "Regulations Concerning Expropriation and Management of Urban Residences" announced by the Communist Party's State Council in 2001, and including the corresponding regulations of local governments at all levels, takes the state ownership of land as its legal foundation. It gives government departments complete authority to use any means they like in doing their expropriations. It further gives them, with developers, authority to set land prices unilaterally when they evict people. It is the magic wand of forced evictions.

Such "legality" is a classic case of bad law. When it commodified housing, the government chose to sell rights to use "state land" to private parties. This amounted to a mutually acknowledged contract between those people and the government, and a contract, by definition, is binding on both sides. When one of the parties—the government—unilaterally tears up a contract, it violates the law. To put the point another way, when a private individual has paid money to the government to buy the right to use land for a set period of time, the government that has received payment in return has no legitimate grounds for using its status as landowner to force a homeowner to sell to a developer.

Even more important is the fact that land has long been recognized as the most important form of property. In today's China, rights to use land are the root of prosperity for farmers, just as, for urban people, rights to home ownership are the foundation for a lifetime of saving. State ownership of land should in no way bestow legality upon forcible eviction; on the contrary, the people's rights to land use should give them legal power to oppose evictions. This is why landgrabs in the countryside and evictions from homes in the cities are first and foremost questions of property rights. Only secondarily are they questions of compensation. Property ownership should be viewed as a basic human right, and forcible expropriation the deprivation of a basic human right.

People throughout Chinese society have challenged the State Council's "Regulations Concerning Expropriation" and the associated regulations of local governments. Not only experts have been skeptical; ordinary citizens have raised questions, too. On August 31, 2003, six Beijing residents submitted a petition to the Legal Work Committee of the National People's Congress arguing that the expropriation provisions in the "Beijing Municipal Procedures Concerning the Expropriation and Management of Residences" and the State Council's "Regulations Concerning Expropriation" seriously contravene Articles 3, 4, 5, 6, and 71 of China's "General Principles of Civil Law" as well as Articles 13 and 39 of China's Constitution. [Article 13 states: "The state protects the right of citizens to own lawfully earned income, savings, houses, and other lawful property. The state protects by law the right of citizens to inherit private property." Article 39 states: "The home of citizens of the People's Republic of China is inviolable. Unlawful search of, or intrusion into, a citizen's home is prohibited."—Trans.]

2. *Without full and secure property rights there are no rights of fair exchange.* In a perfect market, full and secure protection of private property is a prerequisite for free and fair trade. It is what makes the rights of two sides equal in an exchange. With the "half-baked privatization" that we now have in mainland China, the rights of the two sides are severely out of balance, and fair market exchange is impossible. What we have instead is unfree, and even less fair, property seizures, with unilateral determination of prices.

When exchange takes place in China today between two private parties, each of which bears equally defective rights, the exchange can still be roughly equal. But when "exchange" takes place between an ordinary citizen and the government—or a combine of the rich and powerful backed by official interests—the official side enters with absolute land-ownership rights in its pocket while the citizen has only a deficient land-use right. An ordinary person has no alternative but to accept an unfair deal. In the long term this kind of unequal exchange, which is arranged in secret, exacerbates official corruption, damages the authority and dignity of government, and undermines the government's ability to carry out its proper functions.

Once any piece of land in mainland China, urban or rural, falls under a government development plan (be it for urban design, commercial development, or infrastructure such as railways, bridges, airports, or reservoirs), land that is "private" in terms of its land-use rights reverts to land that is "public" because of ownership. People must accept the stronger side's purchase agreements, compensation offers, eviction deadlines, and relocation sites. When the regime wants to bring a private entrepreneur into line, even a large one, simple mention of the phrase "loss of state-owned property" can, in the blink of an eye, turn massive family wealth, accumulated over many years, into a bubble. If victims of such extortion can settle for mere bankruptcy, they are being let off easily; often they have to pay with a prison sentence.

Examples of government use of intimidation to force unjust exchange, and thuggery to force evictions, are legion. Such methods contravene the following articles of the regime's own Contract Law:

> Article 3. Equal Standing of Parties: Contract parties enjoy equal legal standing and neither party may impose its will on the other party.

> Article 4. Right to Enter into Contract Voluntarily: A party is entitled to enter into a contract voluntarily under the law, and no entity or individual may unlawfully interfere with such right.

> Article 7. Legality: In concluding or performing a contract, the parties shall abide by the relevant laws and administrative regulations, as well as observe social ethics, and may not disrupt social and economic order or harm the public interests.

The standard tactics also violate the following article of the Criminal Law:

> Article 226: Whoever buys or sells commodities by violence or intimidation, or compels another person to provide or receive a service, if the circumstances are serious, shall be sentenced to fixed-term imprisonment or criminal detention of not more than three years and shall be fined, or fined only.

These articles clearly establish that forcible commerce is illegal. In particular, forcible buying and selling that resorts to violence or threats should be severely punishable under the law.

Even so, because the regime holds the two magic wands of absolute political power and "state ownership of land," no citizen, no matter how much reason is on his or her side, can resist the force of the bulldozer.

3. *The rights to timely notice, to agreement, to appeal, to fair judgment, and to personal security are all lacking.* When it determines its land development plans, the Communist government at all levels routinely ignores people's basic rights, including the right to be notified. It pays not the slightest attention to public opinion and holds no public hearings. At most it does a bit of "expert testimony" and "open bidding," but ignores the views of the people whose land is being taken away and makes all arrangements inside a black box where unchecked power, official corruption, and the trading of wealth for power are what make things happen.

When it implements its plans, the government and its allies in the power elite proceed basically by force. They disregard the circumstances, opinions, and expressed needs of the people whose land is being taken— and they always win. It is very hard for the people to get their appeals heard, and even when they are heard, they bring no result. The "big-picture interests of society as a whole" lead to the waving of the magic wand of "state ownership"—even though, in reality, these phrases are only outriders for the interests of the government and the power elite.

As the power of government offices becomes daily more bloated, the consequent erosion of individual rights becomes ever more serious, and the result is a situation of extreme injustice in which a tiny power elite reaps exorbitant profits while the vast majority of ordinary people see their interests dwindle. Living in the fear that one's farmland will disappear or one's house will be bulldozed, and with no possibility of legal recourse (or any other recourse), ordinary people invent their own ways to pursue their property rights. Rural people travel to towns and cities where they petition, protest, and sometimes surround government offices. Urban people file lawsuits, demonstrate, and if all else fails take poison or immolate themselves. If people want to pursue their interests, and to find relief from the predations of the rich and powerful, their only alternative is to throw themselves into the "rights-defense movement" that has been growing in China and that offers long-term, gradual popular pressure as a means to force the government eventually to return rights to the people.

Poverty in China today is not just a matter of inadequate resources or supply, but more a poverty of the political system and a poverty of rights. A system that uses "bad law" to deprive people of their basic rights cannot eradicate this kind of poverty, and it is precisely the impoverishment of citizens' rights that lays the groundwork for a system in which avaricious plunder and extreme injustice run rampant. Ever-increasing conflict between populace and officialdom is the only prospect for such a system. If the government wishes to ease or to solve this problem, no temporary carrots or sticks—no *ad hoc* bans or shows of mercy—will do much good. What needs to be done is to redress the enormous asymmetry between the power of the government and the rights of the people. The goal of "returning property to the people," which was announced as part of China's reform and opening, will remain elusive until "returning land to the people" takes place. Inserting the protection of private property into the Constitution and passing the Property Law are merely the beginnings of China's legal progress toward privatization. The crucial breakthrough, yet to occur, will be to abolish "state ownership" of land.

At home in Beijing, April 7, 2007

*Originally published in* Guancha *(Observe China), April 7, 2007*
*Translated by Timothy Brook*

## A DEEPER LOOK INTO WHY CHILD SLAVERY
## IN CHINA'S "BLACK KILNS" COULD HAPPEN

◆　◆　◆　◆　◆

*In May 2007, parents of children who were missing in Henan Province began to report the disappearances to journalists at a local television station. For several years kidnapping of children had been on the rise nationwide, and there were rumors specifically that operators of brick kilns in Shanxi had been kidnapping people to do forced labor. Reporters from Henan television went undercover to Shanxi, found a widespread problem, and reported on it. The news shocked China, reached the international press, and led to government investigations during June and July 2007 in which 570 people in Shanxi and Henan, 69 of them children, were freed from what everyone agreed were conditions of slavery.*

*This article, in which the author concludes that "a ruling group that makes maintenance of its monopoly on power its first priority can never turn around and put the lives of people—even children—in a higher position," was one of six articles adduced at Liu Xiaobo's trial as evidence of his guilt of "the crime of inciting subversion of state power."—Ed.*

IT HAS BEEN NEARLY TWO MONTHS since the news from Shanxi of labor by "child slaves" in "black kilns" shocked China and the world, and yet—compared with the huge public outcry and demands for investigation, compared with the blizzard of official directives, apologies, and dispatches of personnel, compared with the blanket of police enquiries and the announced resolve of Shanxi officials to "completely solve the slavery question within ten days"—the actual results in the case have been perfunctory and superficial.

Slave-labor kilns have proliferated widely during the past decade, but to look at the official response you would think the problem is only a single black kiln in Caosheng Village, Guangshengsi Township, Hongdong County, Shanxi Province. Only a handful of offenders have been charged, and the charges have shrunk to only three: illegal detention, forced labor, and malicious injury. Crimes such as illegal child labor, abduction, kidnapping, and child abuse are passed by. And the verdicts? Brick-kiln supervisor Zhao Yanbing is sentenced to death and chief labor contractor Heng Tinghan, from Henan, to life imprisonment. Others get sentences ranging eighteen months to nine years.

Yet the most glaring examples of perfunctory and superficial justice appear in the ways in which officials have been treated. On July 16, authorities announced a list of officials who were being investigated for either negligence or abuse, and, although the list was long—ninety-five Party members and public officials to be subjected to Party discipline (not criminal charges)—the length of the list masks its threadbare content. All of the names on the list are of people at the lowest levels. The highest among them are a few of what the people call "sesame-seed-sized functionaries" from Hongdong County: County Party Secretary Gao Hongyuan received a "serious warning from the Party"; Deputy County Party Secretary and County Chief Sun Yanlin was dismissed from office, and Deputy County Chief Wang Zhengjun received a "serious warning from the Party" plus administrative dismissal.

That such egregious crimes should lead to such trivial punishments, and that they should arrive so late, is, for the victims, to add insult to injury. It also reveals contempt for the opinions of the outraged public and a radical disrespect for any respectable system of law and justice. No matter how high-sounding words from the central rulers about "caring for the people" might seem, and no matter how sincere the regrets of the Shanxi governor might sound, none of this verbiage will be effective in uprooting the system that gave rise to the widespread scourge of slave labor, nor can it rescue the Communist regime from bankruptcy in its political credibility and moral authority. Specifically, the ways in which the authorities have handled this case cannot possibly stand up to the following six questions.

QUESTION ONE: *Why were official efforts to rescue the child slaves so inefficient?*
On June 5, an appeal entitled "A Cry from 400 Fathers: Who Will Save
Our Children?" appeared on the Internet. It read: "The scandal in Hong-
dong over forced labor has rocked our nation, but is still only the tip of
an iceberg; more than a thousand more are still at risk . . . save our chil-
dren!" But half a month later, most of these fathers, who were from
Henan Province, still could not find their children. On June 20 they
posted another appeal online, this one revealing that their search for
family members had turned up more than 100 children but that most of
these were not from Henan, i.e., were not their own. There obviously
were many more children to be rescued, and some of them had likely
been transported over long distances. The fathers called for redoubled
efforts and that the search be expanded to be nationwide in scope.

Meanwhile, public opinion continued to demand answers from the
government. An editorial entitled "How Can We Be Sure to Rescue
Every Single One?" appeared in the *Southern Metropolis* newspaper on
June 27. It read:

> How can we be sure that no corner of our country is left to
> crime, and that we can rescue every single victim? Simply to rely
> on the high-sounding rhetoric of Shanxi officials is not going
> to do it. The government must—immediately—give itself a far
> more rigorous physical exam. Society must pitch in more aggres-
> sively, and citizens must greatly heighten their awareness if we
> are to have any hope that every single one of the victims of this
> scandal will be rescued—and, more importantly, if we are to
> have any hope that the social environment that allowed the
> blight of slavery to arise will be fundamentally eradicated. All
> of these measures are much more pressing and practical than
> any high-sounding political rhetoric could be.

Nevertheless, as I write this in mid-July, there still have been no re-
newed efforts to find the missing child-slaves. The number that have
been found, as reported in the official media, is a bit over 100, which is
only 10 percent of the more than 1,000 that are missing. From this we
can see that the mighty government, with all of its advantages of vast
resources, is not ready to do battle with the Chinese underworld.

If the rescue efforts of tens of thousands of police, blanketing the area, produce results as pitiful as this, what are we to believe? That the criminal underworld is out of control, or—as I believe—that for this kind of effort the government is dysfunctional?

It is common knowledge that our powerful authoritarian government, with its monopoly on society's resources, presents an odd paradox of competence: when it comes to preserving its grip on power, pursuing its privileges, suppressing people's civil rights, monitoring dissent, controlling the media, converting public property into its own property, or smoothly pulling off corruption, the government and its officials are not just competent but supercompetent. In these matters nothing escapes them; a pack of police in a bevy of cars can focus on a single dissident. But in serving the people, fostering social justice, improving social welfare, or combating social ills, the government and its officials are not just incompetent but super-incompetent. In these matters they are good only at turning a blind eye—even to something like child slave-labor, even as it persists on a large scale and for a long time.

QUESTION TWO: *Why are Chinese officials so coldhearted and shameless?* Let's review the government hoopla over the black-kiln matter that has appeared so far: on instructions from the central government of Hu Jintao and Wen Jiabao, the Hongdong County government dispatched eleven task forces to twelve provinces to deliver letters of apology, missing wages, and reparations directly into the hands of rescued migrant workers. The county office of the Party Discipline Commission launched an investigation into malfeasance by involved officials. On June 20 in Beijing, Premier Wen Jiabao convened a meeting of the State Council at which Shanxi governor Yu Youjun presented the Shanxi provincial government's official examination of the case. On June 22 in Taiyuan, the capital of Shanxi, the State Labor Protection Department, the Ministry of Public Security, and the All-China Federation of Trade Unions Joint Working Group held a press conference at which Governor Yu, speaking for the provincial government, apologized to the migrant-worker victims and their families about the black-kiln matter and offered a self-criticism to all of the people of the province.

Amid this flurry of activity one man, a lone campaigner named Wang Quanjie, who was a representative to the National People's

Congress from Shandong Province, tried to reach deeper. On June 28, Wang sent to Shanxi governor Yu Youjun "A Call for the Resignation of the Chief of the Office of Labor and Social Security in Shanxi Province." Wang wrote:

> In recent days the "black kiln" scandal in Shanxi has shocked the entire country . . . it has led to universal condemnation . . . Shanxi governor Yu Youjun has apologized to the victims and has offered a self-criticism to the people of his province. But officials at the vortex of the scandal, in the Shanxi Provincial Office of Labor and Social Security—the ones who are directly responsible for labor in the province—remain strangely untouched. Not one has come forward to take any responsibility or to offer any apology. All we have are a few "bold attacks" from labor and police offices, but these only push the blame onto others. People of course will ask: How can it be that, when something as big as this happens, nobody in the government's labor offices bears any responsibility? . . . How can the person in charge of "labor and social security" in the province calmly and confidently proceed as director of all the rescue efforts? Article 82 of our country's Law on Civil Servants stipulates that people "who make serious mistakes in their work, or are in dereliction of duty, or cause major losses or adverse social impact, or who bear major leadership responsibility for accidents, should accept responsibility by resigning from leadership positions." The practice of resigning as a way to acknowledge responsibility is a hallmark of a society ruled by law. Public trust can be restored only when officials who are seriously miscreant resign.
>
> Resignation of this kind should be a standard political procedure: it shows an official's respect for his job, his deference to public opinion, and his willingness to accept the supervision of fellow citizens. It should also be a conditioned reflex in any human being who is endowed with a sense of shame. But no, there are those who, girding themselves with the tactics of "shamelessness and cruelty" that have been so useful throughout Chinese history, can bear up under any weight, face down

the denunciations of an entire society, cling tenaciously to the "entitlements of their official position," and not only have no fear for public opinion but lose track of their very senses of shame.

Once again I call upon the Chief of the Office of Labor and Social Security in Shanxi Province, who bears undeniable responsibility in the black-kiln scandal, to face the nationwide public outcry, have the courage to accept responsibility, look squarely at the situation, and bow to the public will. There is but one way he can honor public service, thank his fellow citizens, and put his apologies into concrete form: resign!

In the face of demands as strong as this, and with such a passionate public outcry in the background, how can it be that we have seen not one province-level resignation? Why doesn't the central government step in to call these people to account? How can the state-run media focus attention only on the black kilns of Shanxi and pay no attention whatever to the dereliction of official responsibility in neighboring Henan Province, from where most of the child-slaves were kidnapped? It is hard to avoid the conclusion that the Shanxi governor's self-criticism and apology are nothing but a perfunctory and superficial show.

In Shanxi, where all the attention is focused, only small-fry officials at the county and township levels have been punished. Party and government officials at higher levels have been ordered merely to undergo "inspection." On July 16 chinanews.com reported that the Shanxi provincial committee of the Communist Party instructed the Party committees of Linfen City and Yuncheng City to do a "deep inspection." Within the parallel government bureaucracy, the Shanxi provincial government instructed the governments of Linfen City and Yuncheng City, the Provincial Office of Labor and Social Security, the Provincial Ministry of Land and Resources, and the Provincial Bureau of Industry and Commerce also to do "deep inspections." Leading officials in these cities and bureaucracies followed up with self-criticisms in front of large assemblies of officials. Mere talk.

And of course the people who need to come clean are not just in Shanxi. High officials in Henan must do so as well. Fully two-thirds of the missing children of those 400 fathers who issued the appeal were children from Henan. That so many children could be missing for so long shows how rampant human trafficking in Henan has become. Henan is a main supplier of slave labor. Moreover, when parents fail to find their children even after so long a search—and then see them found not by police but by journalists—it is clear that the public security organs are at best grossly negligent and at worst deliberately looking the other way. Those police organs should be called to account. And Henan governor Xu Guangchun should, at the very least, match Shanxi governor Yu Youjun by offering a public apology to the victims and their families.

The main reason officials at all levels in China are so coldhearted and irresponsible is that they are appointed within a system in which public power is monopolized in the hands of a private group, the Communist Party of China. In order to guard the power of its one-party dictatorship and the vested interests of the privileged elite, the Party keeps a tight grip on the appointments and dismissals of officials at every level. In effect this takes power out of the hands of the people, where rightly it belongs, and turns it into an item of private exchange within the Party. The power of every official at every level comes not from below, from the people, but from above, from higher levels within the structure of private authority. This fact then establishes a pattern: the first priority of officials is always to serve the higher-ups (because, in effect, this serves oneself) and not to serve the people below. The priorities are not even hidden. For example, in a July 5, 2007, interview with *Southern Weekend,* Governor Yu Youjun stated his mission this way: "When Party Central sent me to Shanxi," he said, "it delegated a heavy responsibility to me. When the National People's Congress appointed me governor, it invested high hopes in me. My duty was to protect the territory, to help Party Central shoulder its burdens, and to ease the distresses of the people." Even in rhetoric, the people come last.

Not only has no big province-level official resigned; we don't even have a resignation from any official from Hongdong County or Linfen City—the ones who are in the direct line of responsibility for the black-kiln scandal. No police official from Henan or Shanxi who ignored the reports of missing children for all of that time has acknowledged any fault. (A few chiefs of local police offices have been interrogated, but that's it.) The judicial system—another tool of monopoly Party power—

consistently shows its competence in dealing with citizens and its incompetence in dealing with the official-underworld alliance.

QUESTION THREE: *Why did it take so long for such a huge scandal to come to light in the first place?* In any civilized country, a story about child slavery would be headline news even if only a few people were involved, let alone more than a thousand. But in China, while news from Shanxi sent shockwaves around the world, headlines at home were dominated instead by the comings and goings of the Communist oligarchy. Reporting good news and pushing the government's point of view remain the main tasks of the Chinese news media. The Party's Propaganda Department at all levels, together with bureaucracies like the Press and Publication Administration that handle ideology, are the responsible offices. They are watchdogs that scour the media and force them to be the Party's mouthpiece, simultaneously robbing the public of its right to know and robbing journalists of their freedom to report.

Without freedom in reporting, the media become, over time, tools of the regime in its efforts to lock out certain information and to keep the people in ignorance. As the black-kiln case shows, blocking information can lead to major disasters. Then, after disasters happen, the Party manipulates the media to portray the villains as the saviors, bad government as good government, and the cleanup of losses as political achievements. A blanket of pretty headlines covers the regime's shabby record of performance. So when shocking events in Shanxi are exposed, reports on the treatment and fate of child-slaves are squeezed out by reports about Hu Jintao, Wen Jiabao, and other high officials issuing instructions. Stories of parents searching for their children give way to accounts of the rescue activities of local governments. In the end the regime's monopoly of the media once again works its magic: the words and deeds of officials high and low get all of the attention, while the voice of the victims, if it gets out at all, is only on the Internet.

QUESTION FOUR: *Why is nothing done to stop China's underworld economy, even though it includes the oppression and mistreatment of migrant labor, the use of child labor, and the kidnapping of children?* Abuses of migrant labor, including minors, have been increasing. New cases keep appearing. And they not only continue but have a snowball effect: the more it is seen that such things can be gotten away with, the more attractive they become to entrepreneurs who exploit the weak as means to get rich and to the interest groups, including corrupt local officials, who stand behind those entrepreneurs by providing them with protective umbrellas in return for a slice of the profits. Officials cover what they do with euphemisms like "developing the local economy" and "safeguarding public order." But the truth is that in China the underworld and officialdom have interpenetrated and become one. Criminal elements have become officialized as officials have become criminalized. Underworld chiefs carry titles in the National People's Congress or the People's Political Consultative Conference, while civil officials rely on the underworld to keep the lid on local society.

Officials and underworld bear joint responsibility for the outrages that take place and for the political cover that protects them—yet central authorities seem to have no formula for curtailing anything. It is not always clear whether they cannot intervene or choose not to intervene, but in any case they *do* not intervene—and the joint projects of underworld and officialdom go forth unimpeded in many local areas. It makes one wonder if things aren't just about the same at the highest levels.

QUESTION FIVE: *How can the National People's Congress (NPC) and the people's congresses at lower levels look the other way at official malfeasance as ugly as this?* By law the NPC is the highest authority in the country. Its 3,000 or so delegates are charged with oversight of all branches of the government, and the delegates to all of the people's congresses at lower levels, who number more than 3 million, are supposed to do the same at their levels. Why is it that, with very few exceptions, these people are so ineffective?

Media reports say that a single delegate to the NPC from Hunan, over a period of nine long years, did do his best with the black-kilns problem. But he was alone; no one else in the NPC or any in people's congress at any level joined him. What qualifies people's congresses that behave in this way to say they are organs of public opinion, and how do their delegates have the nerve to say they "represent" anyone?

In the Chinese political system, the lack of supervision by people's congresses goes hand in hand with the abuse of power by government authorities. The two principles have a long history together. Their symbiosis comes about because the people's congresses and the government share a common origin in the dictatorial powers of the Party. Both institutions give priority to serving that power, not the people.

Farmers are 80 percent of the population but hold only 20 percent of the seats in the NPC, while urbanites, 20 percent of the population, hold four times as many. But that imbalance actually doesn't matter, because in fact no one is represented in the true sense anyway. The Standing Committee of the Politburo of the Communist Party of China supplies the chair of the National People's Congress, and Party chiefs chair the people's congresses at all the lower levels. More than 70 percent of delegates to people's congresses are Party or government officials.

Because all authority of the congresses derives from the Party, they become mere rubber stamps for Party power. And when the "people's representatives" at all levels in fact are officials—premiers, governors, mayors, bureau chiefs, county chiefs, town chiefs, village chiefs all the way down—how are they going to "supervise" the use of the power that they themselves hold? There is no separation at all between administrative power and supervisory power. Wang Dongji is a perfect example. Wang is the father of black-kiln boss Wang Binbin in Caosheng Village, Guangshengsi Township, Hongdong County, Linfen City, Shanxi Province. He holds administrative power as the Communist Party secretary in Caosheng Village and "supervisory" power as a two-term deputy in the Hongdong County People's Congress.

QUESTION SIX: *Why is that, ever since Hu Jintao and Wen Jiabao came to power, China has seen such a succession of major crises of a kind that should have been dealt with before they got out of hand?* Examples are legion: the SARS crisis of 2003; the Songhua River water-pollution crisis of 2005; the serial panics of 2006 over toxic food products and fake medicines; plus others. The common factor underlying all of them is the monopoly power of an authoritarian government that neglects to take action and then concentrates on concealing its inaction. Were it not for the efforts of citizens with consciences—publishing on an Internet that the government cannot yet completely block and through that means bringing problems to light and forcing the Hu-Wen government to react—the consequences would have been even more disastrous. The Internet is truly God's gift to the Chinese people.

In the black-kiln case in particular, the Hu-Wen regime cannot foist responsibility onto a local government "different" from itself, because the local government is nothing but an artifact of the central government. Arguments that information was "concealed" or "not received" have no traction. Consider the following story:

On March 8, 2007, Yang Aizhi, who lives in the city of Zhengzhou in Henan Province, began looking for her fifteen-year-old child Wang Xinlei. At the end of that month, she and the parent of another missing child, from Meng County in Henan, set out to Shanxi in search of their children. They visited more than a hundred kilns but did not find them. In early April Yang made another trip to Shanxi, this time with five other parents of missing children, but again they found nothing.

Then, on May 9, Henan television reporter Fu Zhenzhong joined the six parents on a third trip to Shanxi. Fu shot scenes of the black-kiln work sites surreptitiously and then produced a television report called "Cruelty beyond Words, Extent beyond Measure." When the report was aired, more than a thousand more parents approached the television station pleading for help. Later, on June 5, an Internet post on "Great River Forum" in Henan appeared under the headline: "The criminal underworld strikes again! A desperate appeal from 400 fathers of children sold into Shanxi kilns." On June 11, Yang Aizhi mailed her own urgent appeal to Premier Wen Jiabao.

Only after all of this had happened did the national media begin to pay any attention to the problem of slavery in the black kilns. Three full months of time had been wasted between March 8 and June 15, the date on which the Hu-Wen regime finally issued some instructions.

Even more maddening, consider this: As early as 1998, nine years before people in Henan took action, a mayor named Chen Jianjiao in Xinguan Township in Hunan, who was a delegate to the Hunan People's Congress, had been working on the black-kiln problem in Shanxi, Hebei, and elsewhere. Chen had already rescued hundreds of enslaved laborers, many of whom were children. But eventually, overwhelmed by the scale of the problem, he decided to appeal to the central authorities for help. On September 8, 2006, he wrote to Premier Wen Jiabao recommending that there be a comprehensive national project to clear up the black-kiln slave-labor problem once and for all.

But Delegate Chen's letter sank like a stone in the ocean. He received no response from Wen Jiabao or from anyone else. Imagine what could have happened if Wen had done something then. The exposure of the black kilns, the breakup of the mobs that ran them, the rescue of slave labor, and the discipline of negligent officials all could have happened at least six months earlier than it did. Instead of just passing the blame to lower officials, should not the Hu-Wen regime apologize to victims of the disaster for *its own* failure to respond to the letter of this member of a provincial people's congress? And if this is the way they treat an appeal from a person with that kind of prestigious position, need we say anything about the way they treat the appeals of ordinary citizens?

The Hu-Wen regime's favorite performance since it took power has been its "we-love-the-people" show. Look, they say: we repealed the arbitrary detention system called "custody and repatriation," we changed the system that covered up SARS, we have written "human rights" into the constitution, we abolished agricultural taxes, we crisscross the country showing our concern, we help migrant workers get fair wages, we sell peaches for farmers, we spend New Year's Eve in a mineshaft, we wear old sneakers, we weep repeatedly over the sufferings of the people, and so on. Over time, thanks to their monopoly of the media that report their strivings every day, every month, every year, they have indeed built a certain image of caring about people. But this image is what they wear on their faces, and in front of television cameras. Their coldness lies in the bones, and in the deals they make inside black boxes. They are, after all, the highest-ranking members of the country's private ruling group, and their first priority must always be to safeguard the vested interests—the power and the special privileges—of this group. It is impossible for them truly to put mainstream public opinion first—or the suffering of the people, or the overall public interest. For them, the first task of the media is to highlight the Party's political achievements and to show things in as bright a light as possible; it is quite unthinkable that the media should become independent operators, running around uncovering problems. In truth, the black-kiln child slavery affair only illustrates, once again, the mendacity of the regime's pious pronouncements about "getting to the bottom of things" and "putting people first."

The reason the regime is so coldhearted is not that the human be-
ings in it are all coldhearted. The problem is the cruelty of the authori-
tarian system itself. This kind of system cannot adapt to respect life or
uphold human rights. A ruling group that makes maintenance of its
monopoly on power its first priority can never turn around and put the
lives of people—even children—in a higher position. In the end it is
because the system does not treat people as people that such hair-raising
atrocities can come about. Authoritarian power is as cold as ice. It obliges
people to focus on power and power alone, and this makes feelings of
human warmth impossible.

The history of the Communist Party's rule in China shows consis-
tent adherence to this authoritarian pattern. Unless there is a change of
system in China, monstrous episodes like the black kilns will never be
"uprooted"; indeed, not even many of their leaves are likely to fall off.

At home in Beijing, July 16, 2007

*Originally published in* Ren yu renquan *(Humanity and Human Rights), no. 8, 2007*
*Translated by Perry Link*

# THE SIGNIFICANCE OF THE "WENG'AN INCIDENT"

◆　◆　◆　◆　◆

A SERIES OF MAJOR EVENTS in China in this Olympic year of 2008 have been attracting the attention of the world. In March the crisis in Tibet seriously hurt China's Olympic image. Then, in May, a huge earthquake in Sichuan handed the Communist regime a chance to restore its tarnished image by using "earthquake relief" to give the impression of "a new China bursting forth from the quake." But shortly thereafter, another large-scale conflict between Chinese officials and Chinese people emerged to shock the country and the world.

On June 28, 2008, only forty days before the opening ceremony of the Olympics, a confrontation that pitted tens of thousands of people against a local government broke out in Weng'an County in Guizhou Province. Li Shufen, a student only 15 years old, had been raped and murdered, and her body had been thrown into a river. Local police, in handling the egregious case, ruled that the girl had committed suicide by throwing herself into the river. Bypassing autopsy and investigation, they simply released the suspects. The girl's family, who stoutly rejected the police version of events, sent an uncle of the girl to argue with the police, who then not only refused to give the uncle any explanation but decided to give him a good beating as well. They later dispatched gangsters to beat him again, this time sufficiently to send him to the hospital, where, after futile attempts to save him, he died. His wife was beaten, too—enough to disfigure her face.

The outrageous behavior of the police stirred a public outcry. A group of Li Shufen's high school classmates went to the local government offices to demand justice, and before long tens of thousands of local citizens had joined them. An angry mob burned the county-government and police buildings and set fire to a dozen or so police cars. The turmoil began during an afternoon and raged deep into the night, when a large detachment of paramilitary police—who opened fire, injuring one person—finally put it down. The authorities cut off communication with the outside world and blocked reporters who tried to enter the city.

In recent years, if one were to read only the Party-controlled media, one might get the impression that China is prosperous, stable, and headed for an age of "great peace and prosperity." Attention to China from the international community has added to the problem, lending credibility to clamor about "the rise of a great nation." China's rulers have, in addition, both instigated and indulged a wave of popular chauvinism that helps to cover their regime with a veneer of apparent widespread popular support. On the other hand, the glaring discrepancy between official New China News Agency accounts of this "Weng'an incident" and widespread popular opinion on the Internet puts the true face of officialdom into sharp focus. Not only from the Internet but from foreign news sources as well as the internal documents of the regime itself—its "crisis reports"—we know that more and more major conflicts, often involving violence and bloodshed, have been breaking out between citizens and officials all across China. The country rests at the brink of a volcano.

The popular "rights-defense" movement of recent years has sprung from the lowest levels in Chinese society. It arises primarily from the following problems (this list is not complete) that China's dictatorial political system and its unbalanced economy have generated:

—damage to workers' rights and interests when state-owned enterprises are "reformed" into private hands;

—exploitation of migrant workers in sweatshops;

—damage to the rights and interests of retirees;

—forcible appropriation of farmers' land for private "development";

—resettlement and compensation for people who have been displaced by major hydroelectric power projects;

—protests that result when efforts to petition higher authority come to nothing;

—outbursts of public indignation at bullying by officials.

Even more ominous, from the viewpoint of the regime, is that many of the participants in large-scale disturbances in recent years have not been pursuing only their *personal* interests. They have been, to borrow government jargon, "groups whose direct interests have not been harmed." The "Weng'an incident" is a good example.

How, exactly, could the rape and murder of one student lead to a demonstration by tens of thousands of people and eventually to the burning down of a building that housed a police station and other government offices? A brief notice from the official New China News Agency on June 29 offered a stale explanation:

Because of some people's dissatisfaction with the results of the Weng'an public security bureau's identification of the cause of death of a female student in that county, they gathered in front of buildings of the county government and public security bureau. In the process of discussions with the county officials concerned, some people incited the masses, who did not know the truth of the incident, to attack the county public security bureau, the county government, and the offices of the county Party Secretary. Later, a few lawbreakers took advantage of the situation to smash the offices and set fires in many office rooms and some automobiles.

On the Internet, however, people simply ignored this account, choosing instead to look for what local citizens were saying by computers and cell phones. In the popular accounts, the relevant story was that the black-box politics of officialdom had turned a case of rape and murder into a case of "shielding the suspects and beating the victim's relatives to death." Netizens wanted to know how the suspects, if they did not have official protection, could have evaded the long arm of the law.

We, on the other hand, should ask why this conflict between offi-
cials and ordinary citizens escalated so dramatically. How could it have
swelled from an inquiry by a family member of a victim into a huge
public demonstration—unless, of course, local officials had already had
very bad reputations for nasty rule?

This "Weng'an incident" recalls the very similar "Wanzhou inci-
dent" that happened in Sichuan in 2004. Both incidents involved pro-
testers "whose direct interests had not been harmed." In both cases, the
angry citizens in the tens of thousands who surrounded and attacked
government offices were neither direct victims, nor relatives of direct
victims, nor even people who shared material interests with direct vic-
tims. Most did not even know the victims. They came together entirely
out of "moral indignation"—an indignation that could only have come
from experience of a much more general pattern of official abuse.

Let us briefly review this "Wanzhou incident." On the afternoon of
October 18, 2004, a confrontation broke out in the Wanzhou District
of Chongqing. Yu Jikui, a common laborer, accidentally bumped his
carrying pole against Zeng Qingrong, a wealthy lady, dirtying her
dress. Zeng's husband, Hu Quanzong, then used the carrying pole to
beat Yu, breaking his leg. Undaunted at this result, Hu let it be known
that he was a government official and that, no matter what happened, he
could always settle anything with money. Even the *life* of an ordinary
man, he said, would cost him only two hundred thousand yuan. To
make things worse, when the police arrived they were indulgent toward
Hu Quanzong. They shook hands with him, exchanged small talk, then
let him go. Angry bystanders, seeing "official arrogance" and "mutual
cover-up" as blatant as this, gathered in a demonstration in front of the
gate of the Wanzhou District government offices. The crowd grew into
the tens of thousands. Authorities, desperate for control, dispatched
more than a thousand riot police to disperse the crowd, but this only
caused the crowd to counterattack with bricks and stones. They burned
police cars and fire engines, and set fire to a government office build-
ing. The government in Wanzhou was forced to close down for a day.

What the Wanzhou and Weng'an incidents both show is how a
random and relatively minor event can trigger expression of the systemic
and increasingly serious antagonism between officials and the people
that has grown from a long, accumulated record in China of official

tyranny and deceit. It is hardly an exaggeration to speak of "sparks in a tinderbox."

The two incidents also make clear the crucial importance of the Internet, a new medium that official censorship has never been able fully to control. In recent times, whenever large-scale "sensitive incidents" take place, they almost always emerge first on the Internet. It is significant, moreover, that when netizens report these confrontations between the government and the people, they tend invariably to side with the people. Standard government accounts have practically zero credibility on the Web. In other words: if large-scale "incidents" between officials and the people can reveal how deep the antagonism is between these two sides, what netizens' *reactions* to these incidents show is the almost total lack of public trust in official reporting on such matters. This happens because any netizen with an interest in politics or current affairs is already familiar, from his or her personal experience on the Web, with the ways in which the authoritarian regime lies and dissembles. So whenever a conflict breaks out between the government and citizens, Internet opinion reflexively heads for the citizens' side and makes the question "What really happened?" the first order of business.

In today's China, the balance of strength between the government and the people in daily life is slowly but steadily drifting in the direction of more strength for the people and less for the government. The "Weng'an incident" is just another piece of evidence of this trend.

It does remain true that there is no freedom of speech or judicial independence in China and that, therefore, people whose rights and interests are violated can expect no help from executive or judicial authority and no support from public opinion through official channels. The one object of hope that ordinary people still cling to is the "petition system" for appealing to higher authority—but that system, after years of abuse, now exists in name only, as a somewhat freakish appendage of the dictatorial apparatus itself.

On the other hand, the good news is that the Chinese people today are no longer the ignorant and obedient "masses" of old; they increasingly are citizens who are aware of their rights and are ready to act on them. They have limited patience for officials inured to arbitrary power, and they are keenly aware of the forms that official deceit takes. This is why tyrannical authority has been steadily declining and why the deterrent power of government intimidation is far less than it once was. There is no way that popular political currents such as these, or the rights-defense movement that expresses them, are suddenly going to shift direction out of respect for the will of the regime or its associated elites. The question is not whether the government welcomes this trend, or whether such a trend is possible. The only real question is when, and by what means, the trend will shift from a scattered pattern—rising first here, then there, then somewhere else—and turn into a unified pattern like the one we saw during the nationwide protests of 1989.

Whether China's power elite wants to admit it or not, its record over the last two decades of nefarious behavior and violence against ordinary people has already led to a distrust of officialdom and an appetite for political participation that have prepared the ground for this kind of huge 1989-style mobilization. When the people's demands for justice and fairness continue not to be satisfied, or even relieved, and when their appeals for rights and their desires for participation continue to be repressed, then, at that point, more repression leads only to more popular demands, and only makes a major outburst more likely. With society in this sort of condition, an outburst in a major city, *no matter over what issue,* could precipitate a conflagration.

President Hu Jintao and Premier Wen Jiabao are at least somewhat aware of this situation. This is why, as soon as they came to power six years ago, they initiated a policy of "drawing close to the people." But their policy addresses only the symptoms of the problem, not its causes. The Hu-Wen approach has been to grant a few favors from on high without making any changes in the way society works. No amount of shouting "We're getting close to people!" will be able to solve problems like the ever-worsening corruption in China. The only ways in which China's current regime can defuse popular hostility and avoid a comprehensive social crisis are these:

—allow space for flexible political mobilization among the people;

—provide an effective legal order through which popular "rights defense" and political participation can operate, without violence;

—permit political solutions to the vicious cycle of social injustices that China's unbalanced economic reforms have generated; and

—protect the rights of the people and restrain official abuses of power while moving China gradually toward a system in which human rights are guaranteed.

Beijing, June 30, 2008

*Originally published in* Guancha *(Observe China), June 30, 2008*
*Translated by Josephine Chiu-Duke*

# PART II

# CULTURE AND SOCIETY

# EPILOGUE TO *CHINESE POLITICS AND CHINA'S MODERN INTELLECTUALS*

◆ ◆ ◆ ◆ ◆

*This piece, written in New York in 1989 just before Liu Xiaobo returned to China to join the protests at Tiananmen, marks a watershed in his thinking. It is an epilogue to his book* Chinese Politics and China's Modern Intellectuals *(Taibei, 1990) in which he uses Western ideas as standards to criticize Chinese intellectual culture. After the book manuscript was finished, Liu suddenly had some profound doubts about Western culture itself, and with characteristic frankness lays these bare, sparing no one, including himself.—Ed.*

THIS BOOK MAY HAVE SOME VALUE in comparing China and the West, and maybe in the project of reforming China as well. China's present condition, in international comparison, is just too outmoded, too degenerate, too fossilized, and too senile; it *needs* challenge, even "menace," from another civilization; it *needs* a vast and surging, boundless sea to pound it out of its isolation, its solitude, and its narrow-mindedness; it even needs a taste of the humiliation of "falling behind" in order to spur its determination to transform itself. Western culture can serve as a comparison that helps to illuminate the contours, including the many flaws, of Chinese culture, as a critical tool with which to attack China's obsolescence, and as a source of wisdom that can bring new lifeblood to China.

But on the other hand, this book may have no value at all in matters such as the fate of humanity, the future of the globe, or fulfillment in the lives of individual human beings. The problems this book concerns itself with are too shallow and parochial for that; they are problems specifically of China and the Chinese, not of any larger or deeper questions. The book has value only as a kind of cultural detritus; its two greatest shortcomings are the narrow nationalism of its outlook and its blind obsequiousness toward Western culture.

Like everything else I have written about Chinese culture, this book is grounded in Chinese nationalism. It is far from the "wholesale Westernization" for which I have been criticized. One of the main characteristics of Western culture, in my view, is its tradition of critical reason, and to be "Westernized" in a true sense requires one to adopt a critical attitude toward everything—the West as well as China. It also requires concern for the fate of all humanity and for the incompleteness of the individual person. By contrast, the impulse to use Western culture merely as a tool with which to regenerate the Chinese nation is classic Sino-centrism and not real "Westernization." My preoccupation with China has limited my ability to reflect on matters at a higher level. (I believe most Chinese intellectuals have been similarly blinkered. These nationalist blinders explain, I think, why China has produced no world-class intellect in recent times.) I am unable to enter conversation with advanced, global culture over the fate of humanity as a whole, and I am helpless to pursue individual transcendence of the kind that religions offer. I am too practical, too materialist, and remain too bogged down in the backwardness of China's realities and secular concerns.

My fate—that of having no transcendent values, and no God—is perhaps not so different from that of the great Lu Xun (1881–1936). In his vignettes called *Wild Grass,* Lu Xun plumbs the depths of the human condition; what he needed at this stage of his life were transcendent values with which to address his inner schisms. But he could not find any. In the despair of seeing a road that ends only in a graveyard, he needed a hand from God; no secular value would do. He had launched his career from his ability to stand apart from Chinese culture, from where he could deliver withering criticisms of it. From there he moved on to discover disappointment with himself, and then the existential concerns of *Wild Grass*. But ultimately *Wild Grass*, because it lacks a sense of absolute value that can transcend worldly concerns, stands both as the pinnacle of Lu Xun's creativity and as the self-dug grave from which there was no escape for him.

After *Wild Grass* Lu Xun could no longer bear his inner world of isolation, solitude, and despair. He could not tolerate lonely confrontation with the unknown, or the terror of the grave, and could not undertake a transcendent dialogue with his own soul under the attentive gaze of God. Eventually he left those struggles behind and plunged back into philistine China, where he engaged in word wars with some mediocre intellects who were in no way his match. His battles with mediocrity led him, too, into mediocrity. The practical mentality of a traditional herb doctor won out in his mind, and a godless Lu Xun had nowhere to go but down. Nietzsche had influenced Lu Xun deeply, but there was one great difference between the two: Nietzsche, despairing over humanity and himself, could ride on his "superman" notion to a higher level; Lu Xun, similarly despairing over China and himself, could find no such alternative, and fell back into the sordid reality that he had once rejected.

This problem leads me to another question. Why is it that exiled writers, philosophers, and scientists from European countries—not just Western Europe but the Soviet Union and Eastern Europe, too—have been so outstanding while those from China have been so unremarkable? Why are Chinese writers and thinkers who go abroad and live in exile so unproductive? I think it is because their vision is parochial. They care only about China, and are too practical, too materialistic. They have no transcendent impulse, lack the courage to face an unfamiliar or uncertain world, and lack a spirit of the individual standing alone to challenge a larger world. They felt comfortable only on their home turf, where they could hear the plaudits of fatuous multitudes. It was very difficult for them to leave behind their renown in China and start from scratch in a strange land. Back in China, their every action and utterance had drawn attention throughout society, but now, overseas, they do not get this worshipful regard; apart from the enthusiasm of a few Westerners who care about China, no one pays them any heed. Their China-centered mentality, so hard to shake off, can cause them to clutch for dear life to the straw man of patriotism. What they really need, if they are to deal with their isolation, is not support from others but inner strength. No matter how famous they were in China, and no matter how high a status they had, once they are overseas in an unfamiliar environment they have no real choice but to rely on themselves. It is a test of talent, wisdom, and creativity.

This is why I feel that, even while I praise Western culture, and however I use it to criticize Chinese culture in this book, I remain a "frog at the bottom of a well" that actually sees little more than a patch of blue sky the size of the palm of my hand. None of my critical reflections on China's condition or traditions require much intelligence or creativity. All the theoretical tools that I use have been known and widely available for a long time. I by no means "discovered" them. Centuries ago Western literati expressed, with crystal clarity, a number of ideas that Chinese today regard as profound novel truths. These truths are common knowledge in the West, and in terms of "innovation" are actually obsolete. If this is coal, no one needs Liu Xiaobo to carry it to Newcastle.

My own best hope is only to get as deep and accurate a grasp of these things as I can. On a visit to the Metropolitan Museum of Art in New York, I suddenly realized how insignificant the China issues that I have been wrestling with are, if one measures them in terms of true spiritual creativity. Looking at the masterworks, I was struck with how superficial my thinking was, and how atrophied my vitality, after so many years of being cooped up in a benighted environment of what was, essentially, a cultural desert. Eyes kept too long in the darkness do not easily adapt to dazzling sunlight when it suddenly pours through a window. How could I, all of a sudden, face my own situation squarely, much less engage in dialogue with world-class thinkers?

All I can do now is hope to abandon the hollow fame of my past, make a clean start of things, and set out into an as-yet unknown world. Success or failure will depend not just on whether I make use of the large stashes of knowledge that humanity has already accumulated; it will depend, too, on exploration of the unknown, as well as on my intelligence and whether I can muster the courage to be an authentic person. I hope I will be able to endure the pain—not pain suffered for the sake of others, but the pain of extricating myself from a terrible bind. If I fail, at least let the failure be genuine. If it is, at least it will be worth more than all the empty victories I have had.

My tendency to idealize Western civilization arises from my nationalistic desire to use the West in order to reform China. But this has led me to overlook the flaws in Western culture—or, even if I see them, to set them aside intentionally. I have not, therefore, been able to stand apart from Western culture, take a critical view of it, and perhaps get a better view of human frailty more generally. I have been obsequious toward Western civilization, exaggerating its merits, and at the same time exaggerating my own merits. I have viewed the West as if it were not only the salvation of China but also the natural and ultimate destination of all humanity. Moreover I have used this delusional idealism to assign myself the role of savior. In the past I have always despised "saviors"—at least when they were other people. But wittingly or unwittingly, I myself could not help slipping into this role, with all its attendant complacency and grandiosity.

I now realize that Western civilization, while it can be useful in reforming China in its present stage, cannot save humanity in an overall sense. If we stand back from Western civilization for a moment, we can see that it possesses all the flaws of humanity in general. I am reminded of what Zhuangzi (369–286 BCE) said in "The Floods of Autumn":

> However great the river, it is nothing compared to the ocean; however vast the ocean, it still is not the cosmos.

The belief that one can possess all of the beauty that exists is nothing but a dream. And so it is with human civilizations: China is backward compared with the West; but the West is only part of humanity, and humanity itself is tiny within the universe. The mind-boggling arrogance of human beings shows itself both in the complacency of Chinese-style moral pride as well as in Western-style confidence in the omnipotence of reason and science. No matter how strongly modern Western intellectuals may critique Western rationalism, and no matter how harshly they may denounce the West's colonial expansion and the premise of white superiority, they still maintain deep-rooted feelings of superiority toward non-Western peoples. They feel proud of the courage and sincerity with which they do self-criticisms. They easily offer criticisms that they make of themselves, but have trouble listening to criticisms that originate from outside the West.

If I, as a person who has lived under China's autocratic system for more than thirty years, want to reflect on the fate of humanity or on how to be an authentic person, I have no choice but to carry out two critiques simultaneously. I must:

1.  Use Western civilization as a tool to critique China.

2.  Use my own creativity to critique the West.

Neither of these kinds of critique can substitute for the other. Nor can the two be jumbled together. I might point out that the West's overriding emphasis on rationality, science, and money has resulted in the loss of individuality and in a commercialization that overwhelms all resistance; I might also criticize the economic stratification that technological integration has brought about, and I can repudiate the ways in which consumer culture has inured humanity to an unquestioning addiction to affluence and a cowardly fear of freedom. But none of these criticisms can be reasonably applied to an impoverished China, where there is still little awareness of science. We must guard against using the criteria by which we criticize the West to apply to China; that makes about as much sense as playing zither music to an ox or shooting at phantoms. Still less should we use the criteria that we apply to China as the standard that we expect of the West; to do that would be to launch all of humanity on a race to the bottom. Some Western intellectuals, beginning from criticisms of their own societies, have looked Eastward, peering toward mystical Eastern culture in search of solutions to humanity's problems; but this is often fatuous self-delusion of a most ridiculous sort. "Eastern culture" in today's world cannot even come to grips with the problems in its own region, let alone be any beacon for humanity as a whole.

One of humanity's greatest mistakes in the twentieth century, in my view, has been its attempt to escape its predicaments using the civilizations that it has already created. In fact, neither the classics of the East nor modern culture in the West is strong enough to rescue humanity from its plight. The most that we can hope for is that advanced civilization in the West might draw the backward East into its own survival mode; but the larger problem is that the Western pattern itself is tragic. Humanity so far has been unable to conceive a completely new civilization that might solve such problems as the population explosion, the energy crisis, environmental imbalance, nuclear disarmament, and addiction to pleasure and to commercialization. Nor is there any culture that can help humanity once and for all eliminate spiritual suffering or transcend personal limits. Humanity has built weapons that can extinguish all of humanity in an instant, and there is no escape from the fundamental anxiety that results; it has become part of the backdrop of every person's life. The specter of death can render all human effort futile. The best that anyone can do is to face the cruel realities squarely and to stride bravely toward the abyss. Humanity has been seeking a final destination ever since its banishment from the Garden of Eden; Western culture is not that final destination, but merely a stage in the journey.

Even more lamentable, the Western notion of "original sin" has grown weaker over time and general awareness of repentance is in sharp decline. The religious notion of the sacred has come to be little different from rock 'n' roll—more nearly enjoyment than painful self-examination. No one in the years since Jesus was nailed to the cross has again sacrificed himself for humanity, and humanity has lost its conscience. The disappearing awareness of "original sin" has left human life weightless and has led to another fall for humanity, leaving us unlikely ever to recover from the original fall of Adam and Eve. How can people who lack a sense of "original sin" ever hear the voice of God? From the early Middle Ages, when God was a being of reason, to the late Middle Ages, when God was a figure of power, to modern times, when God became even more profoundly subjected to reason, and finally to today's world, where God has gradually become secularized, human civilization has been in descent. By its own hand, humanity in the West has killed the sacred values of its heart.

This is why, after I finished this book, whose guiding principle was to use Western civilization as a tool for critical reflection on China, I suddenly found myself at a loss, trapped in an awkward position, and shaken. It struck me like bolt from the blue that I had been attacking an obsolete culture with a weapon that itself was only a bit less obsolete. I was like a paraplegic laughing at a quadriplegic. Now looking at myself plainly, I suddenly can see that I am no theorist, and no personage of note: I am but a common person who must begin again from scratch. When I was in China, the pervasive ignorance in the social background made my intelligence stand out. But it stood out only in the sense in which my own tenuous health might look good if I were to stand next to an idiot. Here in the West, without that backdrop of ignorance, it is obvious that I am no great mind. Without an idiot standing next to me, my own inadequacies appear in profusion, and they are plain in the friends around me as well. In China, I lived for a fame that was 90 percent puffery; here in the West, for the first time, I have had to face reality squarely and make difficult choices about life. When a person falls from an illusory height into the abyss of reality, he discovers that he had never been at a height in the first place, but in fact had been struggling in the abyss all along. The frustration and despair that seized me when I awoke from my dream caused me to hesitate, to vacillate, and to consider the cowardly alternative of reentering the illusion, returning to the Chinese context that I knew so well, where again I could stand out among the ignorant. Were it not for the Metropolitan Museum of Art, I might actually have done this.

My wife [Liu Xiaobo's first wife, Tao Li—Ed.] once wrote to me in a letter:

> Xiaobo, on the surface you seem to be a rebel within this society, but in fact you have a deep identification with it. The system treats you as an opponent, and in so doing it accommodates you, tolerates you, even flatters and encourages you. In a sense you are an oppositional ornament of the system. But me? I'm an invisible person; I disdain even to demand anything of this society, and don't lose sleep over how I am going to denounce it. It is I, not you, who am fundamentally incompatible with it. Even you cannot comprehend my profound indifference. Not even you can accommodate me.

When I first read these words they went right past me, but now, thinking back, I can see that they hit the nail on the head. I am grateful to my wife. She is not only my wife but also my most perceptive critic, and her criticisms leave me nowhere to hide.

Right now there is no escape for me. Either I jump off the cliff or am crushed to smithereens. The price of freedom is to go to the limit.

Before ending this essay, though, I need to make some unpleasant comments about the ways in which Westerners flatter China. Their interest, and their effusive praise, seems to me rooted in the following sorts of psychology:

1. Some are attracted to Chinese culture purely from personal inclination, temperament, interest, and values. They seek spiritual resources, or a kind of comfort, and there is nothing wrong with that. It is a normal human pursuit. It's just too bad that Westerners of this kind, who are responsible only to themselves, are so few. Indeed, it is too bad that human beings of this kind in general are so few.

2. Some, beginning from criticisms of their own societies, look to China for weapons that they can use to try to transform the West. Their mission leads them to embrace a Chinese political language and conceptual system, to strain it through their own Western thought processes, and thence to come up with a version of "Chinese" culture. These Westerners believe that they are Sinicizing themselves, but in fact they are doing nothing of the sort. They are doing a very Western thing. (In my view cultures usually block out other cultures; we will have to await the birth of a truly transcendent talent if we are ever to see a person fundamentally exit the cage that is native culture.) There is nothing wrong with Westerners idealizing Chinese culture for their personal use; but to idealize it with a view to improving the human condition will only cause humanity to regress. This idea is even more ridiculous than the idea that Western culture itself is humanity's salvation.

3. Some begin with Western superiority firmly in mind and a sense of *noblesse oblige* toward Chinese culture. Their affirmation of things Chinese is like that of an adult who commends a child for handling "big people's language" or a nobleman who praises the loyalty of a slave. Both are mixtures of charity and insult. I have heard plenty of this kind of praise during my current trip abroad. People say things like: "This is the first time I've heard a Chinese say anything like that," or "What an understanding of Western philosophy for a Chinese!" or "How did

China ever produce a rebel like you?!" Such comments are meant as compliments, but each reflects the premise that normally Chinese are dodos. When I hear such praise, it makes me feel as if I am not really a visitor from China so much as a person who has been stuffed into a leather case and loaded onto an airplane to be displayed, as and where my hosts see fit, as a novel object from a distant land. In this pattern we can see how, despite centuries of progress toward democracy and equality, the deep-seated human impulse to master other people has not disappeared, but waits to be resurrected at a moment's notice. The Westerners of this type include those extremely career-minded so-called China experts.

4. Western tourists praise Chinese culture out of their amazement at unfamiliar things. These people—who enjoy modern civilization and would never dream of leaving it—nevertheless thirst for a change of pace and a different flavor, and China, suddenly opened up to them after decades of being sealed off, provides an ideal destination. China's ignorance, backwardness, and primitiveness present sharp contrasts to the culture of Western civilization, and all of this, for tourists, stimulates curiosity and a sense of mystery. The praise that these tourists give to China springs from the satisfaction of their personal curiosity. If their enthusiasm were to stop there, without moving on to broach the great issues facing the world, I suppose no harm would be done. But the problem is that they frequently elevate their personal hedonism to the level of a cultural choice for the entire human race—and this, if I may be blunt, is just too preposterous for words. Their hypocrisy is plain when you consider that they come to China only to sightsee— never to stay—and yet say to Chinese people, "Your civilization is first-rate; it is the future of humanity." Their shift from tourist to savior is not merely absurd; it is cruel. It recalls the gladiatorial games of ancient Rome, where the nobility who sat in the stands of the Coliseum would never have dreamt of joining the battles within the arena, yet could be intoxicated with pleasure at viewing them. It was no doubt true that those savage and bloody spectacles offered novelty, stimulation, and hence a certain kind of pleasure. But how must the cheers have sounded to the slaves who were being torn apart? Another example: viewed from an airplane, the sight of an old buffalo plowing a field produces a feel-

ing of pastoral beauty. But can the viewer therefore say to the tiller, "Stick with your primitive ways; they are charming"? To do so would be to ask a living human being to freeze eternally in a primitive state for the viewing pleasure of another, more comfortable human being. How unjust, how cruel, is that? To use the suffering of others for the pleasure of oneself is the ultimate ugliness. To me, as a Chinese, it could not be plainer that China is not going to be the answer for humanity in the twenty-first century. In a world that is already riddled with divisions and strata, and on an earth that is so limited in its natural resources, how could China, with its population of over a billion, ever be the beacon of the twenty-first century? Even if its self-transformation succeeds in the short term, China cannot rise to the economic level of the U.S. or Japan; our planet cannot bear a superpower so large. This is why I do not look to the flourishing of any race to support my own well-being, do not pin my hopes on any particular group, and do not count on any society's progress to assure my future. I can only rely on my own efforts in contending with this world.

5. A very small number of Westerners view China from a purely academic standpoint. These people, who study China from a certain remove, are relatively objective and clear-sighted. China's virtues and vices are irrelevant to their personal interests, and their views of China, for that reason, are all the more realistic and of theoretical value. These are the Western voices that Chinese should listen most carefully to.

Writing this epilogue has exhausted me.

New York, March 1989

*Originally published by the Tangshan Publishing House, Taipei, 1990*
*Translated by Stacy Mosher*

# ON LIVING WITH DIGNITY IN CHINA

‧ ‧ ‧ ‧ ‧

*This piece, written near the end of the second year of Liu Xiaobo's third incarceration, seems to signal a turning point in his thinking. From this point on he puts heavy emphasis on "human dignity," on the responsibility of each human being to be loyal to that idea, and on the examples of people like Václav Havel, Martin Luther King Jr., Mohandas K. Gandhi, and Jesus Christ, who have shown how this is done. His exaltation of Christ becomes especially strong, but, unlike his younger friends Yu Jie and Wang Yi, who are Christians, Liu has not declared himself formally to be a believer in any religion.—Ed.*

IN A TOTALITARIAN STATE, the purpose of politics is power and power alone. The "nation" and its peoples are mentioned only to give an air of legitimacy to the application of power. The people accept this devalued existence, asking only to live from day to day.

This has remained a constant for the Chinese, duped in the past by Communist hyperbole, and bribed in the present with promises of peace and prosperity. All along, they have subsisted in an inhuman wasteland.

They live without a shred of human dignity, valued only as pawns in a system ruled by fear.

Mao Zedong, echoing Lenin in his famous "Talks at Yan'an" in 1942, exhorted the Chinese people to serve as "cogs in the revolutionary machine." And even though the people have shifted from embracing revolution under Mao's rule to avoiding it since the days of Deng Xiaoping, in both cases they have remained willing cogs.

To live in opportunism is to sink into unabashed wickedness.

To live in hypocrisy is to sacrifice integrity to cynical scheming.

To live in apathy is to become inured to selfish inaction.

To live on one's knees is to settle for charitable handouts.

To live in frivolity is to escape into farce and buffoonery.

To live in tearful humiliation and shame is to stifle one's innate moral capacity with silence.

To live in groveling impotence is to lose faith in the power of principles and righteousness.

To live in resignation and compromise is to let opportunism devour one's principles.

To live in chicanery is to sell one's conscience, to betray others who are heroes of conscience, and eventually to abandon one's sense of shame. A person or nation that lives free of shame can get along quite well.

Rationalizing such ways of life has eroded people's spiritual dimension, inflamed their brutishness and materialism, and degraded them to the level of animals. With the devaluation of faith and the sacred, people are enthralled by carnal desires. Stripped of compassion and a sense of justice, they are reduced to callous, calculating economic beings, content with a life of ease.

In the conflict between survival of the flesh and dignity of the spirit, if we cower to preserve ourselves, we become mere zombies, despite our trappings of prosperity. If we stand up for our dignity, we live nobly, no matter how much we may risk or suffer.

The Chinese people often question the need for dignity, conscience, ideals, compassion, rectitude, and a sense of shame. After all, they contend, such notions won't put food on the table or money in your pocket, and empty blather undermines our national interest. Hiding one's head in the sand, and even resorting to outright ruthlessness, they maintain, are the only ways to survive.

Admittedly, righteousness is weak unless it is backed by power, but power devoid of righteousness is evil. If most people cast their lot with the latter, then evil will prey forever upon humankind, as wolves and tigers prey upon lambs.

But unarmed righteousness fostered by love can overcome weapons and power, as demonstrated by the miraculous triumph of Jesus over Caesar, or Gandhi's and Martin Luther King's victories through non-violent resistance. Jesus is a model of martyrdom because he withstood the temptations of power, wealth, and glamour, and remained steadfast even when threatened with crucifixion.

Most important of all, Jesus exemplified opposition without hatred or the desire for retaliation; his heart was filled with boundless love and forgiveness. Completely eschewing violence, he epitomized passive resistance, serenely defiant even as he meekly carried his own cross.

No matter how profane and pragmatic our world is, we will have passion, miracles, and beauty as long as we have the example of Jesus Christ.

In the labor camp, Dalian, August 1998

*Originally published in* Dajiyuan *(The Epoch Times), July 18, 2004*
*Translated by Susan Wilf*

# LOOKING UP AT JESUS

*For my unassuming wife*

Jesus, do you know me?
a yellow-skinned Chinaman
from where we bribe the gods with bread soaked in human
 blood
we pray to gods and Buddhas solely to exterminate divinity
our gods are burnished in gold
from emperors and sages to soldiers and virgins
countless people have turned into gods
we only beg for blessings and never repent
even a puddle of piss reflects gods upside-down

I don't know you, Jesus
your body is too gaunt and shriveled
each rib assaultingly distinct
your posture on the cross is too tragic
each nerve bearing the suffering
head slightly angled forward
neck crisscrossed with protruding veins
hands, hanging down limp
when their five fingers extended
it was like dry branches in a fire

Humanity's evil is too heavy
and your shoulders are too narrow
can you hold it up, the cross
that was forced upon you?
blood soaking into the wood grain
brews the wine that rears humanity
I suspect you were a bastard child
cruel god tearing the hymen open
he made you sacrifice alone
how could it have been a way to
spread the news of God's love?

Believers who read the Old Testament
are awed by its grammar of command
and terrified by its wrathful God
no questions, no discussion
no rationale at all
belief and disbelief, obedience and disobedience
when He wants to create, He does what He likes
when He wants to destroy, the floods rise high
God has no form
but sows seeds of hate

The creation story is a bit of entertainment
that caused unprecedented evil
our progenitors, the Tree of Wisdom, the snake
make a loop manipulated by God
since the start of humanity's exile
God has become a bottomless trashbin
back then, Jesus
you hadn't been born yet

Between the rural manger and God's cross
a destitute infant
turned a wrathful God into the embodiment of love
continuous repentance and infinite atonement
love

no boundary, no leeway
like the darkness before history

December 26, 1998

*Translated by Nick Admussen*

# ELEGY TO LIN ZHAO, LONE VOICE OF CHINESE FREEDOM

.    .    .    .    .

*Lin Zhao, originally named Peng Lingzhao, was born in 1932 to a promi-nent family in Suzhou. In her teens she ran away from home to join the Communist movement, and with its victory in 1949 threw herself into the Party's land reform campaign. To her, in those years, Mao Zedong was "a red star in my heart." In 1954 she entered the prestigious Chinese Depart-ment at Peking University, where she became known for her literary flair, critical views, and spunky personality. Labeled a "rightist" in Mao Zedong's 1957 Anti-Rightist Campaign, she nonetheless remained unrepentant, continued her critical writing, and was imprisoned in 1960. While in prison she continued to write, using her own blood as ink during times when ink was denied her. In 1965 her sentence was fixed at twenty years, but later, in 1968, was revised to a sentence of death. She was shot in Shanghai on April 29, 1968, following which police presented her family with a bill for five cents to cover the cost of the bullet.*

*Her story came to light in 2006 primarily through the efforts of a filmmaker named Hu Jie. For more on Hu Jie and Lin Zhao, see Philip Pan,* Out of Mao's Shadow *(Simon and Schuster, 2008), chapters 2 and 3.*

*Ding Zilin, who is mentioned at the beginning of this piece, lost her only son in the 1989 Beijing massacre and later founded the "Tiananmen Mothers," whose mission was to tell the truth of the massacre and to help the families of other victims. (See "Listen Carefully to the Voices of the Tiananmen Mothers").*

*This elegy was written on the evening of the Qingming Festival, when the spirits of the dead are honored.*—Ed.

Dear Lin Zhao,

My friend Professor Ding Zilin told me about how, one year, she sought out your grave in Suzhou, your hometown, on the day of the Qingming Festival. As a token of respect, she composed a belated eulogy and left you an offering of flowers.

But was that really your grave? No one knows. In our land of more than three and a half million square miles, where lie your remains? And how many of the 1.3 billion Chinese people are able to commune with your departed spirit?

At the time of your execution, our entire land was a killing ground. This included your acclaimed alma mater, Peking University, where Mao Zedong, the despot who murdered you, had been an assistant librarian during his youth. Later, posing as China's savior, he reigned over this seat of higher learning, relying on the adulation of its fawning celebrities—men like the renowned poet Guo Moruo and the eminent philosopher Feng Youlan—to bleach away the bloodstains on the fleshy white hands that he used to scribble both lyric poetry and execution orders. After shooting a bullet into the back of your head, his regime saw fit only to extract the "bullet fee" from your mother.

Lin Zhao, even though I've spoken out against the madness of that era and the ignominious toadies who knelt down to kiss the executioner's hand, I am just a nobody. Allow me to fantasize for a moment: If I'd been in your class at school back then, I might have had a crush on you, might have sent you letters filled with pledges of eternal love. But could the bullet of evil that blotted out your passion for freedom also have extinguished my ardor?

Lin Zhao, you died so young. I hear the answer to my questions coming out of your empty grave.

Power and money reign supreme in our nation today. Universities count for nothing, and scholarship and ideas count for even less. Love, truth, and sacrifice are meaningless concepts, while betrayal and collective amnesia are taken as a matter of course.

Gasping for breath in this vacuum, I gaze at your lovely face and timidly reach out to remove the cotton plug from your mouth. Your lips feel soft to the touch of my icy, stiff fingers. Your blood is the only spark in the impenetrable darkness, cauterizing my soul—if, comparing myself to you, I can claim to have a soul.

The cold spring rain stings like needles from the heavens as I sit in solitary meditation on this bleak Qingming Festival. Humbled by nature's lament, I feel unworthy to mourn you.

Any tomb, any offering seems too vulgar for a martyr to freedom such as you. Tonight's shower may moisten the parched earth, but it cannot soothe your departed spirit, nor can the stars in the dark rainy sky bring back your beauty.

Your nobility was extraordinary in the China of your day.

From your distant vantage point, this world must seem more absurd than that of Kafka. When cups were raised in toasts to Peking University's hundredth anniversary [in 1998—Ed.], the endless brouhaha about founding a first-rate, world-class university must have elicited a derisive laugh from you. By expelling you, this, the leading educational institution in China, banished itself from academe and reduced itself to a place where court eunuchs convey imperial edicts.

Our motherland is steeped in blood. Wipe! Scrub! Wash! This is real blood! Who can eradicate the blood of a martyr to freedom?

Lin Zhao, you wrote prison poetry in your own blood, but our motherland, which sucked the life from you, has yet to see the buds of freedom.

This disgraceful country that trampled on your devotion and betrayed your sacrifice does not deserve your noble beauty, your blood, or your tears.

Lin Zhao, I choke on the cotton plug from your lips, as if it were a piece of bone stuck in my own throat. I qualify only to listen to your message in dumbstruck silence: your last words, literally written in your lifeblood, are a lone voice of freedom from the China of your day.

At home in Beijing, April 4, 2004

*Originally published in* Guancha *(Observe China), May 3, 2004*
*Translated by Susan Wilf*

# BA JIN

## The Limp White Flag

◆　◆　◆　◆　◆

ON OCTOBER 17, 2005, the distinguished Chinese writer Ba Jin, renowned for his "conscience" and for having lived a full hundred years in this world, finally found his release from it. He took with him his mission, never fully realized, to "tell the truth" about the Cultural Revolution; also his spiritual malaise, which he could never fully dispel, over his own involvement; and finally his proposal for a "Cultural Revolution Museum," which never reached fruition.

On the afternoon of October 24 there was a funeral for Ba Jin at the Longhua Funeral Home in Shanghai. President Hu Jintao and other high-ranking Communist officials sent wreaths. Jia Qinglin, chair of the People's Political Consultative Conference, visited in person to pay his respects. The official media brimmed with high praise for Ba Jin from cultural luminaries.

Given the way language is used in China, the best way to respect the departed soul of this man of the century is neither to blame and disparage him, on the one hand, nor to accord him high praise, on the other. People who have enjoyed his writings will want to grieve, and should; people who have warmed to his calls for "truth-telling," "repentance," and the building of a museum should not only grieve but try to do something about his dying wishes. Where he showed cowardice and blind spots, we should extend our understanding and our sympathy. We must not expect everyone who faces tyranny to be a model of virtue like Professor Ma Yinchu, who spoke out against Mao Zedong's population policy in the late 1950s, and still less can we ask people to be martyrs to principle such as Lin Zhao [see preceding essay—Ed.]. In our society, to criticize someone too much can mean "beating him to death," but pouring on too much praise can also mean "praising him to death." We should do neither to Ba Jin.

The official memorial occasions for Ba Jin were hardly more than performances by the Communist Party to show how the regime "cares" for an eminent literary figure. Calling him a "writer of the people" and a "literary giant," the authorities instructed the Xinhua News Agency to give wide circulation to an article called "Comrade Ba Jin's Remains Are Cremated in Shanghai, Jia Qinglin and Others Visit the Funeral Home to Pay Respects." The report contained 1,126 Chinese characters, and Xinhua's separate account of Ba Jin's burial contained only 222 characters. Neither report said anything about the persecution that Ba Jin suffered during the Cultural Revolution, and neither mentioned his pleas for truth, repentance, or a museum. Instead, the reports used a total of 889 characters to describe the "sympathetic concern" of the regime. Of those 889 characters, fully 583 were the names of high officials.

Meanwhile the glitterati of the cultural world have been praising Ba Jin so highly as almost to deify him. The kudos are nearly unanimous for his "truth-telling" and his "spirit of personal repentance." Wang Meng, a fellow writer and former Minister of Culture, puts him on a big pedestal with terms like "high-flying banner" and "conscience of the century." No one seems interested in things Ba Jin himself had called for: telling the truth and repenting.

The writer Yu Qiuyu says that Ba Jin's call for truth-telling is "most important" and that it constitutes "advice for the century." Shu Yi, the son of Lao She, Ba Jin's fellow writer in the 1930s, says that Ba Jin's little book called *Random Thoughts,* which reflects on the horror of the Cultural Revolution, is "a monument." But we have to note that Yu Qiuyu to this day has expressed no regret for his own "performances" during the Cultural Revolution, and Shu Yi has shown not the slightest sign of repentance for having denounced his own father for the sake of an ideology—to say nothing of "telling the truth" more broadly. Yet these two notables are quite ready to spew fine words for Ba Jin. Praise of this kind is nothing but cynical performance of a kind that by now has become regrettably normal in China.

In my view, to compare modern Chinese literature with modern literature elsewhere in the world is to see clearly that China has no "literary giants." Ba Jin's literary work qualifies him as an influential writer but hardly a giant. College students of my generation who majored in Chinese all know the pantheon of the "six great modern writers"—Lu Xun, Guo Moruo, Mao Dun, Ba Jin, Lao She, and Cao Yu. These six, always listed in that order, squeezed almost every other writer out of the curricula. The list, though, is political. Its dual purposes are to establish the official Communist version of literary history and, secondarily, to attract popular opinion to the Communist "mainstream" by bringing well-known writers into the fold.

Ba Jin's main weakness as a writer is that his language lacks creativity. His contributions to Chinese literature pale next to those of Lu Xun, Shen Congwen, Lao She, and Cao Yu, to say nothing of Eileen Chang and Xiao Hong. Some of Ba Jin's works are simply bad. He wrote several long novels, but only one, *Family*, is worth much note, and that is because of its impact on society, not its literary value. The other novels are long-winded, bloated, and pretentious. They lack authorial control, and their language lacks beauty. When they were assigned in college, I, for one, couldn't finish reading them.

Ba Jin's one hundred years in this world put him in first place among the "six model authors" in longevity. But if we measure the six by literary standards or standards of integrity, it is Lu Xun, who was the first of the six to die, who looks best. By dying in 1936 Lu Xun did not have to turn into a literary vegetable after 1949. There was no way the Communists could push him into the quagmire of "thought reform" and force him to write humiliating self-criticisms, no way they could parade him through the streets in a dunce cap, or confine him in a "cowshed" [in the Cultural Revolution, a makeshift detention room for "cow ghosts and snake spirits"—Ed.], or throw him into a prison or have him beaten to death or shower him with insults until he was driven to suicide. In brief, the early demise of Lu Xun's corporeal self allowed longevity for his spiritual self. It is true that Emperor Mao anointed him as the "stiffest backbone," and true, too, that political hacks used this label as a stick to beat up on others. But that was not the fault of Lu Xun; it was a crime of the autocratic regime.

What about the other five "models"? Guo Moruo, a romantic poet in the 1920s whom people then called a "genius + hooligan," turned into a shameless sycophant after 1949. Mao Dun, formerly a "left-leaning petty bourgeois," turned into a slippery, mediocre survivor within the literary bureaucracy. Cao Yu transformed himself from a genius of drama into a craven bit-playing partner of the regime. Lao She, that master of Beijing brogue, was a "writer of the people" for a few years after 1949 but later, pinched between a cruel regime on one side and an unsympathetic family on the other, surrendered himself as fish food in Taiping Lake. And Ba Jin, the one who lived the longest and who received the most favors from the regime, changed from a prolific writer into a quasi vegetable.

In the early 1950s, when the sensitive Shen Congwen was persecuted to the point of attempting suicide, his old friend Ba Jin watched and said nothing. When Shen then chose to abandon writing and simply to remain silent, Ba Jin busied himself in extolling "the new era" and piling on when the regime attacked the liberal-minded writer Hu Feng. As Hu Feng and his associates were facing prison for their writings, Ba Jin found it in himself to express his "indignation" at them and to write articles crying "I accuse . . . !" in the *People's Daily* and the *Wenhui Daily* in Shanghai. He described Hu Feng's smile as "contemptuous" and compared Hu and his group to "pus" that makes a person retch. In a piece in the *Wenhui Daily* entitled "Their Crimes Must Be Punished Severely" (May 27, 1955), Ba Jin wrote that "we should turn their own methods of all-out attack against them; they are pus, and must be drained!" In the Anti-Rightist Campaign that followed two years later, many of Ba Jin's friends and acquaintances met with disaster while Ba Jin somehow emerged unscathed. This led him to redouble his expressions of fealty to the regime. During the 1959 celebrations of the tenth anniversary the Communist accession to power, he wrote articles, seven of them, with titles like "We Want to Build a Heaven on Earth," "Welcoming the New Light," and "Unsurpassed Glory."

But in the end his genuflecting did not inoculate him from persecution. The Cultural Revolution that arrived in 1966, sweeping all before it, swept into Ba Jin's family, too. We have already noted how it claimed the life of Lao She; for Ba Jin, it brought the first personal experience of what persecution feels like. Marauding Red Guards climbed over the wall at Ba Jin's residence in Shanghai and ordered the entire family out into the courtyard. Then they locked Ba Jin, his two sisters, and his daughter, Li Xiaolin, in a bathroom. Ba Jin's wife, Xiao Shan, was able to sneak away to the police station for help, but the police dared not intervene. Later Ba Jin was detained in a "cowshed" and repeatedly denounced. At a May Seventh Cadre School [a "thought-reform-through-labor" camp for officials and intellectuals—Ed.] he wrote a confession in which he excoriated himself and denounced colleagues as well. His wife died during the Cultural Revolution, and Ba Jin could not be with her at the end.

When the Cultural Revolution was over, Ba Jin wrote a series of essays that he published in a little book called *Random Thoughts*. In it he made pleas to "tell the truth" and for a "spirit of repentance." He wrote a self-dissection on "how a person can turn into a beast." Around the same time Hu Feng, whom Ba Jin had cruelly attacked two decades earlier, was given an official exoneration. Ba Jin was too embarrassed to visit Hu in person, but did write of his feelings of repentance toward the Hu Feng group in *Random Thoughts*. It was there, too, that he issued his call for a Museum of the Cultural Revolution whose purposes would be to look squarely at history's lessons and to avoid a repeat of disasters.

Appearing, as it did, within a flood of post-Mao "scar" literature whose main theme was to blame someone else—various perpetrators of Maoist violence and oppression—Ba Jin's willingness to be self-critical stood out as a rare display of conscience. It led readers to recall the hazy image of a Ba Jin in the pre-1949 years. But it is important to note how he always kept his truth-telling and his repentance carefully within the scope allowed by the Communist regime. He spoke only of events during 1966–1976, which the regime had officially declared to be "ten years of catastrophe." He held his tongue on the Hu Feng affair, which happened in 1954 and 1955, and then broke his silence after the regime announced its "reversal of verdict" on Hu Feng. Later, when the post-Mao regime's own ideological campaigns came along—the campaigns to criticize Bai Hua's "Unrequited Love" (1981), to "Eliminate Spiritual Pollution" (1983), and to "Oppose Bourgeois Liberalism" (1987)—Ba Jin no longer saw fit to "tell the truth." After the Tiananmen Massacre of

1989, and throughout the stultifying 1990s, when China was most in need of some truth-telling, and when it would have been especially appropriate for a big name like Ba Jin to speak out, he opted for golden silence. The noted scholar Zhu Xueqin was right to issue this challenge to Ba Jin a few years before he died: "He says that just three words have helped him to survive the last ten years: *tell the truth*. But there are plenty of truths waiting to be told. How about giving us some? It doesn't have to be a hundred sentences. Can't you give us just one? What could they do to you if you gave us just one?"

In sum, during the second half of Ba Jin's life, his cowardice outweighed his conscience and he uttered more falsity than truth. If we say that the pre-1949 Ba Jin was an independent writer who cried "I accuse!" and became the spokesperson for a generation of idealistic youth, then we should say that after 1949 the independent writer Ba Jin died and what remained was nothing more than a hired gun for the regime and a political flower vase.

From 1999 until the day he died, Ba Jin, the sole surviving "dean" of twentieth-century Chinese letters, lay in a ward inside the famous East China Hospital in Shanghai. (Only after he died did authorities reveal which hospital he was in.) Guards were posted on his floor and at the doors to the elevator that led to it. No one could see him without special permission. The "people's writer" could not talk, recognize people, move his hands, raise his feet, eat, or control his bladder or bowels. Basically in a vegetative state, he may not have been able to feel pain, either. Yet the media carried stories of how Ba Jin smiled and nodded his head in appreciation when high-ranking Communist officials came to wish him a happy birthday. It is rumored that Ba Jin's hospital care cost nearly 30,000 yuan a day, but if so, that would have been a pittance within the booming economy of greater Shanghai. So long as it gave the autocratic Party an opportunity to show off its "advanced culture," this was a small price to pay.

The image of a sick old man controlling a whole country is a specialty of dictatorships. Mao Zedong, in the weeks before he died, could not speak clearly, but just the shape of his lips was enough to wield power. One sentence gleaned from him outweighed ten thousand from anyone else, and he still held sway over hundreds of millions of people. In his very last years, Ba Jin was even more ill than Mao. It is said that on several occasions, when his mind was at least semi-clear, he requested euthanasia but was refused. The Party would not agree, his family would not agree, and "people who loved the great literary master" would not agree. Ba Jin had to accede to their wishes, had to respect a principle greater and more noble than that of his own suffering, and so agreed to "live for all of you."

It was in this condition that he remained chair of the All-China Writers' Association, the pinnacle of the literary corps that served the power elite. He was regularly listed as making "honorary" appearances at major events of political theater. Every year on his birthday, this "dean of the literary world," with the careful assistance of family members and hospital staff, accepted formulaic, reverential visits from representatives of the dictatorship and a coterie of literary pretenders. Birthday congratulations also poured in from across the land, especially from students in elementary and high schools. In 2003, when the whole country marked his one hundredth birthday, and the honorific title of "people's writer" was officially bestowed upon him, Premier Wen Jiabao paid him a bedside visit in person.

There is a long tradition in China of power-holders using cultural figures to buy popular favor to enhance their power. It began more than two thousand years ago, in pre-Qin times, when kings patronized groups of artists. The Communists, though, are number one in the creative application of the technique. They have shown how to use it to maximum benefit, how to execute it with maximum ruthlessness (only Stalin's exploitation of Gorky is comparable), and how to position their own political benefit as the sole criterion for its use. When the regime needs decoration, a famous literary figure is like a priceless antique vase, to be held on high for all to view; when the decorative need has passed, the vase can become a pile of broken shards, fit only to be to cast upon a barren plain. That is why Ba Jin's relatives need to be so super-careful in tending to him. His intrinsic literary value died long ago, but the Communists still see in him a decorative value that they can exploit. This value is, however, a fragile commodity; a careless inadvertency might shatter it.

In 2002, at the annual spring conventions of the Communist elite, official delegates inside the Great Hall of the People in Beijing selected Ba Jin to be vice chair of the Tenth People's Political Consultative

Conference. This was while Ba Jin himself was lying in a semi-vegetative state in a Shanghai hospital. Working overtime to keep Ba Jin's heart beating even as it appointed him to be a national leader, the regime had unwittingly provided an apt metaphor for the moral vacuity of its own rule. "Dead at heart," it continues to exact a price that all of China must pay.

On October 17, 2005, the day after Ba Jin's death, the *Jinling Evening News* in Nanjing carried this message: "We received the bad news of Ba Jin's passing shortly after 7:00 p.m. yesterday. Our reporter rushed to the East China Hospital, where tight security was in place. As more reporters arrived, so did armed police, who blocked the hospital's two gates. Only city government vehicles were allowed to enter or leave, as municipal leaders one after another went to pay their last respects to the venerable writer. As reporters gathered outside the gates in ever larger numbers, the police presence grew in kind."

So there you have it: tight security, government officials allowed to enter, everybody else blocked out—the very picture of the regime-kept Ba Jin at the end. Far from "the conscience of the century," he ended as a mirror of the intellectual in the totalitarian state: mediocre in literary work and timid in character, yet owner of a bizarrely outsized reputation. In these regards he is a fitting representative of others among the regime's kept intellectuals. To make things worse, the lavish words that officials and fellow litterateurs have heaped upon his recently departed spirit only highlight the humiliating incongruity between the reality of Ba Jin and the myth. What words like "master," "conscience," and "banner" in fact show is not that the intellectual world respects the old man but only that it sees advantage in playing the hypocritical language game that has become part of its culture. In truth, this game hurts a person. The regime's airtight security, its exaggerated solicitude, and its whispers of "heartfelt" concern only underscore the utter servility of the person who lives in the keep of the powerful. And extravagant praise, flamboyant exaggeration, and cynical hypocrisy from the pens of literati only magnify the humiliation.

Understanding these things, one can see clearly that insistence on Ba Jin as a "high-flying banner" is, in fact, tantamount to insistence that the Chinese intellectual world continue to hold a white flag of surrender to the political autocracy. It is tragic that Chinese intellectuals, despite all the disasters they have survived and all lessons they have learned, can look at a white flag, as it hangs limply, and somehow see a "high-flying banner" dancing in the sky.

At home in Beijing, October 25, 2005

*Originally published in* Minzhu Zhongguo *(Democratic China), October 27, 2005*
*Translated by Perry Link*

# ALONE IN WINTER

*To Xia*

The solitude of a winter night
is the blue of a blank computer screen
simply, obviously visible, and also nothing
so just think of me as cigarette
now to light, now to rub out
go ahead, smoke!
you'll never finish

A pair of bare feet crush into the snow
like an ice cube falling into a glass
drunkenness and madness
are the drooping wings of a crow
beneath the borderless shroud of earth
black flames sob in silence

The pen in my hand suddenly snaps
a sharp wind skewers the sky
stars disintegrate, then meet by chance in dreams
curses, dripping with blood, write lines of verse
the tenderness of skin remains
a gleaming light again shines on you

Solitude, plain to see
towering above the tears of the cold night
touches the marrow of the snow
and I
not smoke, not wine, not pen
am nothing but an old book
much like
poison-toothed *Wuthering Heights*

January 1, 1995

*Translated by Perry Link*

# VAN GOGH AND YOU

*For Xiao Xia*

Your penmanship puts me to shame
in your letters (each stroke a paragon)
who'd catch the hint of despair?
at the calluses where you grasp the pen
Van Gogh's sunflowers bloom

How precious that empty chair!
not for reading and writing, but for remembering
each shift of the shoulders calls up another time
you endure the raids with equanimity
and savor Van Gogh's images alone

With your heart in your mouth
each step may be your last
sensing obstacles ahead, you pick your way
across the opposite of love
and on the other side of death
where Van Gogh's Sower comes to grief
amid his sprouting seeds

For you, a single room is Heaven
returning home, deliverance
now, when everyone's become a singer

and there's none to mourn the dead
you alone keep still
beside that empty chair

Bloody deeds remembered grip the throat
words are salty, voices dim
neither round-the-clock surveillance
nor the watcher in your mind
can snatch away your pen
and the blizzard in the painting

Van Gogh's severed ear takes flight
seeking the right tint for you
the clumsy stride
of muddy peasant shoes
shall bear you to Jerusalem's wailing wall

August 14, 1997

*Translated by A. E. Clark*

# THE EROTIC CARNIVAL IN RECENT CHINESE HISTORY

◆　◆　◆　◆　◆

IN THE YEARS SINCE THE TIANANMEN MASSACRE, the rampant materialism of the power elite's moves to privatize wealth has given rise in China to a consumer culture that has grown ever more hedonistic, superficial, and vulgar, and the social function of this materialism has been to bolster the dictatorial political order. Sarcasm in the entertainment world has turned into a kind of spiritual massage that numbs people's consciences and paralyzes their memories; incessant propaganda about "the state drawing close to the people" reinforces the notion that the government is the savior of the people—who accordingly are its servants. Meanwhile an erotic carnival of products in commercial culture invite entry, real or fantasized, into a world of mistresses, prostitutes, adultery, one-night stands, and other forms of sexual abandon.

The craze for political revolution in decades past has now turned into a craze for money and sex. Mao Zedong, that most exalted icon of the revolutionary era, has gradually lost his halo to some very non-Maoist values, and even his own legacy has become a commodity. At the same time, the shameful truth about the tyrant's private life has become ever more clear. Stories about the peccadilloes of Mao and other high-level Party leaders of the past not only feed popular jokes today, but also serve officials of all ranks by offering them examples of how adultery is done. Thus the ghost of Mao not only helps the political "left" by supplying it with ideological language for stimulating narrow nationalism but also is of service to today's business elite, who get pointers on how to enjoy wealth and power.

The glorious dream of overnight riches has come to include a thirst for sex that happens night after night. When lust, long-suppressed during the Mao years, is suddenly released, it looks everywhere for action: "keeping mistresses"; "whoring"; what have you. The joys of adultery and the screams from the bed are then packaged as cultural products. Countless soap operas and blockbuster movies feed on the "flesh explosion" that is happening everywhere. Literature has entered the era of "writing the body." First came the "pretty-girl writers," who sold accounts of their personal sexual adventures, and then came the "pretty-boy writers," who did about the same. Next we saw the erotics of the white-collar bar, followed by the confessions of prostitutes, followed by straight-forward records of fact known as "diaries from the waist down." Next a woman, who claimed to hold the M.A. degree, posted nude photographs of herself on the Internet. "Sex literature" has boomed on the Internet and has deteriorated into bald expression of sexual appetite and fleshly encounter. No wisp of shame is visible.

## A Steady Rise in Exposure of Flesh

### 1. Eros That Broke through Government Restrictions in the 1980s

In the midst of China's passions for "liberation of thought" in the 1980s, commercial culture, largely from Hong Kong and Taiwan, seeped into the mainland and challenged the dictatorial status quo on two levels. First, it helped to undo Party culture. It helped people to get out of the "class struggle" mentality and turn toward more natural human feelings. Second, it helped to dismantle cultural elitism. It broke the hegemony of cultural elites and led to variety in the cultural marketplace and variety in the tastes of audiences. When popular culture like songs from Hong Kong and Taiwan, the martial arts fiction of Hong Kong writer Jin Yong, and the love stories of Taiwan writer Qiong Yao spread through the mainland, not only did people stop reading things that preached the Party line; they also turned quickly away from elite magazines like *People's Literature, Poetry,* and *Harvest* and the "serious" literature they contained. In short, popular culture performed a wonderful service in causing the Party-directed "great unity in culture" to collapse. It brought major divisions into the cultural market, where three main kinds of literature—official, elite, and commercial (or popular)—now existed in parallel. People were no longer limited to the forcible messages of official culture or the sermons of the intellectual elite; now they had other cultural products to choose from.

These new cultural products naturally involved the topics of love and sexual desire. Erotic liberation in the 1980s began with Hong Kong and Taiwan popular music, hand-copied novels, and Japanese films, with Japanese films and love songs of Taiwan crooner Teresa Teng leading the way. For an older generation of mainland listeners, who were accustomed to the "iron melodies" of state socialism, Teresa Teng's soft, velvet-throated sobs about the joys and pains of romantic love seemed to be nothing but decadence that eats away at revolutionary resolve. But her voice intoxicated the younger generation, the one that grew up after the Cultural Revolution. Even under the pressure of the "Anti-Spiritual Pollution Campaign" of 1983, Teresa Teng's songs remained popular all across China. They not only charmed listeners but inspired imitators, thereby planting seeds for later popular music on the mainland. In a similar way, the elegant long hair of the heroine of the Japanese movie *Pursuit,* and the undying devotion of the lovers in *Love Is a Many-Splendored Thing* dominated the nighttime erotic fantasies of urban youth.

By the middle 1980s, there were three main ways that Chinese people satisfied their erotic hunger. One was to consume foreign literature in translation, like the erotic novels of D. H. Lawrence. A second was to watch pornographic videotapes in secret; to gather at the home of a friend who had a VCR and watch "skin flicks" had become one of the more intimate modes of friendship. A third, for those who had the good luck to travel abroad, was to make tourist stops at the "red light districts" of the capitalist world. People returning to China from such trips were always happy to tell their buddies everything.

In literature, the erotic liberation that "reform and opening" allowed to China's writers did not extend to description of lust or the human body. Political strictures required that such topics still be packaged as "love." Zhang Jie's 1979 short story "Love Must Not Be Forgotten," famous for breaking political taboos, showed how totalitarian government can devastate human love, but the lovers in the story do not even hold hands. Romantic love was also important in the non-governmental, underground literary works like those that appeared in *Today* magazine; Shu Ting's poem "To an Oak" is a good example. Later in the 1980s, literary depictions of romantic love gradually added more sexuality. One reason Zhang Xianliang's 1984 novella *Mimosa* caused a stir was that it described sexual attraction between the male protagonist, a "rightist" intellectual banished to wander in the countryside, and a humble but healthy village woman who takes him in. But Zhang's broaching of sex was only a minor part of his ideological critique. His broader purposes were to widen the scope for creative freedom by breaking down restrictions on writers and, beyond that, to highlight the hard fate of intellectuals in contemporary China. He also expressed a faith, which he shared with other intellectuals at the time, in "the proletariat-as-God": his village woman from the lowest rungs of society offers her pure love and her lush body to save a down-and-out scholar, who finally gains official reprieve and "ascends" to a red carpet at the entrance to the Great Hall of the People in Beijing, where he is to attend a meeting. The 1986 film *Hibiscus Town* is another indictment of the Anti-Rightist Campaign. Its love story between a hard-luck scholar and a shrewish village woman won China's most coveted film prize. The example shows that, by that time, clandestine love between a repressed "rightist" and a "fallen woman" could already be viewed as a healthy sign of normal human feeling. Even the authorities accepted this view, as shown in their willingness to award a prize.

During the same years, Freud's theories on sexual desire spread on the mainland, and theories of the subconscious influenced the ways in which writers handled the topic of sex. It became stylish for writers to "begin with a concept." Wang Anyi, for example, wrote three novels about sexual attraction in 1986–1987, nicknamed the "three loves," which once again showed the distortion of sexuality under totalitarian rule. When I read these works, I had the feeling the author was taking Freud's *Three Essays on the Theory of Sexuality* as her guide to write about subconscious sexual drives. The reason Zhang Yimou's film *Red Sorghum* (1987) was such a hit was that it drew so freely upon the themes of raw sexuality and adultery. Its theme song, "Sister, Be Gutsy, Go Forward," was an unbridled endorsement of the primitive vitality of lust. Against the backdrop of fire-red sorghum in desolate northwestern China, under the broad blue sky and in full view of the bright sun, bandits violently abduct village women, wild adultery happens in the sorghum fields, bandits murder one another in competition for women, male laborers magically produce the widely renowned liquor "Six-Mile Red" by urinating into the heroine's brewing wine, and so on. All of this dramatic plot arrangement and character design not only sets the scene for marvelous consummations of male and female sexual desire; it creates a broader dream vision that carries magical vitality. That *Red Sorghum* could win prizes symbolizes a change in national attitudes toward sex: erotic display had come to be seen as "exuberant vitality."

The mysterious fusion of political taboo and clandestine eroticism found an even deeper and more artistic expression in Wang Xiaobo's novel *Golden Age*. The most affecting part of this story is the description of the life of the main character, Second Wang, a young urbanite who is sent to the countryside during the Mao Zedong era. The great dictator had directed that these "rusticated youth," as they were called, "receive re-education from the poor, low, and middle peasants." But part of what they actually learned was the rudiments of sexual awakening— plain, coarse, unrestrained, and laced with the excitement of consuming forbidden fruit. High school students who had not quite dared to hold hands in the city, once they answered the call of the Great Leader and went to the countryside, with its "communal living" and militaristic "brigades," suddenly found themselves in close proximity and with nothing to relieve the boredom except the presence of the opposite sex. Feelings of shame or wrongdoing associated with sex melted away. This led Wang Xiaobo to describe those "broad open skies," where rusticated youth were supposed to "do great things," as their place to "do great sex." The empty fields of rural China provided a wide-open playground for a generation of young people who were escaping years of sexual repression in the cities. In the Mao era, sentimental love among spoiled urbanites had been viewed as part of a "capitalist lifestyle" that had to be eliminated.

Secret sex was an even more monstrous crime, especially for a woman. Caught in a "private connection," a woman could be labeled a "broken shoe," and there was nothing more despicable than that. As they prepare for sex out in the fields, Second Wang and Chen Qingyang, the male and female protagonists of Wang Xiaobo's *Golden Age,* discuss the question of "broken shoes." The local people already view Chen as a broken shoe, but she can set the label aside. (She was not a broken shoe, by the way, until Second Wang's sexual aggression made her one.) Political prohibitions and ethical prejudices could still cause fear, but the thrill of eating forbidden fruit always remained as a counterweight.

Before the Cultural Revolution, no one would ever have dared to call the wife of a top leader a "broken shoe"; but during the Cultural Revolution, Red Guards hung a sign reading *"Broken Shoe"* around the neck of Wang Guangmei, wife of President Liu Shaoqi, who had come under vicious attack from Mao Zedong. When the Cultural Revolution was over, Liu Shaoqi and his widow were officially exonerated, and around the same time the term "broken shoe" also began to lose its connotation of evil. It became almost morally acceptable, and could even be applied to positive characters in novels. The change seemed to usher in an era of indulgence in which "sex" was redefined. The "broken shoe" label that people had once avoided like the plague had turned into a middle-class dream of prowling for "new shoes." On popular television shows on the mainland today, it is easy to hear lines like this: "Marriage is like a pair of shoes. Only those who wear them once or twice can tell if they really fit."

### 2. Enjoyment of Eros in the 1990s

In the nineties, popular culture came increasingly to be dominated and controlled by the market, and this spelled the end of its utility in undermining Party culture. Elite cultural figures, in pursuit of profit, rushed to join the new commercial culture, and as a result popular culture and Party culture began to converge. On the one hand, Party culture began more and more to rely on the trappings of pop culture to bring its messages to audiences. In an era of rising prosperity, the political dictatorship had special new needs for commercial entertainment with which to decorate its "happy" new order. And for its part, popular culture needed increasingly to rely on an authoritarian marketplace; it needed the major official media as platforms on which to sell its wares. Obsequiousness became the key to success in the mainland culture business. Each year the Party threw its extravaganza for Lunar New Year, and entertainers fell over themselves to appear on the show because they

knew it was the biggest of possible stages on which to advertise them-
selves. At the same time, the sexual elements in cultural products,
which originally had to have at least a bit of political flavor, began to
lose all of it and became out-and-out sex for sex's sake.

On January 26, 1991, I left Qincheng Prison in Beijing [having
served a nineteen-month sentence for "counterrevolutionary
instigation"—Ed.] and was escorted back to my home city of Dalian.
When I got off the train, and was browsing through the book stalls near
the station, an especially eye-catching magazine cover grabbed my at-
tention. It showed a beautifully curvaceous nude woman, semi-reclined.
The caption below read "Hot Enough to Wake the Dead." Headlines on
some of the other covers read "Exposé of China's Biggest Sex Abuse
Cases," "Secrets of the Oral Fixation," "Perverts Wandering Our Cam-
puses," "An Overwhelming Lust for BDSM," and "I'll Tell You the Se-
crets of Enjoying Sex." There was even a headline for "Mao Zedong and
His Second Wife He Zizhen."

I was astonished. This was less than two years after the Tiananmen
Massacre; Deng Xiaoping had not yet made his 1993 "Southern Tour,"
which is normally viewed as the event that opened a second round of
economic reform and restimulated China's material appetites; the gov-
ernment was still shouting itself hoarse about "opposing liberalization
and peaceful evolution [toward a Western model—Ed]." Two of the
main points in the ongoing campaign to "oppose liberalization" were
to squelch the private economy and to wipe out pornography. But as the
books and magazines on the stands before my eyes quite clearly showed,
the anti-pornography campaign had been useless. Not only had noth-
ing been wiped away, pornography had grown wildly and had now far
exceeded where it had been in the 1980s. Later, browsing through other
book markets in Dalian and Beijing, I learned that nothing was selling
better than sex and violence; a third kind of best-selling materials fo-
cused on secrets of the private lives of top Communist officials.

During the same years the works of the "serious authors" moved to-
ward the sensationalism of "sex literature," and the response was thun-
derous. Jia Pingwa's *Abandoned Capital* and Chen Zhongshi's *White
Deer Plain,* both published in 1993, were big hits. Zhang Yimou's film
*Judou* (1990) spotlighted "incestuous passion," and his *Raise the Red
Lantern* (1991) laid bare the rampant jealousies among a bevy of wives

and concubines and, under the dim light of red lanterns, their toe-curling sexual climaxes as well. The new prurience was visible even in the way the adultery theme in the American novel *The Bridges of Madison County* captured the imaginations of countless middle-aged wives in China. An uglier manifestation was the way the mainland media ballyhooed the news story from New Zealand about how the Misty poet Gu Cheng murdered his wife and then killed himself.

Cases such as these can be viewed as a roaring revival of Chinese literati traditions of "sex interest" among long-repressed mainlanders. Serious literature became the site of an "erotic carnival" within the newly emerging commercial culture. Passion for topics like adultery, incest, and polygamy, and exquisite appreciation of the finer points of extramarital love came to pervade the sexual cravings of the educated elite. The scholar-official's desire for more than one wife was imaginatively transformed into the desire for a palatial home in which a red lantern would be lit each night. It is hard not think of the great seventeenth-century erotic novel *The Plum in the Golden Vase,* the late-Ming popular stories of Feng Menglong, or the modern fiction of Eileen Chang or Zhang Henshui.

The scholar-official's dream for more than one wife could turn into real-life tragedy. Gu Cheng had both a wife and a mistress, but when the mistress left him and his wife asked for a divorce, his life fell apart. Anxiety—or call it madness—overwhelmed him and he murdered his wife with an axe and then killed himself. And what was the response of the mainland media to these events? It was to stir up a whirlwind of prurient interest. No one looked squarely at the brutal murder, or took the side of the murdered wife, Xie Ye. The spin was to see Gu Cheng as a romantic poet who "died for love." A few people actually took advantage of the media frenzy to promote themselves. These included Gu Cheng's mistress, a former lover of the mistress, and even Gu Cheng's father, the poet Gu Gong. In popular lore a murder case—a husband had killed a wife—turned into a tale of love's purity, and then into best-selling books that brought fame and riches to certain people.

### 3. A Carnival of Flesh in the Twenty-First Century

At the turn of the twenty-first century, women writers took over from men as the leading writers of eros. Even before the appearance of the "pretty-girl writers," Lin Bai, a woman, made a splash by describing sexual experience among very young girls. Then the middle-aged writers Zhang Kangkang and Tie Ning began to publish erotic stories like "Love Gallery" and *Woman of the Great Bath* that became best-sellers. An Dun's *Absolute Secrets,* purporting to record unfiltered accounts of female sexual experience, was popular for a time as well. But it was the younger generation of "pretty-girl writers" who hit the jackpot by "writing the body."

The first of these was Wei Hui, author of *Shanghai Baby* (1999), which exposed the name-brand panties of a beautiful upper-middle-class girl while attesting to the special strength and vigor of foreigners' erections. Drawing on old, colonial Shanghai, Wei Hui captures the mood of "good liquor and strong coffee"; drawing on the new Shanghai, she adds the pleasures of sex that were available to white-collar types in the toilets of bars. Sex in Wei Hui is a completely Westernized thing. Everything about the female protagonist, from her routine daily life to her pursuits of pleasure, is a knockoff of Western "cool": Western brand-name clothes envelop her body; Western-style bars absorb her night life; Western-style music sets her moods; Western-style decadence marks her decline. Even the ways she has sex—her excitements, her orgasms—are the products of a Western lover. In the end, the ultimate expression of her self-love comes from lesbians—who are also foreigners. At each chapter head there is a quotation from a Western author, poet, philosopher, nun . . . The feeling I get from reading her book is rather like recovering from a Valentine's Day of debauchery at a mainland Chinese bar.

In the novel *Candy* (2000), pretty-girl writer Mian Mian howls out an extended erotic confession and introduces us to the sensual landscape of Beijing's Sanlitun bar street and the southern boom-city of Shenzhen. We meet young bohemians and celebrities of the rock music world, sex predators and lonely white-collar beauties, all accompanied by wild music inside the black night, sipping Western liquor and coffee, and shooting illegal drugs. The pleasures of casual flirting and one-night stands produce a decadent, hippie-esque mood. The sexual indulgences of this social elite included a reversal of the classic pattern of "the old ox eating tender grass," i.e., the male-dominated tradition of rich old men looking for fresh-faced girls. Now, in China's age of prosperity, there were also rich old women looking for virgin boys to educate; in some bars, the customers who kept coming back hunting for sex were wealthy middle-aged women. By this time, fleshly desire and spiritual decadence had lost the quality of rebellion against official ideology that it had had in the 1980s; now it was just hedonism, hedonism, and more hedonism.

After *Candy* came the autobiographical work *Crow* by Jiu Dan. Her crude style and subpar narrative ability put her a world beneath Mian Mian and Wei Hui, but that did not stop the press from touting her as another of the pretty-girl writers. Jiu Dan had nothing to offer readers beyond a raw exposé of the lifestyle of mainland prostitutes in Singapore, peppered occasionally with some reflections on the hardships of selling flesh in a foreign country. Jiu Dan hyped her book with the phrase "the absolute truth" and considered the "contrived flesh" of other pretty-girl writers to be beneath contempt.

While Wei Hui, Mian Mian, and Jiu Dan were trying to outdo one another to be the best pretty-girl writer, another competitor, Muzi Mei, came reeling across the sky and made them all look pale by comparison. Muzi Mei's online publication *Love Letters Left Behind* lays all her private secrets bare, with special attention to the lower quarters. In diary form, she records the whole process—all the techniques, and every one of her squirms and groans—with all the men who have visited her bed. She rates each one for sexual ability and skill, and in one case even supplies the name of a male musician she has slept with. In the "Zippergate" case of former American president Clinton, it seems that the pressure of public opinion is what forced the woman, Monica Lewinsky, to release the evidence of semen on her dress; Muzi Mei, by contrast, is quite open about exposing every trace of her sexual activity to everyone on the Internet. The sex craze that Muzi Mei kicked off was enough to attract even China Central Television; its program *Moral Observer* interviewed Muzi Mei, allowing her to explain her obsession with one-night stands in terms of "human nature."

These pretty-girl writers, engaged as they were in a "flesh-writing competition," disparaged one another in interviews, and their squabbling itself became a hot topic in the press. Just as victory in battle goes to the brave, the relative stature of these writers in the public eye turned on whose self-exposure was most daring, most naked, most truthful.

Each new arrival on the scene had to—and did—outdare the last. Muzi Mei's sex diary eclipsed what had gone before, and the year 2003 went out as "the year of Muzi Mei." She once quipped, "If a male reporter wants to interview me, he first needs to come to my bed; the number of minutes his love-making can last is the number of minutes he'll have for questions."

Not long after Muzi Mei's interview on Central Television, a woman who said she was a graduate student emerged under the alluring bourgeois-romantic pen name "Green Eyes in Bamboo Shadows." She had been writing on the Internet for some time, but had got nowhere in attracting readers. Now, inspired by Muzi Mei's lower-body writing, she opted for a more radical method of body exposure—uploading nude photos of herself to the Internet. But this young litterateur still seemed a tad timid: she covered her sex with a palm leaf and cropped her head from the photos, leaving only her svelte limbs for view. It was just like a line from the poem "Song of the Lute Player" by Bai Juyi (772–846 CE): "Yet half-hiding her face with her lute." The coy occlusion only accentuated the sex appeal, of course. The headlessness and the palm leaf lent a certain air of mystery, a space for the accommodation of sexual fantasy from netizens. What kind of face went with this body? Did the body really belong to "Green Eyes in Bamboo Shadows," or was it a transplant from elsewhere? Is the missing part the face of an angel, or the stare of a frog?

Pornographic writing on the Internet has actually gone well beyond what the pretty-girl writers have done. It is easy to find examples that are more bald, brazen, and perverse; it's just that the media have not made as much of them. The writers who use the pen names "Little Spiffy" and "Your Slave," for example, have many works on group sex and mother–son incest. "Bourgeois-Bohemian" tells us about drugged rapes, peeping Toms, wife-swapping, incest, bestiality, science fiction sex, and more. Some specialize in "old men and virgins," others in "old women and boys." One has a special skill for depicting young men infatuated with women over 45. Many address the hot topic of sex between rich city men and young housekeepers from the countryside. Such works offer a smorgasbord of extras as well: drug fantasies, violent conquests, sadomasochism, and fetishes for feces and other excretions. There is even pornography written as children's stories.

Many of these authors are masters of producing works in series. Critics divide them into different schools: the "promiscuity school" that specializes in wild oats and incest; the "brute school" that focuses on sadomasochism and other violence; the "exchange school" that covers adultery, multiple partners, and wife-swapping; and the "fantasy school" that explores sexual fantasies (science fiction sex fits here). Another way they are categorized is by fictional setting: "the campus school," "the officialdom school," "the marketplace school," "the martial arts school," and more. Erotic literature on the Internet now has its own set of critical prizes. There are prizes for best author, best new author, most improved author, most popular author, best work (long- and short-form), and most innovative work. There are awards for contribution to the community and for cumulative achievement. All of this activity happens on privately managed websites. The circulation of works, the commentary, and the critical prizes have nothing to do with the government.

### The Pretty-Girl Economy Blossoms Everywhere

On television and in other media, literary descriptions of the female body have turned into the exposure of bodies on screens. The "pretty-girl economy" of the early twenty-first century is not just underground sex services at dance halls, hair salons, and expensive hotels; it reaches far beyond that. Commercial advertisements of all kinds adorn themselves with pictures of beautiful women, and girls in pursuit of overnight fame rush to big cities looking for opportunities. Packs of young women register for schools in the performing arts, pushing tuition at such places ever higher. "Star classes" that fraudulently promise entrées to stardom have popped up everywhere. Women who have had sex with famous directors and producers, and then have felt cheated when their expected rewards did not arrive, have sometimes decided that indignation outweighs embarrassment and revealed all. One of these women let the world know about director Huang Jianzhong and demanded compensation for his failed commitments to her. Another woman, named Gu, took Zhao Zhongxiang to court, also demanding that he compensate her for the payment she made to him with her body.

Turn on TV today and you can find a cornucopia of slim bodies and pretty faces: innumerable beauty contests, fashion model contests, singing contests, and "Super Girl" contests—all vying for viewers. The honored male guests who bestow the awards (mostly high officials, rich businessmen, or celebrities of the entertainment world) have beautiful young girls on their arms. The contestants on stage wear less and less clothing, ever thinner and more revealing, and add flirtatious speech and coy body language.

Sometimes romantic middle-aged women, people of some social repute, get up on stage as guests, bringing family members to cheer them on, and flaunt their private history with no sense of taboo: sexual awakening in childhood, first romantic love, the bittersweetness of marriage, their criteria today for choosing another partner, the pleasures and anxieties of single womanhood, the excitement and inevitability of adultery. When she reaches the point of greatest passion, the special guest's eyes glimmer with tears, and the host chokes back a sob. The audience is moved, too, and everybody joins the "reality show."

Today's television dramas all include at least one of: a love triangle, an extramarital affair, a mistress, or whoring. It doesn't matter if the topic is ancient history, martial arts, business, officialdom, anticorruption, military affairs, police chases, or small-town life, the bed of the mistress is the site of the downfall of a corrupt official. A love story cannot happen these days without some display of the body of the "other woman"; even dramas whose theme is nostalgia for the Communist revolution are laced with extramarital dalliance. Only the backdrops are different. In recent times, most of the clandestine sex happens at sites of high-level consumerism: Western restaurants or bars at expensive hotels; or the clubs, swimming pools, racetracks, or (the increasing favorite) golf courses of the power elite. Couched in environments of soft music and fresh flowers, one finds coffee to sip, cigars to smoke, Western liquor to savor, sweets to eat, limousines running to and fro, and expensive diamonds for use in flattery. Interspersed with the scenes of luxurious consumption, which are shown in color, we often see flashbacks, which are shown in black-and-white, to the way things used to be in the years of poverty: roadside stands, the barracks-style apartments of the socialist work units, plain clothes and simple food, cheap engagement presents, love held in the stranglehold of politics, and so on.

Of all the possible methods of castrating the human spirit, to feel fully satisfied by performance of fake intimacy must be the cruelest.

The reason for the explosive popularity of the new movie *Cell Phone* is its revelation of the private dirt of China's urban elite today. Here the age of sexual chaos and the age of high tech fly wingtip to wingtip; the cell phone, an indispensable tool of the adulterous husband, turns into a double-edged sword as the wife uses it to monitor the wayward spouse. The excitement and joy that the husband's affair brings to him gradually gives way to fear and embarrassment that the wife will track him down. The potential that either flirting or terror can emerge from the cell phone drives the husband to panic and constant falsity: each sentence he speaks is a lie, each facial expression a tawdry fraud. A mask of virtue covers a private world of secret motives, foul behavior, and perpetual jockeying to maintain the mask. Every conversation is a lie. The marriage is a lie. Each attempt at diversion is a farce, because the adulterous affair is a lie, too. Disgusting faces tell the lies, lascivious voices do the flirting. The film draws its material from the dark side of the human spirit, but in so doing gives us an honest account of the cynicism that pervades the life of the urban elite in China today. It shows not only how they hide their true thoughts from public view but also the duplicity in the ways they treat people in private. In its plot design, characters, dialogue, and music, *Cell Phone* is a comedy; but the ways in which it reveals the moral squalor of our society are hardly funny. It dresses in a well-pressed suit of clothes, but these cannot cover up people's sickness or the ruthless ways in which they treat one another. It highlights the moral contrast between children in the mountains, before the age of the telephone, and the movers and shakers of the cell phone culture in China today.

Outside of film, in the real world, and taking advantage of the new fungibility of power and money that pervades our society, the sex industry has burgeoned. Across the country, in rural and urban areas alike, streets are lined with shabby barbershops, foot massage parlors, Karaoke clubs, video parlors, small hotels, little restaurants, and motels— many offering sexual services on the side. In the big cities, high-class hotels, nightclubs, bars, and social clubs provide nights of sex for rich and influential men. Vacation getaways and seaside cities offer "mistress villages" and "lovers' gardens." Prostitution remains illegal in China, but

rough estimates put the number of prostitutes in the country some-
where above six million, making us number one in the world. Commer-
cial competition and the fungibility of money and power have created a
category of women who are packaged mainly as gifts for clients: lover-
secretaries, hired "public relations" consultants, and banquet escorts. It
has become common courtesy when doing business to invite clients to
"float" [the Chinese term is a homonym for "enjoy sexually"—Ed.] these
women.

When adults are increasingly open about sex, the attitudes and be-
havior of the young naturally fall in line. Offspring of the urban elite
are frequently single children who have grown up in the lap of luxury,
with no brothers or sisters to provide competition. They are "little em-
perors" at home, and outside the home struggle to present themselves
as "new-era types," "bourgeois-Bohemians," or the like. In matters of
sex, they seek early and immediate pleasure and like to follow their
impulses into one-night stands and "Internet romance." They feel no
shame about premarital sex and favor postponement of the responsi-
bilities of marriage and family. The Chinese Planned Parenthood As-
sociation did a survey of 196 research studies and found that 60 percent
of people have had sexual experience before marriage. A saying that
circulates among young urban Chinese says, "Going to bed before mar-
riage is as simple as going to the toilet." Reports of young women aban-
doning infants are increasing. A recent newspaper headline tells us:
"Young Girl Has Sex with Her Pet Pekinese."

The fashions of sex have brought innovation even to the restaurant
business. We have already seen the "gold banquets" designed to shower
good luck on customers and the "infant soups" that are supposed to
bring them longevity, but we now we see "female body banquets" that
deliver erotic rewards. A nude female human being reclines on a table
and waits as her body is piled high with sumptuous dishes. Presto! A
multifaceted feast for the senses. A famous restaurant in Shenzhen,
which sells a dumpling that it calls a "humpling," is hardly alone in in-
venting sexually charged names for its delicacies. Here are some other
new names for dishes: "Hooker Grabs a John," "Thrice Tricking the Mis-
tress," "Love That Viagra," "The Beauty Disrobes," "The Little Secretary
Comes to the Boss," "Beauty Exits the Bath." Even the order of presenta-
tion of dishes can follow the order of lovemaking: a meal begins with

"Love at First Sight" and moves to "Exchange of Flirting Glances" and then to "Fooling Around"; next we get "Glued as One," after which comes "His Pleasure, Her Joy"; finally, at the sweet sorrow of parting, everybody is served a dish of "Lover's Tears." Especially stunning is the fact that cultured people—literary people—can view this kind of blatant "sex banquet" as a form of high culture. They quote the poetic line "With bodies warm and stomachs full, thoughts next turn to sex" and cite the Chinese sex craze as evidence that the society is achieving middle-class prosperity. Cuisine is "three parts flavor, seven parts culture"—and that is very high-class. China today is beyond subsistence worries, and it is only right that lust-culture should be next. This is progress, an advance, even a kind of spiritual and moral pursuit.

### The Eroticization of Nationalist Hate on the Internet

The erotic carnival on the Internet expresses more than sex alone. Nationalist extremists, who call themselves "patriots," borrow sexual language to express hate. When their targets happen to be women, misogynist language does double duty. In the furor over reports that a group of Japanese men bought Chinese prostitutes in Zhuhai, for example, the "patriots" not only heaped teeth-clenching anger upon the Japanese; they also directed verbal violence at the Chinese girls who had sold themselves.

On April 4, 2004, on a bright, warm Sunday in Beijing's Yuyuantan Park, crowds came out to enjoy the "cherry-blossom festival." When two young Chinese women, dressed in Japanese kimonos, were taking photos under the cherry blossoms, they ignited the ire of a group of "patriots," who surrounded the two and beat them. Onlookers gathered, but no one intervened. In fact the crowd began to taunt the victims: "Being Chinese isn't good enough for you?! You have to go be Japanese?! You deserve it!" When news of the incident hit the Internet, a few voices did decry the violence, but many others said the beating was exactly right. Chinese women who "adore Japan" like this not only should be cursed and beaten; their beaten bodies should be shipped off to Japan, to brothels, where they can "adore Japan" all they like.

Around the same time, "patriotic" netizens showered sexually laden invective upon Central Television anchor Zhang Yue after she wore a scarf that seemed to bear the "rising sun" of the Japanese flag. The tough guys of the "angry youth" took offense. Eventually Central Television released a clarification: Zhang Yue's scarf was a famous Italian brand, and had nothing to do with Japan.

But of all the examples of how hooligans attack Chinese women in the name of "patriotism," none beats the "Japanese Flag Clothing Incident" that befell movie star Zhao Wei. In 2001, in making an advertisement for a clothing company, Zhao wore an item that bore an image that resembled something in a Japanese military flag. Someone noticed, pointed out the resemblance, and posted photos on the Internet. Nationalist passions immediately gushed from across society. Heaven-rending, earth-shattering denunciations and curses filled cyberspace. The self-righteous invective originated not just from ordinary netizens but from so-called scholars and experts as well. Under immense pressure, a helpless Zhao Wei could only apologize. But that did not prevent the "Japanese Flag Clothing Incident" from surviving as a hot topic on the Internet, right to the present day. A call to denounce Zhao Wei still pops up near the top of search-result lists at NetEase, where, as of mid-2004, it had received more than 40,000 clicks, more than any other item.

With popular nationalist passions cresting higher and higher, and with the government, which needs nationalism in order to ease the crisis of its moral legitimacy, in no mood to cool things down, netizens are free to wield the blade of patriotism any way they like. The continuing Internet attacks on Zhao Wei include denunciation, demands that she make further apologies, and demands that the film industry ban her from work. But they go further, to include language of obscene violence. The *People's Daily*, which is the Communist Party's flagship newspaper, runs an Internet chat room called "Strong Nation Forum" where a great deal has been said about what kind of physical punishment Zhao Wei deserves for being a traitor and a whore for soldiers. Should her breasts be cut off first, or should that privilege go to her nose and ears? At Web portals like Sina, NetEase, and Sohu, people debate which kind of male animal should rape Zhao Wei. Which would be most satisfying to watch?

Zhao Wei's purpose in wearing the clothing company's clothes had been purely commercial, but the eyes of the "patriots" saw much more. To them, she had been supporting Japanese militarism, and that was treason. Such treason turned her into a "sex chick" for the Imperial Japanese Army, in essence a high-class comfort woman. A shameless hussy like that? If the little Japanese soldiers can do her, why can't we patriots do her? It was not enough, either, to attack Zhao Wei alone. Her female forebears had to be got as well: "Fuck eight generations of her ancestors!" as one put it. The venting of hatred led to an explosion of obscene language; "patriotic" passion led to unbridled sexual violence.

Patriotism is generally viewed as a moral position sufficiently exalted that no one questions it. Add to this the fact that the Internet provides people with nearly perfect anonymity, and the combination leaves Internet "patriots" utterly free to spout opinions as they like, brimming with confidence and with no inhibition from either fear of repercussion or the fetters of conscience. To put it bluntly, patriotism provides a cover of legitimacy for sexual abuse on the Internet. Vulgar verbal violence against a female movie star can dress up as something right and proper—a way to express everybody's nationalist passions—at the same time that it allows hooligans a way to indulge in fantasy about inflicting sexual violence on a beautiful and famous woman. It is just one more item in the erotic carnival we have been considering, except that this one takes place under the veil of patriotism. Next to the crude body-writing of the "pretty-girl writers," however, this kind of hiding eros inside stately arches of patriotism is more shameless, more vulgar, and more brutal. Patriotism has become the moral cover under which bullies carry out verbal assassinations and indulge animal desires, even as they pretend to be passing moral judgment on others. It is not merely the last refuge of political scoundrels; it has become a cudgel in the hand of moral scoundrels, too.

This perverse "patriotism" not only confuses right and wrong but carries to an extreme that distortion of true patriotism that says "better to be a slave at home than to suffer a single insult from abroad." In a television drama *Fragrant Flowers of May,* the Chinese characters are callous, deceitful, scheming, and cruel—hardly better than wolves—in the ways they treat other Chinese. But don't worry, the film director can rescue their moral status by showing us how "patriotic" they all are. He can do this because, although Chinese people cheating other Chinese people may be immoral, Chinese people cheating foreigners shows ethnic solidarity and the integrity of patriots. The boss of an antique shop can oppress his fellow Chinese into agony and death, but because he blocks the flow of national treasures out of the country, he is a paragon of patriotism. In principle this is no different from the way Mao Zedong is credited, right to the present day, as savior of the nation, the one who let "the Chinese people stand up." Mao never came close to treating the Chinese people themselves as human beings, but that somehow is beside the point.

### The Place of the Erotic Carnival in the Society and Politics of China Today

From fiction to real-life diaries to graphic language, the pursuit of eros in China in recent decades has brought ever more audacious exposure of the human body, and the vast, borderless Internet has helped to make the spread easier and more open. Most of the millions of Chinese who use this new high-tech medium use it for pleasure, and, among the pleasures, sexual titillation and fantasy have reached to unprecedented extents. The spiritual emptiness of China today is now clearly visible from the angle of sex.

How should we understand this spread?

Many point their fingers at the marketization and globalization of our society, and there can be no denying that many of the modern modes of exploitation of the female body for commercial purposes have come to China from the West. Western women who have marketed exposure of their bodies by daring to create "live nude shows"—such as Madonna walking down the street naked, or Italy's porn-starlet politician "La Cicciolina"—have made sensational entertainment news in China. Our country's pretty-girl writers may have been influenced by their examples. In an age of commerce, when reputation becomes a commercial commodity, body-writing is not purely about sexual release, sexual fantasy, or sexual pleasure; it is also an extremely powerful and practical way in which to become well known. Especially in China, a patriarchal society where political power is the most important kind of power, if an unknown young woman wants a shortcut to a better position in the world, it is only natural that she make use of her specifically female resources and sell her appearance in exchange for wealth, status, or attention. The shortcut that mistresses take is to market themselves among the male power elite, competing to see who can hook the highest-ranking and richest man. The shortcut that the pretty-girl writers take is to sell their bodies to the public in literary form, tearing down one taboo after another in a competition to market the body by seeing who can expose more of it.

In my view, however, to attribute China's spiritual and moral emptiness to marketization and globalization is superficial. The "New Left" also blames marketization and globalization for China's polarization of wealth and its mind-boggling corruption, but this explanation, whether we speak of sex or corruption, diverts attention from much deeper causes. It ignores the obvious fact that China's system itself is antihumane and antimoral. The biggest and most destructive shamelessness in China today is political shamelessness. The best way to understand sexual shamelessness is to look at how political shamelessness caused it.

Step one is to understand the utter bifurcation between pretense and reality in these matters. In its language, officialdom still presents the noble face of "rejecting the slightest hint of corruption." Traditional ethical norms still stand, in their immaculate dignity, and the Communist Party officially opposes corruption and prohibits the power elite from keeping mistresses. At the same time, though, officials everywhere, including those charged with the anticorruption efforts, slip into debauchery. One needn't rely only on ubiquitous rumor for evidence. Why, if sexual corruption were not such a problem, would the new "Party discipline" rules that have just been announced be so specific in their prohibitions? No "keeping mistresses," no "hunting for lovers," and no "whoring," say the rules.

In its public stance, the regime calls itself a "representative of advanced culture." It sometimes cracks down on prostitution and has no taste for the competition in literature to see who can get their pants off first. It prevents Chinese women from doing "live sex shows"—they can be nude only in writing or photographs. Meanwhile, at the personal level, no one actually cares about ethics. Just as in matters of revolution, political power, patriotism, fame, profit, and many other things, in matters of sex, too, the end always justifies the means. This makes it possible for government departments in charge of stamping out pornography to open dance halls; for law enforcement agencies to shelter underground prostitution if they want; and for officials who denounce corruption during the day to slip into the beds of their mistresses at night.

The roots of this cynicism and moral vacuity must be traced to the Mao era. It was then (an era that "leftist" nostalgia today presents as one of moral purity) that the nation's spirit suffered its worst devastation. During the Cultural Revolution people "handed their reddest hearts to Chairman Mao." Why, after doing that, would one still need one's own spirit? Anyone who declined to hand his or her heart to Mao was—for that reason—"counterrevolutionary." The cruel "struggle" that Mao's tyranny infused throughout society caused people to scramble to sell their souls: hate your spouse, denounce your father, betray your friend, pile on a helpless victim, say anything in order to remain "correct." The blunt, unreasoning bludgeons of Mao's political campaigns, which arrived in an unending parade, eventually demolished even the most commonplace of ethical notions in Chinese life.

The pattern has abated in the post-Mao years, but it has far from disappeared. After the 1989 Tiananmen Massacre, a campaign to "test loyalty" forced people to "display a correct attitude" about the "counterrevolutionary riot." A decade later came a comprehensive, no-holds-barred campaign to eradicate Falungong, and once again people across society were forced to betray their consciences in public shows. If China has turned into a nation of people who lie to their own consciences, how can we possibly build healthy public values?

Everyone knows that the profit motive has come to dominate Chinese society in the post-Mao years. It is no longer a crime to be self-interested, and there has been a certain expansion of individual space. Still, compared to the immense power of the dictatorial state, the individual remains minuscule. People who rely solely on themselves to make it in the Chinese world—no matter how outstanding, intelligent, or even unscrupulous they might be—can never do better than those who make it by ingratiating themselves into Party-dominated power elite. The pretty-girl writers can garner some rewards by selling their private secrets or by writing about their bodies, but in the end—unless they have a powerful backer in the Party-state—they pay a price for their offense to the establishment that they challenge. The regime has denounced Muzi Mei and banned her works. Her days as a famous pretty-girl writer, out in the open, have passed, as fleeting as a mist. Hong Ying's novel *K* has recently been banned as well, ostensibly for its "pornographic description." *K* is a fictional version of the love affair between Julian Bell, a nephew of Virginia Woolf, and the Chinese writer Ling Shuhua, who was married at the time of the affair to Chen Yuan, a famous professor of Chinese literature. The most absurd aspect of the ban on *K,* and the reason it shows what happens when one offends the power elite, is that the ban came not from any government office in charge of ideology but from an Intermediate People's Court in Changchun City, Jilin Province, where the well-connected daughter of Chen Yuan and Ling Shuhua sued Hong Ying for libel of her parents and won, even though the parents were both long deceased.

The resources that the pretty-girl writers have relied on in their efforts to get somewhere inside this hypocritical, patriarchal system that we inhabit have been, in the final analysis, their own bodies. From this perspective their work, whatever else one says about it, is authentic self-expression and does say something about personal freedom. It is "outside the system" and expresses one kind of genuine humanity. I say this in order to point out that, in the context of the shameless and unscrupulous patterns of China's power elite today, and set against examples of other famous women in our society—women who have relied on official power to gain and hold the wealth and fame that they enjoy—the ways of pretty-girl writers actually look remarkably upright and clean. Famous women who rely exclusively on resources "inside the system" wear masks of spotless propriety and reap much greater "success." Consider Yang Lan, the extremely wealthy television hostess. When the scandal of her husband Wu Zheng's fake diploma was exposed, she offered no apology, nor did he, but that was only the beginning. She did everything she could to cover up her husband's disgrace by preventing reports of the fake diploma from reaching the domestic and foreign media and by employing the foulest of tactics to intimidate the people who had exposed the fraud. None of that repressive behavior hurt her, though. In this morally bankrupt system we live under, Yang Lan continues to enjoy the prestige of a position as anchor for Central

Television as well as a role as an "Ambassador for the Olympic Bid." Protected both by the system and by her great wealth, she stands pristine as ever, enveloped in glory. In China, to be a pretty-girl writer is "illegitimate," both politically and morally; to be high in the power elite is to be impervious, both politically and morally.

That said, we must not conclude that blackballed pretty-girl writers reap no harvests at all. Official bans and societal censure combined cannot completely suppress their popularity or strip their body-writing of its profits. There are several reasons for this. One is that the popular appeal of official ideology has dwindled to almost nothing. Another is that a growing contrarian spirit now often turns banned books into best-sellers, which become all the more popular precisely because they have been banned. Such books can spread through the so-called second channel of publication, which is composed of outlets that are technically state-sponsored but sell books outside the official Xinhua Bookstore and are not easy for officials to regulate. Muzi Mei's *Love Letters Left Behind,* for example, had an initial print run, at an official press, of 100,000 copies; then, after it was banned and the unsold copies were confiscated, its appeal to readers skyrocketed. A pirated edition, which was easy to find on streetside book stands and corner bookstores, sold several hundred thousand copies. Normally, pirated editions of best-sellers sell for much less than the official versions, but this was not the case for *Love Letters Left Behind,* whose official version sold for 20 yuan and whose pirated editions sold for 22 or 25 yuan.

In addition, China's opening to the outside world in recent decades has made new markets available to "rebellious" Chinese writers and their banned books. Whether we speak of the political writings of dissidents or the literary works of unruly authors, anything the regime censors tends to attract attention from Westerners. Among the pretty-girl writers, the luckiest in this regard was Wei Hui, the first to be censored. The regime's ban on *Shanghai Baby* became an advertisement for it around the world, and it sold well. We can't exactly say Wei Hui became the "Oriental pet" of the great Western world, but she did see a tidy sum in royalties.

Moreover, some of the "success" of the pretty-girl writers went beyond money. Their reputations inside China, although negative on the whole, were not entirely so. A few literary critics, some feminist scholars of sexuality, and many young Internet users welcomed Muzi Mei for the controversy she created. Her radical self-exposure was more than a celebration of her personal sexuality; it was a subversion of male dominance in sexual matters and a realization of true independence from male power. It is not clear whether Muzi Mei consciously intended this effect or not, but what she did amounted to an attack on the traditional system of male authority.

## Conclusion

China has transitioned from politics-are-everything in the Mao era to money-is-everything in the post-Mao years. A totalitarian society dominated by politics has turned into a post-totalitarian society where the economy is king and "stability" is the government's top priority. But a commonality—amorality—has underlain the two periods and has been there all along. The extreme political hypocrisy of the Mao years has blossomed, in post-Mao times, into a bouquet of hypocrisies in the several spheres of public life: officials are cynical about their governing duties, businesses are cynical about product quality, and scholars are cynical about academic standards. The whole society seems to have tossed integrity aside, as fakes and counterfeits sweep the nation. In this sea of counterfeits, the mightiest of them all—counterfeit democracy—is precisely the area that the current regime is most loath to let anyone talk about. In short, the inhumanity of the Mao era, which left China in moral shambles, is the most important cause of the widespread and oft-noted "values vacuum" that we observe today.

In this situation, sexual indulgence becomes a handy partner for a dictatorship that is trying to stay on top of a society of rising prosperity. Chinese people were so repressed during the Mao era, sexually and otherwise, that when ideas about freedom trickled in from the outside, many of them had great appeal. But while ideas about political freedom—speech, assembly, elections, and so on—could have led to a liberation in the Chinese people of humanity's best qualities, and could have brought dignity to individuals, the idea of sexual freedom did not support political democracy so much as it harked back to traditions of sexual abandon in China's imperial times. It siphoned interest in freedom toward thoughts of concubinage, elegant prostitution, and the bedroom arts as they are celebrated in premodern pornography. This has been just fine with today's dictators. It fits with the moral rot and political gangsterism that years of hypocrisy have generated, and it diverts the thirst for freedom into a politically innocuous direction.

At home in Beijing, June 13, 2004

*Originally published at the website of Chinese Pen, http://chinesepen.org/Index.shtml*
*Translated by Nick Admussen*

# YOUR LIFELONG PRISONER

*To Xia*

*My dear,*
*I'll never give up the struggle for freedom from the oppressors'*
*jail, but I'll be your willing prisoner for life.*

I'm your lifelong prisoner, my love
I want to live in your dark insides
surviving on the dregs in your blood

inspired by the flow of your estrogen

I hear your constant heartbeat
drop by drop, like melted snow from a mountain stream
if I were a stubborn, million-year rock
you'd bore right through me
drop by drop
day and night

Inside you
I grope in the dark
and use the wine you've drunk
to write poems looking for you
I plead like a deaf man begging for sound
Let the dance of love intoxicate your body

I always feel
your lungs rise and fall when you smoke
in an amazing rhythm
you exhale my toxins
I inhale fresh air to nourish my soul

I'm your lifelong prisoner, my love
like a baby loath to be born
clinging to your warm uterus
you provide all my oxygen
all my serenity

A baby prisoner
in the depths of your being
unafraid of alcohol and nicotine
the poisons of your loneliness
I need your poisons
need them too much

Maybe as your prisoner
I'll never see the light of day
but I believe
darkness is my destiny
inside you
all is well

The glitter of the outside world
scares me
exhausts me
I focus on
your darkness—
simple and impenetrable

January 1, 1997

*Translated by Susan Wilf*

# FROM WANG SHUO'S WICKED SATIRE TO HU GE'S *EGAO*

## Political Humor in a Post-Totalitarian Dictatorship

◆　◆　◆　◆　◆

*In the essay that follows, Liu Xiaobo has much to say about* egao, *a term that is almost impossible to translate. E is "evil" or "wicked," and* gao *is a colloquial and highly flexible word whose meanings range across "do," "make," and "work on," but often carry a somewhat negative flavor, rather like "mess with" in English. Liu did not invent the compound* egao. *It arose in the online game culture of the Chinese-language Internet, apparently first in Taiwan, where players adapted it from a Japanese term. When it reached mainland China, it spread well beyond the gaming world and took on a range of new meanings.*

*Depending on context, any of the following can be used to translate* egao *as a verb: satire, debunk, parody, skewer, lampoon, mock, expose, tear down, upset, invert, dismantle, make fun of. As a noun, one might use* spoof, hoax, farce, *or* prank. *To choose among these terms every time* egao *appears in Liu's essay would be a challenge. And even if the challenge were met, the thread of unity that runs through the essay because of the repetition of the term would be lost. Accordingly we do not translate* egao, *but settle for romanization.—Ed.*

FOR THE PAST TWO YEARS, egao has been popular on the Chinese Internet. It uses parody, twisted meanings, and odd juxtapositions to produce an "air of absurdity" that pokes fun at tradition, authority, famous people, fashions, and major public events. Big names in film and television have been favorite targets, and so have cultural icons, current fads, and the Mao-era "red classics." Recent searches on my computer yield some startling results: more than 300,000 egao on film director Chen Kaige; more than 900,000 on the Super Girl sweepstakes and nearly 200,000 more on the Fine Boy sweepstakes; 110,000 on the red classics, and a total of more than 2.7 million on the World Cup.

The examples that are truly creative, truly subversive—the ones that people credit with "cold humor"—often go viral. This famously happened when Hu Ge, an ordinary netizen, produced a short film called *The Bloody Case That a Steamed Bun Caused,* which was a parody of *The Promise,* a blockbuster film by the illustrious director Chen Kaige. Hu's short piece stirred up a storm when it appeared on the Internet in late 2005, and Hu became a celebrity overnight. It almost seemed as if the two artists, the nobody and the great director, were standing side by side in the pantheon of Chinese filmmakers.

Very soon thereafter, the egao fad had spread all over the Internet. When Ang Lee's *Brokeback Mountain* won an Oscar, 200 parodies of it popped up. The day after the release of Huang Jianxiang's "Three Minutes of Passion" about World Cup soccer, more than thirty parody versions were on the Web. Soon every website worth its salt had its own "egao specialists," and analysts had identified five distinct schools of egao artistry: the "Fools," the "Steamed Buns," the "Braggarts," the "Fans," and the "Flashers." They all have their egao websites and they classify their efforts by category: those that "egao MTV," "egao big movies," "egao the famous," "egao idols," "egao the classics," "egao photographs," "egao the theater," and so on. A few days ago I searched "egao" on Baidu and got 11.4 million results. No wonder we hear the popular sayings, "No egao means no fun," and "If it doesn't egao, it's not a website."

An astute critic observed in 2006: "Egao has mushroomed in recent years, both inside China and among Chinese living abroad, and has become especially spirited in the past several months. It reaches every aspect of life and all the senses of sight, hearing, and touch. It started in two dimensions and moved to three. It appeared first on posters and moved all the way to Adobe flash. Last year we had the explosive *Steamed Bun* video, and now we see the spoof of *Sparkling Red Star,* the Communist classic for children. The nature of egao is to use absurdity to generate humor—a cold humor that mocks phenomena in society. Egao also liberates and celebrates the rich imagination and creativity of netizens. An age of entertainment that really does belong to the nation as a whole has finally arrived."

## Wang Shuo's Sarcasm in Fiction Paves the Way for Online Egao

The blossoming of egao of course owes a great deal to the vast new access to information and the broad new platform for popular expression that the Internet provides. The era in which intellectual and political elites in China could monopolize public expression is gone forever. The Internet makes room for popular expression that is quick, convenient, anonymous, and public, and so has become an ideal playing field for fearless sarcasm, a place to let everything hang out.

But it would be a mistake to conclude that egao is purely the offspring of the Internet. Its spirit can be traced to the 1980s, when the first signs of its distinctive kind of sarcasm appeared in the "quasi-hippie" culture of the post-Mao years. The songwriter Cui Jian showed it in his articulation of the voice of rebellious youth. Cui's song "Rockin' and Rollin' on the New Long March" was a forerunner of today's egao of the red classics. His interpretation of the red song "Nanniwan," in particular, threw stalwarts of the old left like Wang Zhen into fits of rage. Slightly later, at the end of the 1980s and the beginning of the 1990s, Wang Shuo's literary sarcasm suddenly appeared and created a major stir. Wang's fiction satirized the Party's ideological language and undermined the authority of its officials, and can be seen as the maturation of the egao spirit.

With the emergence of Wang Shuo, the rebellious spirit of a younger generation of Chinese turned away from the suspicion and shouting that anger generated and toward the sarcasm and insults that jokes make possible. This was the generation that had grown up with solemn lines like "I do not believe!" in Bei Dao's poetry and "I have nothing to my name . . ." in Cui Jian's lyrics. With the 1989 Tiananmen Massacre, this generation saw its passions for freedom impaled on bloody bayonets and its youthful idealism crushed into moans beneath the treads of tanks. In the early 1990s, in the gloom of the terror that followed the massacre, and with nowhere to release its shock and anger, this generation was forced into general despair and a sense of helplessness. There could be no outlet for them at the level of the official discourse, because the Communist Party's assiduous opposition to "Westerniza- tion" and "peaceful evolution (in a Western direction)" made any serious discussion of questions in the humanities impossible. Popular amuse- ments were almost the only possible outlets for these young people, and the result was a huge outpouring of sarcasm—mocking others and pretending to mock themselves—in phrases (many of which were the inventions of Wang Shuo) such as "Whatever you do, don't view me as a person;" "I'm a philistine, too;" "Not a tad of seriousness here;" or "I'm a hooligan, so who am I afraid of?" In short, Wang Shuo's sarcasm— and Wang Xiaobo's humor after that—enabled people at least some escape from the suffocating effects of the pervasive terror that followed the Tiananmen Massacre.

Wang Shuo is a gifted storyteller and is especially good at using "cold" humor to evoke the pains and joys in the daily lives of little people. His heroes, who accept the label "riffraff" that the elites give to them, mock themselves, "play" with life, satirize pompous authority and enjoy ripping masks off gentlemen. Wang is, moreover, a wizard of linguistic chemistry. He can take the argot of hooligans from the alley- ways of Beijing and brew it together with pretentious Communist jar- gon to produce his own special kind of language. He applies the black wit of the Beijing dialect to a red Beijing whose odor has already begun to change from spoilage. He uses alleyway vocabulary to needle self- proclaimed avant-garde literary heroes. His smart, frank, biting humor brings the fraudulent edifice of official pride crashing to the ground and shows that the "modern" pretenses of the intellectual elite, once the lids are removed, amount to practically nothing. In short, Wang Shuo invented a "new Beijing dialect" that devastates political and intellec- tual pretensions with equal flair.

During the 1990s, Wang Shuo's influence quickly permeated the entire cultural scene. It showed in television, film, literature, art, and criticism.

Wang Shuo's "Stories of the Editorial Office" led the way in satiric television and film. The family comedy "I Love My Home" by Ying Da and Liang Zuo was an early imitator, and then came a plethora of spoof-ridden historical dramas. Next came "Tall Tales of the Journey to the West," starring Zhou Xinchi, and a number of Feng Xiaogang's Chinese New Year comedies. In 2006, Ning Hao's film *Crazy Stone*, although low-budget, was a huge box-office success.

In the area of art, Wang Shuo's sarcasm and Western pop combined to give rise during the 1990s to a "Chinese pop" that fed on mockery of the red classics. Wang Guangyi's Cultural Revolution series, Liu Xiaodong's "Joke" series, Zhang Xiaogang's Mao-era "Extended Family" series, and a variety of performance and installation art are all examples of this trend. But the painter Fang Lijun is the best example in the art world of the spirit of egao in the years after Tiananmen. On the principles that "ugliness is beauty," "stupidity is wisdom," and "insult is elegance," Fang created his "bald idiot" series, a wickedly incisive portrayal of China's mood after the massacre. He shows imbecilic smiles as responses to shock, eyes that have glassed over from extreme trauma, and the self-abasement and self-taunting of people who are powerless to resist. [See, for example, his painting *Howl*, easily available on the Internet.—Ed.]

In the early years of the twenty-first century, "sex-writing" [in Chinese, *segao*, which rhymes with *egao*—Ed.] took a lead in the mushrooming trend toward satire. Among the urban young, Wang Shuo's "playing for thrills" gradually turned into "playing it cool," and some of the best at playing it cool were the so-called pretty-girl writers such as Wei Hui, Mian Mian, and Muzi Mei, who highlighted sexual indulgence, spiritual decadence, and name-brand consumerism. Their coquettish language, fashionably sprinkled with Western-language terms, set a trend among the urban upper middle class. Muzi Mei's sex diary and Jiu Dan's documentary accounts of prostitution competed for popularity and set off an explosion of "sex-writing" on the Internet. Then the S-curves of Sister Hibiscus entered the scene, and the competition in sex-writing turned into one of the most conspicuous marks of the times.

Sex-writing, which went hand-in-hand with "keeping mistresses"—another fashion of the times—startled people, but it also provided them, as they surfed the Web for diversion, with something they could easily laugh at. The young women writers who were addicted to their own sex-writing had blind spots that gave them a flamboyant kind of courage. They somehow imagined that they had been born with figures that would give nosebleeds to any male who laid eyes on them. They dared to present ugliness as beauty, dissipation as purity, and crudity as elegance. They dared to hawk their lower bodies as if oblivious of the self-mockery that it implied. In many ways *segao,* in my view, was just another version of egao. The main virtue of *segao* was that it exposed the secret that "men are bandits and women are whores"; it broke taboos about sex and upset the traditional notion that men must be dominant in sex. It threw all the old notions about young ladies and gentlemen into a trash bin—and, in passing, begged the question of whether there still are any young ladies and gentlemen in China these days.

Sex-writing was not just a matter of Muzi Mei or Sister Hibiscus selling their lower quarters; it affected even the "zeal for the red classics." In remakes of Mao-era classics like *Shajiabang, Tracks in the Snowy Forest,* and *The Red Detachment of Women,* trendy touches of the martial arts or sex—especially sex—just had to be added. The male heroes had to have macho sex appeal, and the heroines had to reclaim the "full feminine flavor" that Mao had not allowed. Lovers not only were wildly consumed by passion; they inevitably struggled with love triangles as well.

Not long ago, officials became furious when they learned that netizens were planning to egao Lei Feng, the People's Liberation Army (PLA) soldier whom Mao Zedong had once elevated to be China's foremost hero. In the Mao years Lei Feng had been "Chairman Mao's good soldier" and a "good model for all the people of the nation." The little book called *Lei Feng's Diary* spread almost as widely as did *Quotations from Chairman Mao.* Now, three decades later, netizens were imagining a story about Lei Feng's private life and preparing an online film that they wanted to call "The Girl in Lei Feng's First Love." When some of Lei Feng's former comrades-in-arms got wind of the plan, they were outraged and petitioned the General Political Department of the PLA, who, naturally, viewed the question as one of utmost gravity and took it immediately to the Administration of Radio, Film, and Television and to the General Administration of the Press and Publication. Faced with an angry inquest from the PLA, the two bureaucratic offices were in no position to dawdle. An order to kill "The Girl in Lei Feng's First Love" went out immediately.

Another case of Internet egao—one that drew attention both in China and around the world—was the "Case of Liu Di" in 2002. Liu Di was a student in the Psychology Department at Beijing Normal University, where she had begun to write on the Internet under the unforgettable alias "Stainless Steel Mouse." The authorities arrested her on November 7, 2002, "on suspicions of publishing reactionary opinions on the Internet and of forming a secret organization." Thanks in part to international pressure, she was released a year later, on November 28, 2003, "on bail pending trial."

Liu Di had been very active on the Internet. She moderated popular chat rooms and ran a website called "West Temple Alley" that made an important contribution in the growing trend toward egao. Netizens drawn to satire of the pompous language of the Party-state formed a chat room at her site that they called "*The People's Daily* Reading Group." It attracted some posts of very high-quality egao. Its masterpiece in creativity was an online game called "Always Follow the Party." This got too political, though, and involved too much risk of prison—as Liu Di's own imprisonment shows.

Among her friends, Liu Di was always known for her distinctive brand of humor. She was adept at satirizing rivalries inside the Communist Party—or the "meParty," as its own idiom, and Liu Di, liked to put it—and her friends always looked forward to the laughs that she could provide. Her article "West Temple Persimmon Oil Party's First National Congress Convenes at Nanjing," for example, was a delicious spoof on the First Party Congress of the Communist Party of China. After Huang Qi, founder of "The Skynet Center for Missing Persons," a website founded to track victims of human trafficking, was thrown into prison in 2000, Liu Di wrote another post, announcing that "Persimmon Oil Party Networms Collectively Appeal to the Party and the Government." Her sardonic essay could not have been sharper in its indictment of the regime's persecution of Huang Qi, but what she called for, in form, was that all networms in the Persimmon Oil Party, throughout the country, immediately turn themselves in to local organs of Public Security if they had ever posted anything "reactionary" on the Internet.

Liu Di's most famous article of this kind was yet another, one called "Let Us Take to the Streets to Spread Communism!" It exhorted netizens to bring "The Communist Manifesto" to the streets and preach its virtues. "Bring it to the people and get them to sign it!" she wrote.

"Or you can do what those people passing out advertising flyers do—if there really is no one who will take them, then stuff them into the baskets of bicycles, or paste them onto telephone poles." Liu Di's year in prison for forming an unapproved organization did nothing to diminish her sense of humor. When released she punned on the English word *party*: "we can throw one, but not form one."

Egao as it has emerged today should be seen as an expansion of the Wang Shuo mode of literary sarcasm onto the vast new medium of the Internet.

## Political Humor in a Post-Totalitarian Dictatorship

Some intellectuals are of two minds about things like Wang Shuo's sarcasm and Hu Ge's egao. They like the fact that egao subverts official ideology, but worry that it exacerbates cynicism. They are afraid that something that debunks the sacred and subverts authority, but does nothing more, is only destructive, not constructive. If such a trend spreads out of control, the price of sweeping out pompous authority will be creation of a moral wasteland.

There is some truth in this. Egao in post-totalitarian China is a symptom of spiritual hunger and intellectual poverty at the same time. It can be seen as a kind of psychosomatic drug, something that works hand-in-hand with the vacuous comedy shows that the official media present, except that it can be even more effective than those in its power to anesthetize. People can get drunk laughing at one political joke after another that tells about suffering, corruption, and unhappiness. Jokes on such topics can become mere commodities to enjoy—as in "That's a good one!" One could even say that the laughter egao induces is a heartless kind, something that buries people's senses of justice and their normal human sympathies.

But what might be done about this? What is the way out? China's spiritual poverty certainly cannot be repaired by governmental order; it can come only through the availability of better-quality intellectual fare. Only when there is a free marketplace for ideas and values will true and false, and right and wrong, emerge for everyone to see, and only then can morality take hold and sophistry wither away. Only when differing value systems can coexist, cooperating where they have common ground and respecting differences where they do not, can society's full creativity be achieved. We need to remember how the moral vacuum in China came about: it is the result of a systemic pathology, the determination of a dictatorship to suppress free speech, to instill official lies, and to enforce the biases of the rulers. It is these policies—not anyone's laughter—that are the roots of the spiritual wasteland we see in China today.

In my view, those who see the subversion in egao as merely destructive, not constructive, do not see deeply enough. I see political humor as an important and widespread form of popular resistance in post-totalitarian society. It played a similar role in the Soviet Union and Eastern Europe before the great change-over that occurred there. (Hundreds of Soviet and Eastern European political jokes still circulate on the Chinese Internet, by the way.) After the Tiananmen Massacre, political satire (we might also call it "soft politics") in Chinese popular culture has shown a creativity, and an authenticity, that the solemn face of officialdom lacks. The people's jokes spring from grassroots wit. Official discourse not only provides contrast for popular humor, but can be seen as its primary cause as well: the bland, oppressive face of official culture forces people into laughter, be it an idiotic grin or a wicked dagger of wit; the more serious the face of the government, the more people (can only) laugh.

In a 2001 book called *Carnivalesque Poetics: A Study of Bakhtin's Literary Thought*, Wang Jian'gang presents the views of the famous Russian literary critic Mikhail Bakhtin on "cultural carnival," including the role of jokes in society. "Carnival," according to Bakhtin, has two sides: it is fraudulent, heartless, and vulgar; but it also expresses authentic feeling, feeds real creativity, and brings rebirth and renewal. In dictatorships, where control of daily life relies importantly on fear, it is especially important for rulers to maintain the threat that a solemn public atmosphere embodies. It is an atmosphere that makes official rule seem fixed, legitimate, even sacred. When "carnival" comes along, according to Bakhtin, the people at the grassroots, accustomed to their place at the receiving end of scoldings, suddenly become "fearless." They produce a spontaneous logical inversion of the base and the noble, of up and down. They use parody, mockery, ridicule, and insolence—sarcasm of several forms—to vent their sentiments, but these are not simply negative sentiments aimed at knocking something down. Satire of what is wrong implies that something else is right; it tears things down for the sake of rebirth.

In short there is no doubt in my mind that the benefits of egao outweigh the costs. It is useful to look more closely at what the experience of the Soviet Union and Eastern Europe shows on these questions.

After Khrushchev's de-Stalinization brought "thaw" to the Soviet Union, the Soviet empire fell into what Václav Havel has called "the era of post-totalitarian dictatorship." Resistance now came from two different sources: a handful of political "dissidents" issued bold and open challenges, while a silent majority brooded more quietly and occasionally pressed the borders of what was allowed. In the case of Czechoslovakia the difference can be seen by comparing Václav Havel and Milan Kundera. Havel was a hero of the "Charter 77" group that stood up to Soviet tanks, openly promoted a movement to "tell the truth," became the symbol of popular resistance to dictatorship, and for these efforts won tremendous worldwide honor. Kundera, on the other hand, used subversive jokes to express the sour mood of resistance within the silent majority. Kundera's first major work—*The Joke*—hit Czechoslovakia's literary scene in 1967 like a bomb. It led the best-seller lists for a full year, seeing three reprints and selling several hundred thousand copies, before the regime banned it.

Some people say that political humor tore the Iron Curtain down. This may be giving it a bit too much credit, but there can be no doubt that truth-telling and joking-making have worked hand-in-hand to dismantle post-totalitarian dictatorships. Both are crucial in "antipolitical politics." Truth-telling politics is the open challenge offered by a few fearless people of conscience; joke-making politics is the private digging away at the base of the wall by the silent majority. Without the truth-tellers, there would be no open expression of popular resistance or of moral courage; without the jokesters, the words of the truth-tellers would fall on barren ground. If we say that Havel's resistance exposed the inhumanity of dictatorship, lifted human dignity to a level where it had no fear of violence, and played an indispensable role in awakening the Czech people and mobilizing international pressure, then we must also say that the political jokes that circulated among the silent majority proved that people's consciences were still alive, exposed the rot of post-totalitarian dictatorship for everyone to see, and made it plain that, sooner or later, the political decay would lead to an avalanche-like collapse of the dictatorship.

Some will still say that, compared to the ways in which open truth-telling confronts a dictatorship, the indirect effects of private joke-telling leave something to be desired. Jokes can seem to be merely cynical venting, nothing that changes reality very much. But it is important to see how far-reaching the corrosive effects of political humor can be. They can reach everywhere that the political rot itself reaches, and that means into almost every nook of society. They show the true directions of popular opinion. They prepare the ground for things like "velvet revolutions."

Moreover, if and when a political collapse or major transition does occur, the fact that political humor has already been around for a number of years will likely ease the transition. In China, political jokes have already been making it clear for some time now that the legitimacy of the dictatorship is unsustainable; this means that an end, when it comes, will not be so much of a shock. People will be able to take it more easily in stride, and this will have the benefit of reducing anxieties and lessening the likelihood that people will seek violent revenge. Because jokes had been letting them blow off some of their anger all along, they will have less accumulated anger to deal with. And in addition to all that, the positive values that have underlain political jokes (satire of what is wrong implies that something else is right, as we noted above) will be available for use after the transition.

In a post-totalitarian dictatorship, the grins of the people are the nightmares of the dictators.

At home in Beijing, September 18, 2006

*Originally published in* Ren yu renquan *(Humanity and Human Rights), October 2006*
*Translated by Teresa Zimmerman-Liu*

# YESTERDAY'S STRAY DOG BECOMES TODAY'S GUARD DOG

◆　◆　◆　◆　◆

CHINESE PEOPLE ARE TALKING EXCITEDLY these days about the rise of China as a great nation. First we spoke of an economic rise, then a cultural rise; we started spreading money around the globe, then exported soft power. There have been fads for reading the classics, for honoring the memory of Confucius, and for promoting Confucian ethics. China Central Television (CCTV), pressing to reestablish an orthodoxy in China, has used its program *Lecture Hall* to touch off a fad for reading *The Analects*. The government has put big money into "Confucius Institutes" around the world in an effort to spread soft power. The dream of ruling "all under heaven," repressed for a century or more, is now resurgent and is taking Confucius the sage as its unifying force. The craze for Confucius grows ever more fierce.

In my view, the government's real goal in promoting Confucius is not to give new life to an ancient culture but to restore the tradition of venerating Confucius as a sage, a restoration that fits hand-in-glove with the promotion of radical nationalism. In the years since Tiananmen the government has used a two-pronged strategy of mounting campaigns against liberalization and "peaceful evolution" on the one hand while whipping up "patriotic" sentiment and channeling it in support of itself on the other. This "patriotism" has become a new pillar of the regime's ideology, and the Party's advertising of what it calls a "Golden Age of prosperity" swells the nationalist tide. This could not be more clear than it is in the concluding lines of the official "Address at the Ceremony to

Honor Confucius at the 2005 International Confucius Cultural Festival in Qufu, China," which read: "Prosperity is at hand; Great Unity is the dream; revel in our Golden Age and the glory of strong nation." Is this Confucius? Or a paean to nationalism and the new Golden Age?

Over the past year the promotion of traditional culture in CCTV's *Lecture Hall* has helped to turn Confucius into a commercial product—to become, in Lu Xun's phrase, a "sage in vogue." (Much the same thing happened in the Mao Zedong fad a few years ago.) Today books on Confucius in a variety of genres are making big profits for publishing houses, and adult education classes on traditional Chinese culture and the Chinese classics have been highly profitable as well. At Tsinghua University, a course on traditional Chinese culture costs 26,000 yuan; at Fudan University, it costs 38,000 yuan, and the fee for an after-school course on the classics for children is even more astronomical.

The CCTV program has also helped to turn pseudoscholar Yu Dan into a national celebrity. Yu Dan has been hawking Confucius with a sales pitch that combines tall tales about the ancients with insights that are about as sophisticated as the lyrics of pop songs. Her often arbitrary and always shallow interpretation of Confucius injects a bit of the narcotic of pop culture into the current Confucian renaissance. The take-home message of her book *Confucius from the Heart* is that Confucius teaches that we can all have peachy lives if we just live like cynics: no matter what befalls us, if we just smile at our troubles and do not complain, we can get along and live in bliss.

Just as the Yu Dan–inspired fad to "read Confucius" was taking off, Peking University professor Li Ling published a book called *Stray Dog: My Reading of "The Analects."* Li uses his own research to "exorcize nonsense" about Confucius and to try to capture the philosopher in his original form. Li writes in his preface:

> My book is the product of my own ideas about Confucius. I do not repeat what others have said. I do not care what Mencius, Wang Anshi, or any of the other greater or lesser scholars have said. If something is not in the original text, then sorry, I reject it ... If we want to know what Confucius himself thought, we have to read the original texts ... I am not out to join intellectuals in their squabbling, nor am I out to pander to popular taste.

And Li concludes:

> After reading *The Analects*, I find it most fitting neither to put Confucius on a pedestal nor to drag him through the mud but to say he resembles Don Quixote.

Li's rejection of both idol worship and favor-currying debunks the two-thousand-year-old habit of venerating Confucius as a sage. He writes:

> In this book I explain to my readers that Confucius was not, in fact, a sage. The Confucius to whom emperors paid homage in dynasty after dynasty was not the real Confucius, but a "manufactured Confucius." The real Confucius, the one who actually lived, was neither a sage nor a king—much less, as the popular phrase has it, "inwardly a sage and outwardly a king" . . . [He was] a mere mortal, a man of humble birth who believed that the ancient aristocracy (his "true gentlemen") set the standard for how one should conduct oneself. He loved antiquity, studied it assiduously, and never tired of learning. He was an indefatigable teacher who transmitted the culture of the past and encouraged his students to read classic texts. He had no power or status—only morality and learning—and dared to criticize the power elite of his day. He traveled around lobbying for his policies, racking his brains to help the rulers of his day with their problems, always trying to convince them to give up evil ways and be more righteous. He was bighearted and dreamed of restoring the reign of Zhou so that peace could come to everyone in the world. He was tormented, obsessed, and driven to roam, pleading for his ideas, more like a homeless dog than a sage. This was the real Confucius.

In both research and interpretation, Li Ling goes well beyond the shallow and careless Yu Dan as a reader of *The Analects*. More importantly, he feels a strong empathetic connection with a fellow intellectual of two thousand years ago. He notes that Confucius himself thought of himself as a sort of homeless dog:

Confucius was in despair about his homeland and, with disciples in tow, set out on foot to travel far and wide, living among strangers. He met dukes and princes, but got nowhere with them, and in the end returned to his place of birth, where he ended his days brokenhearted. Before he died he lost a son and others who had been near to him—his disciples Yan Hui and Zhong You—and wept until his tears ran dry. He died at home—but in another sense had no home. He may or may not have been right in his teachings, but in either case his life does illustrate the fate of Chinese intellectuals.

When Li Ling tossed his stray-dog comment into the midst of the popular discussion about Confucius and traditional Chinese culture, it was like tossing a big rock into a pond: it caused huge waves of protest from the new Confucian defenders of the Way. Li became the target of sputtering vitriol and curses from those whose shame turned to humiliated rage. He was denounced as a "prophet of doomsday" and (oddly, given what he stood for) an "angry youth." People who had not read his book nevertheless felt qualified to judge it "garbage." All this happened because he had called Confucius a stray dog. It shows that the Confucius fans of today have taken their reverence for the Master to the point where nothing actually meaningful can be said about him. Thank goodness the fans do not have much political power; if they did, we would be back to an era in which (as Lin Biao said of Mao Zedong) "every word is true, every word is worth ten thousand words from others."

Li Ling, as a serious historian, writes that "I regard *The Analects* as a subject for historical inquiry, not as a sacred book." When he calls Confucius a stray dog, he is reminding us that during China's Spring and Autumn period (770–476 BCE) intellectuals lived lives of uncertainty, even fear, because their talents were often unwelcome, and in that context "an idealist who can find no spiritual home" does resemble a stray dog. In my own view, to say that Confucius lacked a "spiritual home" is already giving him too much praise. The truth is that he was roaming the land to look not for a *spiritual* home but for a place where he could go to work for someone who held power. His cherished goal was to be the teacher of a king, and in that he failed. He was a stray dog who lacked a master. Had he found a ruler to take him in, the stray dog would have become a guard dog.

Li Ling was not the first to call Confucius a stray dog. Scholars of antiquity have evaluated him that way, too. The biography of Confucius in the *Records of the Grand Historian* by Sima Qian (145?–86 BCE) states that, at the age of 40, and having accomplished nothing, Confucius wailed, "My Way has reached its end!" and "There is no place in the land for me!" According to the biography in the *Records,* people in Confucius' own time noticed that he was "haggard and worn as a stray dog," and Confucius, hearing of the remark, allowed that the comparison was apt. Today's "true defenders of the Way" claim that when Confucius made his acknowledgment he was in fact hinting at some abstruse and profound truth about cultivating humanity and governing countries. For Li Ling to take the response more literally, in their view, is heinous heresy and enough to make his book garbage not worth reading. Some "angry youth" went so far as to say "Professor Li is insane!"

Today's Confucius worshippers can heap all the scorn upon Li Ling's book they like, but it remains true that what he writes about Confucius, especially in his plainspoken and captivating preface, far surpasses anything that Mr. Jiang Qing and the other "new Confucian thinkers" have to offer. An impressive range of well-known scholars have given *Stray Dog* high praise.

In an essay called "On the Feasibility of Benevolence and Righteousness: A Review of Li Ling's *Stray Dog,*" historian Wu Si writes, "Li Ling has done a fine service. Cultural projects of the future must be based on reliable core texts. In my view Li Ling, in his work on *The Analects,* does even better than Zhu Xi (1130–1200)." In a similar review essay, Professor Qian Liqun of the Department of Chinese at Peking University writes, "Li Ling's reading of *The Analects* stands out for its powerful 'heart to heart' empathy with Confucius, one intellectual to another. This empathy allows him to see the 'stray dog' problem clearly . . . When I saw the 'stray dog' phrase, I sensed a touch satire in it, but more than that I sensed Confucius's perseverance, and his sorrow." In an interview, Liu Mengxi, director of the Institute of Chinese Culture at the Chinese National Academy of Arts, praised Li Ling's conscientious textual research, his critical attitude, and his dispelling of myths about Confucius.

Professor Qin Hui of Tsinghua University, in an article entitled "How Did *The Analects* Become a Classic?" writes that "nowadays there are those who would elevate *The Analects* to the status of a Confucian Bible, just as, once upon a time, people elevated a thin little book called *Quotations of Chairman Mao* to the status of a 'pinnacle' of Marxism. Did the fervor for *Quotations of Chairman Mao* enrich Marxism or wreck it? Does the fervor for *The Analects* advance Confucianism or run it to ruin?"

China has a long tradition of reverence for sages, and in the eyes of the defenders of the Way, be they ancient or modern, Confucius is not to be questioned; he is a venerable "uncrowned king," the bearer of truth and the teacher of rulers through the ages; he is the Complete and Perfect Sage and King of Culture (a title actually given him in the fourteenth century) to whom emperors must bow. For Kang Youwei (1858–1927) and his Confucian Association, Confucius was the founder of a religion and a god; for the "new Confucians" of today, he is the symbol of Chinese culture. For them, every maxim in *The Analects* expresses astounding insight into either the management of state affairs or the cultivation of a person's innate morality. In ancient times the most outlandish claim was "half *The Analects* can govern the world"; its rival today is "Confucian teachings have governed the world for five thousand years and are ready for five thousand more." Some even say, "If you don't read Confucius, you are not really human." Today's "Confucians" go so far as to make up eye-catching fake news—such as the story, spread during the recent fad, that in 1988 seventy-five Nobel Prize winners from around the world gathered in Paris to name Confucius as the greatest thinker in human history. (Does someone covet the approval of Westerners?)

Today's fans are so smitten with their sage that they have lost the ability to distinguish ordinary human life from sainthood and ordinary language from ritual worship. Pardon me, good people, but Confucius was a human being, and must have farted. Are you sure those, too, had deep meaning? Could it be that the words of *The Analects* are common sense, not mystical wells of unfathomable wisdom? Let's look again at the two modest, clear lines that begin *The Analects:* "Is it not a pleasure to make frequent use of what one has learned? It is not a joy to have friends visit from afar?" Where, exactly, is the mind-bending abstruseness that warrants more than two thousand years of annotation and explanation? Zhou Zuoren (1885–1967), in his "Notes on *The Analects*," had it right: "*The Analects* tells how to be a good person and how to interact with the world . . . It can be useful a guide for future generations, but we must not take it as immutable truth or moral dogma, and still less should we claim it to hold brilliant political philosophy that can regulate nations and bring peace to all under heaven." The great German philosopher G. W. F. Hegel considered *The Analects* to be no more than a collection of daily-life truths.

It was when Emperor Wu of the Han (156–87 BCE) announced his ruling to "venerate Confucianism alone" that the man named Kong Qiu posthumously turned into Master Confucius. The skeleton of that stray dog sprang back to life as a guard dog to defend emperors and the Chinese autocracy.

When the autocrats realized how useful Confucian principles could be, the position of court guard dog began to offer excellent job security; once in place, the incumbents stayed for more than two thousand years. The moment when the paragon of China's intellectuals was elevated by political powerholders to a place of exalted honor, the moment statues of the paragon were gilded and placed inside the ancestral temple of the imperial clan, was the moment Chinese intellectuals arrived in hell on earth, because now they were nothing more than handmaidens to power. An early example was Sima Tan, father of Sima Qian. Both men had served as "grand historian" at the Han court. When Sima Qian was castrated—his punishment for offending Emperor Wu—he wrote a lament to his father:

> My father achieved nothing that merited any mention in the imperial records. He was responsible for astronomy and the calendar, which was mere fortune-telling and communion with the dead. The emperor used him for personal amusement and treated him like a court musician or other performer, and the common people never took him seriously.

During the nineteenth and early twentieth centuries, when the Western powers forced China to open itself to the world, China's imperial system and its ideology fell into sudden and rapid decline. In 1911, when a revolution finally brought an end to centuries of imperial dictatorship,

Confucianism, which had been the ideology of the dictatorship, lost its institutional support. The Confucian scholars who had been guard dogs went back to being stray dogs. Yuan Shikai (1859–1916) did manage to get himself appointed emperor in January 1916 and did make a big show of reviving the Confucian rituals, but that farce was short-lived. Yuan died six months later. By that time, the complete collapse of traditional institutions and their supporting ideology had become inevitable.

This felt dreadful, of course, to the Confucian scholars who lost their imperial doghouses and were put back out onto the streets. But from another point of view, the transition was a great blessing. It was an opportunity for Chinese scholars to become modern intellectuals, to leave behind the authoritarian props they had been depending upon and to venture into a new world of independent, critical thought. The opportunity was upon them whether they welcomed it or not. Unfortunately, this era of being "stray dogs by necessity" lasted only about fifty years. Once the Chinese Communists brought their totalitarianism to China, it was hard for Chinese intellectuals to be anything quite so comfortable as stray dogs. Most became whipping dogs, the targets of persecution and violent attack, while a fortunate few secured positions as guard dogs for the Mao regime. Guo Moruo (1892–1978), who earlier had dared to make open criticisms of Chiang Kai-shek, after 1949 turned into Mao Zedong's lap dog.

The fate of Confucius's reputation in the twentieth century would likely have puzzled Confucius. Twice he was made the target of major political campaigns, once during the May Fourth movement that began in 1919, and once when Mao Zedong launched a campaign to "criticize Lin Biao and Confucius" in 1974. In the years since Tiananmen, a trend in Chinese intellectual circles has opposed "radicalism," and some people have lumped the radical anti-traditionalism of May Fourth and the radical anti-traditionalism of Mao together, rejecting the two as a package. But these two "anti-Confucius" campaigns were radically different things.

First, the prime movers of the two campaigns could not have been more different. May Fourth was a spontaneous, bottom-up movement by people who were making demands on the government. They were mainly independent intellectuals who had been influenced by new ideas, values, and strategies from the West, and were using Western yardsticks to try to understand why China had fallen so far behind. They had transcended the thinking of the late nineteenth century, which held that "catching up" was merely a matter of technology—or perhaps of government form—and had concluded that the problem was deeply involved with culture. "Confucius" needed to be uprooted. In sharp contrast, the 1974 campaign to "criticize Lin Biao and Confucius" was a top-down political movement launched by a dictator, Mao Zedong, who held absolute political power and who had ensconced Mao Zedong Thought in the sole position of honor in China's world of ideology. No other ideas, whether from China or elsewhere, were permitted.

Second, the goals of the two campaigns were radically different. The Confucius whom the modern-minded intellectuals of May Fourth were attacking was not the wandering philosopher of the fifth century BCE but Sage Confucius, that artifact of Emperor Wu, the man who had embalmed Confucianism as the "only thought to be venerated." The new intellectuals wanted to drive off a guard dog and root out an entrenched way of thinking. Mao Zedong's campaign against Confucius, by contrast, had nothing at all to do with any effort to improve or renew culture, and in fact had nothing to do with Confucius, either. Its purpose, purely and entirely, was to aid Mao Zedong in his power struggles at the top of the Communist Party of China. The point was to utterly demolish the image of Lin Biao and to draw a line in the sand for the "chief Confucian in the Party," Zhou Enlai.

How much different, in their fundamental natures, could these two "anti-Confucius campaigns" have possibly been? One originated with modern intellectuals who had no political power, the other with a traditional-style despot who held absolute power; one was spontaneous and bottom-up, the other engineered and top-down; one was an effort to find a way forward for the nation, the other an effort to solidify autocratic power for a dictator.

This is why I continue to endorse May Fourth's anti-Confucius campaign and continue to condemn Mao's. It is hardly a close call.

In a 1935 essay called "Confucius in Modern China," Lu Xun denounces the tradition in imperial China of sage worship. He writes:

> The ones who put Confucius on a pedestal, who made him a sage, were powerholders and would-be powerholders. This sage-making had nothing at all to do with the common people.

Sage-worship—a product of the joint efforts of kings, emperors, and their hired scribblers over many centuries—in my view is the most impressive piece of mythmaking in all of Chinese history. The Confucius who has been dubbed "sage" long ago lost any connection to the historical Confucius and is nothing but a shoddy counterfeit.

If one actually does some conscientious reading of China's pre-Qin philosophers, it is not hard to see that Confucius was relatively mediocre. He lacks the grace, ease, and elegance of Zhuangzi (369–286 BCE), has none of Zhuangzi's gift for powerful language, or beautiful flights of fancy, or genius for unconventional, arresting philosophical insight, and falls far short of Zhuangzi's clear-eyed understanding of the human tragedy. Compared to Mencius (372–289 BCE), Confucius is no match in boldness of vision or breadth of mind, to say nothing of the ability to stand up to authority with dignity or to show genuine concern for the common people. It was Mencius who said, "The people come first; the social order next; the rulers last." By comparison with Han Feizi (281–233 BCE), Confucius seems pretentious and crafty; he lacks Han Feizi's gift for straightforward, trenchant, satirical commentary. As for Mozi (ca. 470–391 BCE), Confucius does not have his talent for logical rigor or the faith in humanity that undergirds his ideal of universal equality.

The sayings of Confucius, by contrast, are clever but contain no great wisdom. They are extremely practical, even slick, but show no aesthetic inspiration or real profundity. Confucius lacked nobility of character and breadth of vision. He ran around trying to get a position at a court, and when this failed he became an expounder of the Way. He enjoyed telling people what to think and how to behave, for which the sage-makers have credited him as "an indefatigable teacher of men," but what it actually shows is a certain arrogance and small-mindedness. His famous principle of "engaging the world when it is orderly and withdrawing when it is in chaos" is, if you think about it, a formula for irresponsible opportunism. How costly has it been for the Chinese people that this particular thinker—this most sly, most smooth, most utilitarian, most worldly-wise Confucius, who shied away from public responsibility and showed no empathy for people who suffer—became their sage and exemplar for two thousand years? A people is reflected in its sages, and a sage can mold people in his image. I fear that the slave mentality in the Chinese people today came entirely from this source.

In addition to the serious intellectual project of uncovering the original Confucius, Professor Li Ling seems to have had some other targets in mind in publishing his *Stray Dog* book. Today's ultranationalism was clearly one of them. Li is challenging the fads for "reading the classics" and "worshipping Confucius" and indirectly is raising questions about the "rise of China as a great nation" as well. His reference to Confucius as a homeless dog "spiritually adrift in the world" is aimed at the "new Confucians" who are promoting Confucius as a worldwide savior. Li comments, "I can imagine nothing more pointless than planting the flag of Confucius all over the world . . . Confucius could not save China, and he cannot save the world."

A second target of Li Ling's critique is the tradition among Chinese intellectuals of cozying up to power, and the critique is timely because the Confucians of today are falling over themselves to do just that. They honor Confucius and spout Confucian teachings, but their purpose is not to use Confucianism to revive the ethics of the nation; it is to reassert the principle that mastery of Confucianism qualifies a person to be a ruler. In stressing that Confucius was an adviser to kings and emperors (even "the teacher of the nation"), in advocating that Confucianism resume its place as the nation's orthodoxy, and in hoping that the government will use its authority to make these things happen by decree, what the new Confucians are actually doing is showing their own ambitions to be the advisers to the modern-day kings and emperors—or maybe even to be Plato-style philosopher-kings themselves, holding power in their own hands. In giving Confucius his latest makeover they are, in essence, sending China back to the era of Emperor Wu. They are hoping for a resumption of the days when Confucianism was venerated and all other schools of thought were banned—indeed, when *all* thought was banned, including Confucian thought, because you don't need thought when unquestioning worship of a sage takes its place.

Li Ling sees the record of history as showing that China's intellectuals, with all those utopian ideals bulging in their heads, have done good for China only when they find themselves out of power, taking stands as critics of authority. When they have power in their hands, it can spell danger, even disaster, for the nation. "Intellectuals, with their sharp eyes and keen minds," he writes, "can be more autocratic than anybody. Put the executioner's sword in their hands and the first to lose their lives will be other intellectuals." This happens because of the habitual conceit of the Chinese intellectual that *his* morality, *his* ideals, and *his* insights are necessarily superior to anyone else's. He accords himself the pedestal of being "first in the world to assume its worries, last in the world to enjoy its pleasures" [from Fan Zhongyan (989–1052 CE)—Trans.] and believes he can help to save the people from calamity and build a paradise on earth. Zhang Zai (1020–1077 CE) summed up the goals of the Chinese intellectual in four sentences: "Establish morals in the world; establish livelihood for the people; transmit the lost teachings of the sages; bring peace to the world for thousands of years." Today many Chinese intellectuals still exhibit this mentality, which shows just how deeply the ancient literati traditions of arrogance remain engrained.

Li Ling wants today's Chinese intellectuals to take lessons from history, to stand apart from power, to give up their ambition to be the teachers of kings, and to stop politicizing the ancient classics with ideological readings. At the end of his preface, Li writes:

> We must approach *The Analects* coolly and objectively—without any politicizing, moralizing, or sermonizing. Our sole purpose should be to fill the need we have for the real Confucius, a need that is particularly acute in this age when, to paraphrase Confucius himself, "the rites have been lost and the music at court is disordered."

If China's intellectuals ignore this advice, their fate, like that of their predecessors, will be to serve only as running dogs for others. A stray dog that finds favor with no one and a guard dog prized by its master both are dogs.

In my opinion the greatest tragedy in the history of Chinese culture was not the famous "burning of books and live burials of scholars" for which the First Emperor of the Qin (259–210 BCE) is famous, but Emperor Wu's "banning all schools of thought and venerating Confucianism alone." This latter decree led to Dong Zhongshu's (ca. 175–105 BCE) reinterpretation of Confucianism, which substantiated the theory that the imperial system (in fact founded and maintained by violence) was a manifestation of the Way of Heaven. Dong's principle, cited in his biography in *The History of the Former Han,* that "if the will of Heaven does not change, then the Way does not change" was an assertion that the cosmos endorses imperial rule. It wrapped a violent military dictatorship in the dress of benevolent rule. Emperors of course saw the utility of this disguise, were happy to continue upholding Confucianism as the "uniquely venerated" official ideology, laying out a path by which the literati could master Confucian orthodoxy and use it to flourish as lackeys. Mao Zedong got the intellectuals just right when he invoked the saying "With the skin [i.e., the state] gone, what can the hair [the intellectuals] hang onto?"

The most important responsibility of Chinese intellectuals today is not to defend sage-worship that an autocratic political authority supports but to pull free from reliance on and service to such authority. We should inherit and promote the May Fourth tradition, which Professor Chen Yinke (1889–1969) captured in the phrase "independence of thought and autonomy of person."

Beijing, August 18, 2007

*Originally published on boxun.com/hero/2007/liuxb/63_2.shtml, September 2, 2007*
*Translated by Thomas E. Moran*

# MY PUPPY'S DEATH

*To my beloved Pinkie*

*From time to time in Communist China, beginning in the early 1950s and extending into the 2000s, officials have issued orders to kill all the dogs, including pets, in designated areas.*—Ed.

My love, my puppy died
while I was out one afternoon
killed with Dad's belt
and Red lies

My love, its name was Tiger
my closest childhood friend
it brought me far more joy and sorrow
than anything

That afternoon was special
Dad bought me a movie ticket
always making revolution
he'd never touched my heart before

I only got ninety minutes
then cruel lies ripped me to shreds

my puppy died
while I was first feeling a father's love

Its flesh handed out to the neighbor boys
its hide nailed to the back of our door
Tiger, once so full of life
now splayed across the stiff cold wood

With its death
my childhood vanished
my only words for this dark world:
I'll never believe anymore

My darling Xia, can you
bring back my puppy?
I believe: you can
I'm sure you can. I'm sure!

November 14, 1996

*Translated by Susan Wilf*

# LONG LIVE THE INTERNET

◆　◆　◆　◆　◆

MORE AND MORE CHINESE are using the Internet. This year, 2006, the number has exceeded one hundred million. [When this book went to press the number had passed 450 million.—Ed.] The Communist regime, always obsessed with media control, has been frantic to keep up with Chinese Web users. It tries this, tries that, fidgeting and twitching through a range of ludicrous policy contortions in its attempts to stay on top of things. Its fundamental dilemma is this: on the one hand, its imbalanced economic reforms may well collapse if high growth rates cannot be sustained, and the super-efficient Internet obviously is a money machine. On the other hand, dictators always fear open information and freedom of speech, and the political possibilities of the amazing Internet can be terrifying to them. In fact, the Internet in China has already done much to spread awareness of rights and to support specific rights-defense projects, and this record only adds to the regime's consternation. It is no wonder that controlling what gets onto the Internet has moved to the very top of the regime's agenda in ideological matters. It has spent huge amounts since 1998 in building its Project Gold Shield [popularly known as "The Great Firewall"—Ed.] and in recruiting armies of Internet police. It coerces Western Internet firms into accepting its restrictions as the price of doing business in China.

From my own experience, though, I can attest that the contributions of the Internet to freedom of expression in China have been immense, indeed hard to overstate. Despite the escalation in blocking information on the Web and despite the increasing numbers of people who have been sent to prison for what they have posted, the Internet remains a tremendous boon to China's civil society.

It has meant a lot to me personally as well. On October 7, 1999, I came home from a three-year stay in prison to find a computer already set up in my home. A friend had given it to my wife, and she was already using it to learn typing and to go online. She showed me how to use it. In the days that followed, nearly every friend who came to see us advised me to get on the computer as fast as I could. I tried a few times, but composing sentences in front of a machine just did not feel right. I resisted, and for a while went on writing with a fountain pen. Gradually, though, as friends continued to offer their patient advice and their free demonstrations, I got used to the computer, and before long I could not do without it. The first essay I wrote on it came in fits and starts, and it took a week. Later—after my first submission to a publication by email got a response from the editor within only a few hours— the marvelous power of the Internet suddenly struck me, and I decided to master the computer as quickly as possible. The machine had originally belonged to my wife, but after I took it over she rarely touched it.

In my precomputer days, it took a lot of time and effort to work with handwritten drafts. This was not just because editing by hand is onerous; it was also because delivery costs were high. My writing was banned in China, so I could publish only abroad. The post office would intercept my manuscripts if I tried to mail them overseas, so, to prevent this, I used to travel from the east side of Beijing to the west, where I burdened a foreign friend with sending out my essays by fax. These high transaction costs inevitably took a toll on both my efficiency and my motivation. I was doing pretty well if I published one or two pieces a month.

Now, with my computer, I am connected with the entire world in a way that used to be inconceivable. The computer makes information gathering, consultation with others, composition of essays, and submission of manuscripts all much easier. The Internet is like a magic engine, and it has helped my writing to erupt like a geyser. Now I can even live off what I write.

This is what the Internet has done for me personally. For Chinese society as a whole, it has provided a channel of information that dictators cannot completely control and a platform on which people can exchange opinions and organize, in cyberspace if not in real space.

Open letters by individuals or groups have always been one of the most important ways in which civil society confronts dictatorship and seeks freedom. Two canonical texts in this tradition are the open letter that Václav Havel wrote to Czech dictator Gustáv Husák in 1975 and Charter 77, which Havel and a number of other Czechs signed and published in 1977. When a group like this signs an open letter, it is more than an expression of political opinion; it is a beginning in the formation of organized citizen power.

Open letters began to make a difference in China during the run-up to the 1989 pro-democracy movement. The famous astrophysicist Fang Lizhi took the lead by submitting an open letter to Deng Xiaoping in January 1989 in which Fang called for the release of political prisoners, including the "Democracy Wall" leader Wei Jingsheng. Soon two more open letters appeared, from groups of intellectuals numbering thirty-three and forty-five, respectively. These three open letters have been seen as the prelude to the major nationwide uprising of 1989. During the movement's high tide, other open letters were popping up like spring shoots after rain. Nearly every sector of society was coming out with public statements in support of the protesting students.

After the massacre, especially in the mid-1990s, there were many more public statements and open letters; but this was before the Internet arrived, and it took a lot of work to organize them. As a veteran of those efforts, I look now at the computer screen before me, on which I do emails so easily, and sigh to remember what I used to have to go through.

The public statements of the mid-1990s had titles such as: "Declaration of the Alliance for the Protection of Labor Rights," "Recommendations on Abolishing the System of Re-education-through-Labor," "Recommendations to Combat Corruption," and "Learn from the Lesson Written in Blood and Push Democracy and Rule of Law Forward: An Appeal on the Sixth Anniversary of Tiananmen." These statements all were related to the protection of human rights. Their signatories came from three generations of intellectuals and included both "dissidents" and people "inside the system."

The year 1995 in particular gained a reputation as a peak year for the rights-defense movement. A series of open letters appeared around the June anniversary of the massacre that year. The most influential among them, one called "Welcoming the U.N. Year of Tolerance and Calling for Tolerance in China," had been initiated by the distinguished physicist and veteran Party liberal Xu Liangying. The famous nuclear physicist Wang Ganchang led the effort to collect signatures, which he got in abundance from cultural luminaries and members of the Chinese Academy of Sciences, such as Yang Xianyi, Wu Zuguang, Lou Shiyi, Zhou Fucheng, Fan Dainian, Wang Zisong, Ding Zilin, Jiang Peikun, Wang Ruoshui, and others. 1995 was also the first year—in what was to become an uninterrupted annual effort over the next decade—in which the Tiananmen Mothers sent an open letter to the National People's Congress. It was also the year in which Professor Bao Zunxin and I mobilized a group of intellectuals to call for medical parole for Chen Ziming, who was serving a thirteen-year prison sentence for being a "black hand" behind the 1989 Tiananmen demonstrations. The signatories to our statement included Ji Xianlin, Tang Yijie, and Yue Daiyun from Peking University and He Xiquan, Tong Qingbing, and Wang Furen from Beijing Normal University.

It is hard for people who have done all their rights-defense work in the Internet age to appreciate how much time and effort it took to organize an open letter in 1995. In order, for example, to time a letter so that it would appear near the anniversary of the massacre, one had to start about a month in advance. It took time to find someone to be the lead signatory and to bring others in; then it took several days (at the very least) to reach consensus on questions of content, wording, and timing. Next, one had to find a place where the handwritten letter could be typeset and printed. Then copies had to be made, for which one usually had to go impose on foreign friends in the diplomatic quarter. Most taxing of all was the task of collecting signatures once the final version had been hammered out, printed, and copied. Normally the organizers would divide this task and set out in person. We did not dare to use telephones, because we knew the government tapped the lines of us "sensitive" people, so we ran around Beijing by bicycle or bus. In 1995, in order to get signatures on my open letter from my friends Mang Ke, the famous poet, and Li Xianting, the famous art critic, I first had to cross to the eastern edge of the city, then head to the northern quarter, visiting their homes and talking with them in person. It took me a full day to bring in a modest harvest.

But if it used to take many days to bring in just a few dozen signatures, today, with the Internet, one can gather hundreds, even thousands, in a short time. Then one can send the statement to the whole world almost instantly.

There are four important ways in which the Internet has been a boon to civil society in China.

1. The Internet has given rise to "Web-based Rights Defense." Because the Internet is fast, inexpensive, convenient, and able to reach all sectors of society, it makes organization of rights-defense efforts vastly easier than before. Activity has grown by leaps and bounds compared to what was possible in the bicycle-and-telephone era of the 1990s, and the new advantages have greatly lowered costs in time and effort. With the Internet, all of the major steps in producing an open letter can be done on a computer: drafting, discussion, editing, printing. A few clicks of a mouse, the exchange of a few emails, and it is done. Signature gathering, which used to be the hardest part, can be done through group email and at websites. A group email might pull in dozens or hundreds of signatures immediately, and a website dedicated to the receipt of signatures can gather names from across China and around the world. After that, all that one needs is oneself or another volunteer to maintain an updated list of signatures, collate comments and other incidental information—and the result is a rights-support effort that can have considerable reach, staying power, and influence. This process has given rise to many rights-defense websites, as well as to the important network called "Chinese Human Rights Defenders."

2. The Internet has brought new strength to public opinion. The convenience, openness, and freedom of the Internet has given rise in recent years to a lively new kind of public opinion that can serve as a check on official behavior. Public opinion on the Internet tends to swell every time a major disaster arises, and these swells have effects—larger or smaller, as the case may be—both on the traditional media and on the attitudes of officials. The government is good at keeping the scandalous aspects of stories out of the traditional media, but it cannot keep them off the Internet, where news spreads quickly and public opinion usually follows close behind. Raging public sentiment can force the government

to make at least some concessions to what the public demands; it can, in addition, force the traditional media to do better reporting, lest they fall behind what the Internet has to offer and lose credibility with the public. Whether a newspaper or television station can keep up with Internet news and opinion is already a standard by which the public evaluates the media.

One of the standard ways in which the government responds to Internet pressure is to release a limited amount of information on some topic. Higher officials often look for scapegoats among lower officials to take the rap in public opinion, and then those lower officials need to make open apologies to the families of victims and to the general public. The 2003 SARS crisis, a number of major mining accidents, and the 2005 chemical spill on the Songhua River all illustrate this pattern. More rarely, a very high official makes an apology himself. The first clear example of this pattern occurred in March 2001 at the annual meeting of the National People's Congress. Shortly before this grand meeting occurred, forty-one people died in an explosion that had become famous on the Internet as "The Tragic Case of the Fanglin Elementary School." The public outcry was sufficient that Zhu Rongji, China's premier, made a public apology in his own name.

3. The Internet has made possible a kind of "freedom of assembly" in cyberspace. Unregistered groups are "illegal" under China's current regime, and if the rulers see such groups as rivals to their power, they crush them. This is why Internet websites perform an important role in allowing people—virtually, if not physically—to come together, share ideas, debate, and hammer out consensus of the kind that benefits from the presentation of different points of view. "Virtual meeting" of this kind can also build a camaraderie that is impossible when people are kept atomized or are allowed to meet only in Party-approved gatherings. The camaraderie grows stronger when a virtual group takes up one or another case of injustice—perhaps only a small case, involving just one or a few people—and champions the victims. Such activity not only brings the pressure of public opinion to the aid of victims; it can also help the group itself by bolstering its spirits and its sense of mission. This happened, for example, in the 2003 "BMW Case" in Harbin

[a parked BMW suffered a scrape from a farmer's onion cart, after which the BMW owner used the car to run down and kill the farmer's wife and to injure twelve others—Ed.]. It also happens when relatively unknown writers are sent to prison for what they write, as in the cases of cyberdissidents Du Daobin, Lu Xuesong, and Liu Di [on Liu Di, see "From Wang Shuo's Wicked Satire to Hu Ge's *Egao*," pp. 177–187].

4. The Internet has generated "stars" outside the Party-state system. Before the Internet era there was only one avenue to public prominence in Communist China, and that was through the official Party-state system. Now, with the Internet, "stars" can appear in a variety of fields. Not only are there entertainment stars like the exhibitionist antiheroine "Sister Hibiscus"; we also have "rights defense stars," "opinion leaders," "moral exemplars" and "truth-telling heroes." Some of these are middle-aged intellectuals—people who were famous before the Internet—but now they can extend their influence to a degree that would have been unimaginable before. (I am thinking here of Liu Junning, Xu Youyu, Qin Hui, Cui Weiping, Zhang Zuhua, and others.) In addition, a new generation, such as the charismatic writers Yu Jie and Wang Yi, are now prominent on the Internet. So are popular heroes such as Jiang Yanyong, the doctor known for his courageous truth-telling about the SARS epidemic; the farmer-turned-entrepreneur Sun Dawu, who was imprisoned on opaque charges, then released after a popular outcry; the rights-defense leader Feng Binxian; outstanding journalists like Cheng Yizhong, Lu Yuegang, and Li Datong; university professors Jiao Guobiao and Lu Xuesong; and, perhaps most important, China's rising cadre of rights-defense lawyers, including Zhang Sizhi, Mo Shaoping, Pu Zhiqiang, Zhu Jiuhu, Gao Zhisheng, Guo Feixiong, Teng Biao, Xu Zhiyong, Li Baiguang, Li Heping, Li Jianqiang, and others. All these people owe their "stardom" to their rights-defense work and to the Internet. The appearance of so many larger and smaller stars in the Internet firmament does much to promote diversity of opinion in China's society at large.

Chinese Christians say that even though Chinese people today generally do not have strong religious feelings and not many believe in a God that has been introduced from the West, still the universal grace of God has been extended to all Chinese in our suffering. After all, they say, He has given us the Internet. What better tool could we have for throwing off slavery and pursuing freedom?

At home in Beijing, February 14, 2006

*Originally published in* Minzhu Zhongguo *(Democratic China), February 18, 2006*
*Translated by Louisa Chiang*

# IMPRISONING PEOPLE FOR WORDS AND THE POWER
## OF PUBLIC OPINION

❖    ❖    ❖    ❖    ❖

### I. County-Level Bullies and What They Do

China has a rich tradition of persecuting people for their words. Victims are strewn across Chinese history from the First Emperor of Qin (259 BCE–210 BCE) and his famous "burning of books and live burials of scholars" to Mao Zedong's 1957 Anti-Rightist Campaign and 1966–1969 Cultural Revolution. In these pogroms even family members and acquaintances of victims have been punished. Today, thirty years after the beginning of "reform and opening," at least eighty journalists and online writers are in prison in China. The "glorious" 2008 Beijing Olympics are drawing near, but accounts of the imprisonments are banned from China's media. Still, even with the ban in place, cases keep coming to light on the Internet. Here are some examples:

*The Pengshui Poem Case*   In August 2006, Qin Zhongfei, a clerk in the Personnel Department of the Education Committee of the Pengshui County government, in the municipality of Chongqing, wrote a poem set to the rhyming scheme of "Springtime Seeping through a Fragrant Garden" in which he satirized county officials. He sent it out as a text message on his mobile phone, and that was enough for Communist Party Secretary Lan Qinghua and County Chief Zhou Wei to throw Qin into jail on charges of "fabricating rumors and libel of county leaders." After a public outcry, and with help from rights lawyers, Qin was released and awarded 2,125.70 yuan in compensation.

*The Jishan Article Case*    In April 2007, Nan Huirong, Xue Zhijing and Yang Qinyu, three technology officials in Jishan County, Shanxi Province, wrote an article that expressed discontent with the situation in Jishan, criticized County Party Secretary Li Runshan in a number of ways, and adduced evidence to back their complaints. They sent it to thirty-seven local government departments, and ten days later police arrested them. Again the charges were "rumor-fabrication and libel." The Party Secretary went so far as to require more than five hundred officials at the level of section chief and above to attend a "public warning meeting" at which the three authors of the offending piece appeared in handcuffs and were forced to criticize themselves and to confess.

*The Danzhou Lyrics Case*    In July 2007, two high-school teachers, surnamed Li and Liu, who opposed the decision of the government of Danzhou City, Hainan Province, to move the senior high school grades of the Nada Number Two High School to the Dongpo branch of Hainan High School, wrote a folk song in the Danzhou dialect criticizing the move. The local police put the two teachers under administrative detention for fifteen days "on suspicion of personal attacks on city leaders and libelous defamation of city leaders."

*The Gaotang Internet Post Case*    In December 2006, Dong Wei, Wang Zifeng, Hu Dongchen, and others in Gaotang County, Shandong Province, posted comments about local governance in the "Gaotang" entry on the Internet site Baidu, and later the three were criminally detained "on suspicion of insulting and libeling County Party Secretary Sun Lanyu." After a public outcry and help from rights lawyers, officials in the Gaotang county government decided on January 21, 2007, to withdraw the arrest warrants and release the suspects. The three later filed for compensation and were each awarded more than 1,700 yuan.

*The Mengzhou Book Case*    In December 2007, six farmers in Mengzhou City, Henan Province, reported financial malfeasance at a village-owned brewery. They printed and distributed a booklet called *An Ap-*

*peal for Justice* in which they criticized the deputy mayor of Mengzhou, the former deputy director of the United Front department of the Mengzhou Municipal Party Committee, and a few other officials. The six farmers heard no answer to their "appeal for justice," but they did hear a judge at a local court sentence them to six months in jail for "libel." Worse, they were escorted through the streets—twice—in the kind of public-shame parade that was standard in China's imperial era.

*The Zhu Wenna Case*   On January 1, 2008, *People of the Law*, a magazine published in Beijing by the state-owned *Legal Daily*, carried an investigative report by Zhu Wenna that criticized County Party Secretary Zhang Zhiguo in Tieling City, Xifeng County, Liaoning Province. On January 4, public security personnel from Tieling traveled to the offices of *People of the Law* in Beijing to detain Zhu on "suspicion of libel." Later, after a strong public outcry, Tieling County Public Security withdrew its charges and issued an apology. The Tieling Party Committee announced that Party Secretary Zhang's involvement in the decision to "go to Beijing to detain the reporter Zhu Wenna" and to file charges against her had shown "weak awareness of the law" and that Zhang had direct, inescapable leadership responsibility for the incident. On February 4, 2008, Zhang was obliged to acknowledge that responsibility. He wrote a thoroughgoing self-criticism to the Tieling Party Committee and resigned.

These examples of imprisoning people for words result from two factors: the primitive nature of our political system and the deterioration in quality of the officials who inhabit it. China's autocratic political system has endured for millennia, and right up to today there has been no fundamental change in it. In ancient times the one who ruled "all under heaven" was an emperor, and challenging him was out of the question. (There were, to be sure, a few enlightened emperors who abolished laws that treated words as crimes. Emperor Wen of Han [202 BCE–157 BCE] abolished the crime of "black magic libel," for example.) In today's autocracy, it is the Party that rules "all under heaven," and Party rule at times has been even tighter than premodern autocracy in its annihilation of dissent. High Maoism defined the extremes in treating words as crimes, and today, even after thirty years of reform, there is no change at all in the principle that Party power reigns supreme. The dominant official at every level of government, without exception, is the Communist Party secretary. Once a decision is made, people are free to applaud. In this the popular jingle gets it right:

> The Party points the way,
> The people all say "yea!"
> The rulers make a move,
> The ruled all say "approve!"

Local officials have always made "holding onto the scepter of rule" their highest priority in governance, and in recent years they have been growing more aggressive and arbitrary in their obsession with personal power. They launch large construction projects—which are riddled with corruption and wasteful of public resources—in order to accumulate records of "political performance." The pursuit of boondoggles, in turn, entails that great effort and energy must be spent on "shutting people up." The ostensible mission of "building wealth in a locale" turns into "going berserk in a locale" and finally into "bringing disaster to a locale." Anyone who exposes corruption needs to be packed off to jail. Even if corrupt officials are caught and punished, it is rare for anything good to happen to a whistleblower.

The local bullying happens, moreover, in a context where the bully monopolizes all the resources. The media are not free, the judiciary is not free, and the police work for the "head honchos." The country's constitution states that citizens enjoy the right to free speech, but Article 105 of the Criminal Law provides that "inciting subversion of state power" is a crime, and when the two principles collide, Article 105 wins. This fact makes any criticism of the Communist Party or its officials at any level into a high-wire act and ensures that China's prisons remain well stocked with prisoners of conscience. Even the Party Secretary in a peanut-sized county is an emperor on his own piece of turf, where he can block the sun with one hand if he likes. Offend this little emperor and you can go to prison.

Because Communist ideals have become completely hollow during the "reform" years, the Communist Party has turned into nothing more than a coalition of profit-seeking interest groups. Officials are corrupt and the quality of governance is in steady decline. The marriage of government and business is already well established, and in recent times we have seen an alliance between government and the underworld as well. In some locations this alliance is so tight that the two are practically indistinguishable. The underworld buys the government with bribes, and the government borrows the underworld to control troublemakers. Party officials increasingly behave like underworld godfathers who reject any kind of criticism or dissent. They can use the machinery of state power to cut your throat or their underworld tools to shut your mouth.

## II. The Power of Public Opinion in "Low Sensitivity" Cases

In the eighteen years since the Tiananmen Massacre, China has seen many cases of "prison for words," and they have occurred at many levels of government. Most of the victims have been either political dissidents or rights defenders, two categories about which China's rulers are extremely sensitive, and for that reason news of their cases is routinely sealed from the media inside China, making it almost impossible for the public to come to the aid of such victims. The tiny number of political prisoners who do get released are normally the famous ones, because theirs are the cases that major Western countries know about and can complain about. "Hostage diplomacy" has by now become a standard practice in the Chinese government's negotiations with other countries.

The persistence of political prisons in China might seem depressing, but there is a brighter side to this issue as well. China has come a long way since the Mao era of "one voice fits all." Today we live in a posttotalitarian state where values are more diverse than before and a hubbub of different voices grows louder day by day. "Rights awareness" is on the rise, civil society is growing, the space for expression of opinion is expanding, and concrete acts of rights-defense are popping up with increasing frequency. Now that we have the Internet, which provides both information and a platform for expression that ordinary people never had before, the hunger to say one's piece has grown stronger, too. It looks for every crevice it can find, and when public opinion comes together on an issue it can gush forth in a great wave.

In recent years the Chinese public has been moving toward a consensus that sending people to prison for their words is wrong. The issue of freedom of expression was once something that only intellectuals and journalists worried about, but now it has spread to many other parts of society, where opinions are getting stronger every day. Absurd behavior by local officials (in the cases we noted above, for example) actually serves a useful purpose in building public consensus on the question of treating words as crimes. The consensus can be built because the victims in the grassroots cases are not big-name dissidents or rights defenders of the kind the regime brands as "enemy forces," making people afraid to identify with them. The grassroots victims are just regular government clerks, run-of-the-mill reporters, and other ordinary citizens, and their criticisms are aimed not at the whole Communist system or its high-level officials but at county bosses and local government. In order to voice complaint about the treatment of a famous dissident, a person has to "jump the Great Firewall" of Internet censorship and do his or her talking out in international cyberspace; by contrast, these low-level cases, with their low political sensitivity, can be the basis on which ordinary people satisfy their hunger to express anger at officialdom, and they can do it inside the firewall. When they begin to do so, an additional benefit emerges, which is that the question of imprisoning people for words comes to seem a more normal issue, less "sensitive," and in the long run this is a good thing for the big-name dissidents as well, because public opinion now begins to hold that "prison for words" is just plain wrong, regardless of the level at which it occurs.

All this could not happen without the Internet, which is where ordinary Chinese now go when they want to know what "really happened" in stories that they see in the state-run press, and is also where they go to say something if they want to. No major event in recent years in China has escaped frank public commentary on the Internet.

The public outcry in the cases that I listed at the beginning of this essay could not have happened without the Internet. Those instances of outcry led, in turn, to long reports and commentaries in some of the more open of the official Chinese media, such as *Southern Metropolitan Daily, Southern Weekend,* and *China Youth Daily.* Even one of the Party's standard mouthpieces, Xinhuanet, has published sharp words about the criminalization of speech. When an article called "Why Are the Culprits in Prison-for-Words Cases Always County Party Secretaries?" appeared on Xinhuanet under the pen name Wang Ping, many top websites scrambled to republish it. A search today on Baidu for comments on county-level imprisonment-for-words yields more than 100,000 results. The Wang Ping article alone gets 5,580.

Any case of prison-for-words, whatever the details, draws a torrent of public comment if it ever hits the media, and public attention of this kind can provide protection for victims. The protection is not guaranteed, to be sure, and it does nothing to bring perpetrators to a court of law, but it can get certain other things done. It can spare the victims a trip to prison, and occasionally can leverage compensation from the government as well—as shown in the Pengshui Poem Case and Gaotang Internet Post Case, noted above. It can force perpetrators to retract decisions and make public apologies. Sometimes it can even oblige higher levels of government to impose punishments on offending officials, as in the Zhu Wenna Case, in which Party Secretary Zhang Zhiguo was ordered to resign.

Governmental controls on public expression loosen and tighten from time to time in China, but the pressure from below for more free expression does not fluctuate. It just keeps growing. In the 1990s, petitions that protested cases of prison-for-words typically attracted only a few dozen signatures, and often less than that. A decade later, thanks mostly to the Internet, such letters get hundreds of signatures and sometimes thousands. In 2004 the open letter that was posted in the "*Southern Metropolitan* Case" [editors in that case were fired and criminally charged after exposing government cover-ups—Ed.] attracted more than three thousand signatures among media workers alone. Public pressure—including international pressure—eventually grew strong enough that two of the victims, Deng Haiyan and Cheng Yizhong, were released on grounds of "insufficient evidence" while the other two, Li Minying and Yu Huafeng, both saw the charges against them sharply reduced and their prison sentences greatly shortened. Li was released in 2007 and Yu in 2008. None of this would have happened without public pressure.

The growing popular opposition to prison-for-words has been crucial in the rising "rights defense" movement. In an obvious sense, of course, opposition to prison-for-words is precisely about freedom of speech, but the importance of the issue goes beyond that. This is because the expression of public opinion, besides being good in itself, has become an indispensable tool in pursuing almost everything else in the rights movement. Rights in our authoritarian society are not protected by legal or administrative structures, so the role of public opinion becomes especially important. In a sense it doesn't matter whether a fight is over a nasty law that affects everyone or just a single person's case, because the side-effect of a controversy is always to raise popular awareness of rights. This is why step one for rights defenders is to expose facts to the light of day and let people know that they have the right to comment. This simple step can bring important results in relatively "unsensitive" grassroots cases. It can even do some good in cases of very high sensitivity, such as those of Liu Di, Du Daobin, Sun Danian, and "Freezing Point."*

The Chinese government has been doing everything it possibly can to control the Internet. It constantly announces new regulations and laws, sinks vast sums into building its "Great Firewall" against "anti-China" content, hires an ever-larger army of Internet police, and has been paying people to go online to write posts to "guide" public opinion in pro-government directions. And yet, despite all of that, it is losing. It cannot repress the burgeoning spread of citizen-run websites. Liberal-minded intellectuals, in particular, make good use of the Internet, where they run unofficial and semi-official websites of many kinds. Even websites of the mainline state media—"Building a Stronger China," "New China Forum," "China Youth Online," "Southern Media Web," and others—contain much criticism of China's governing system and of policy decisions that top leaders have made. In short, an online civil society is taking shape, whether the government likes it or not.

Moreover the regime's efforts to block overseas online media are losing ground. "Wall-jumping" software has become easier to get in recent years, and the Chinese today enjoy a broader range of information than they have ever had before. International opinion is also beginning to influence Chinese popular opinion in unprecedented ways.

---

*Du Daobin was arrested in October 2003 on charges of "inciting subversion of state power" on the Internet. Sun Dawu is a businessman sentenced in November 2003 for illegally accepting public funds. "Freezing Point" is the name of a supplement to *China Youth Daily* that was shut down in January 2006 for its criticisms of Communist Party officials and its support for non-Party interpretations of history. On Liu Di, see "From Wang Shuo's Wicked Satire to Hu Ge's *Egao:* Political Humor in a Post-Totalitarian Dictatorship" (pp. 177–187 above).

Even the opinions of Chinese dissidents are reaching people inside China more than before because they are rechanneled back into China through international websites.

Clever officials, perceiving the utility of the Internet in building public opinion, have begun to use it to burnish images of themselves as "caring for the people." During the huge blizzard in winter of 2008, for example, several hundred thousand people became stranded outside the Guangzhou rail station, and the issue began to attract considerable attention in the media. On February 3, in an effort to soothe popular frustrations, Guangdong Provincial Party Secretary Wang Yang and Provincial Governor Huang Huahua used a news website called "Olympics First Net" to publish "A Letter to Our Guangdong Netizen Friends." The letter showed unusual tolerance, even approval, of netizen criticism of the government, and was sprinkled with fashionable net-lingo to boot. You netizens, it said, are "well-informed, thoughtful, enthusiastic, and spirited." You have offered many good opinions and suggestions about what to do in this unusual, disastrous blizzard, and your opinions "have become an important foundation that supports our decisions . . . We are willing to 'rap on' with you on topics of common concern. As for the imperfections in our decisions and our work, we are happy to see you 'let it fly.'"

The Chinese political system remains so untransparent that it is hard to say in any quantifiable way exactly how much the new prominence of public opinion actually affects government decisions. But the trend is certainly upward. On the Internet, 2007 was dubbed "the inaugural year of Chinese public opinion" because of several well-known cases in which the pressure of public opinion obviously had a major effect. These include the "Toughest Nail House Case," in which one solitary family held out against forced demolition of their home; the "Brick Kilns Slave Labor Case" [see pp. 94–106 above]; the "Nie Shubin Case," in which a young man was executed for a crime that (it was later shown) he did not commit; the "Pengshui Poem Case" and "Zhu Wenna Case," both cited above; the "City Patrol Beating Death Case," in which a man named Wei Wenhua was beaten to death after photographing police violence; and the campaign to abolish "Re-education through Labor."

In China today, control on expression by an authoritarian regime and pressure for greater latitude from an increasingly pluralistic society are both realities. It is a mistake to ignore either of them. Among the forces pushing for more freedom, there are heroic acts that challenge government power, but these are rare; much more common, indeed the mainstream of the resistance trend, are the low-key, practical ways in which people everywhere keep making small differences. These people have the principle of free expression in mind, but they are also tactically astute. They know how to get things done even as they devise clever ways to protect themselves. They are aware that the political regime is not going to change any time soon, so do what they can in their immediate environments. To purists, they can seem to be making too many compromises, but there can be no doubt they are a major part of the overall quest. The best hope for the future lies in the way civil society on the Internet continually eats away, inch by inch, at the government controls.

In sum, the power of public opinion in China today is much greater than it was in the 1990s, to say nothing of the Mao era, and it is unlikely that China will ever revert to a situation where only the government speaks and everyone else shuts up. But we must recognize that the power of public opinion is not yet a formal part of the political system. It works here and there, now and then—and more and more—but only freelance, as it were, outside of the system. The regime can still simply "declare" an activity to be illegal whenever it wants to. We must look forward to the day when the rights of the people will have institutional guarantees. That day will come.

At home in Beijing, February 19, 2008

*Originally published in* Ren yu renquan *(Humanity and Human Rights), March 2008*
*Translated by Louisa Chiang*

# PART III

# CHINA AND THE WORLD

# BEHIND THE "CHINA MIRACLE"

• • • • •

IN THE YEARS FOLLOWING the Tiananmen Massacre of June 4, 1989, China saw economic growth that far surpassed what happened in the 1980s. Deng Xiaoping was attempting to recoup his authority and to reassert his regime's legitimacy after both had melted away because of the massacre. He set out to build his power through economic growth, justifying the move with the slogan "development is the bottom line."

As the storm clouds cleared and the economy began to flourish, powerful officials saw an opportunity to make sudden and enormous profits. Their unscrupulous pursuit of profit became the engine of the ensuing economic boom. Their greed also set an example. It stirred a nationwide popular fever to get rich quick and to amass huge fortunes, and this dream of rags-to-riches fueled abnormally rapid growth. Growth rates of over 9 percent annually were called a "miracle," and indeed they were, in a way.

## "Chinese Characteristics"

The economic "miracle" happened because of marketization and privatization. Here "marketization" does not mean creating markets under the rule of law; it means marketization of political power, that is, allocating capital and other resources through political authority. And "privatization" has been neither lawful nor ethical; on the contrary, it has meant a robber baron's paradise, a free-for-all. The opening of the real estate market created a platform on which tycoons did landgrabs, and "reorganization" of state-owned enterprises has allowed the power elite to serve themselves heaping portions of communal property. The most highly profitable of the state monopolies have fallen into the hands of small groups of powerful officials, and the government-manipulated financial markets have become a playground on which the power elite romps. In short, the changes in economic policy have opened a host of opportunities for the political elite, who can amass instant fortunes. It also created a group of young millionaires who, if not part of the political elite, were beholden to them.

The income of the Communist regime has skyrocketed, far exceeding the growth rate both of the country as a whole and of the average citizen. High officials have begun to throw their weight around and to scatter money across the globe. Their private hoards could make those mighty capitalists of the Industrial Revolution look shabby. Stories of fabulous overnight wealth pervade the upper reaches of the power elite.

## An Extremely High Price

The "miracle" came at the price of disregard for personal freedoms and the public good. The main beneficiaries of the miracle have been the power elite; the benefits for ordinary people are more like the leftovers at a banquet table. The regime stresses a "right to survival" as the most important of human rights, but the purpose of this truncated notion of rights—call it "human rights with Chinese characteristics"—in fact is to serve the financial interests of the power elite and the political stability of its regime.

The Communist Party will stop at nothing to defend its power. Now that orthodox Marxism has fallen by the wayside, it has adopted a philosophy of sheer opportunism by which any action can be justified if it upholds the dictatorship or results in greater spoils.

## Governing Strategies

The Communist Party in the post-Tiananmen era has consolidated its power using five interrelated strategies:

First, it has used nationalism as its new public ideology.

The Party has fused its rhetoric about "the rise of a great power" with anti-American, anti-Japanese, and anti-Taiwanese sentiment. It also idealizes the imperial glories of China's past so that now the good-old-days of the dynasties have become a central theme in popular culture.

It presents economic growth following years of severe turmoil as a chance for people to recuperate; it depicts the "modest living standard" of the future as sufficiency in food and clothing alone. Hu Jintao's "harmonious society" is offered as an ersatz copy of the Pax Sinica of the past, and his "Eight Virtues and Eight Shames" ("Love the country, do it no harm . . . Observe law and discipline, be not chaotic or lawless," etc.) are an appeal to the Confucian ideal of "rule by virtue."

Second, it has encouraged raw capitalism.

Under the pressures of a devil-take-the-hindmost race to make money at all costs, the interests of the Party have crumbled into factional interests, national interests have broken down into the interests of various privileged groups, and those interests themselves have further divided into the interests of families and even individuals in the power elite.

Profit-seeking is no longer taboo, and the Party has no compunctions about representing big capital. The drive for profit has replaced ideology as a social glue, and profit has become the standard by which government officials are judged. Abuse of power for personal gain is rampant, and has become a cancer within the body of the Party.

"Money is the most important form of political power." This has become the new guiding tenet of the Party. Only money can guarantee the stability of the regime and the interests of the power elite. Only with money can the Party maintain control of China's major cities, co-opt elites, satisfy the drive of many to get rich overnight, and crush the resistance of any nascent rival group. Only with money can the Party wheel and deal with Western powers; only with money can it buy off rogue states and purchase diplomatic support.

Third, the Party has encouraged extravagance in consumerism and frivolity in culture.

Consumerism has been invigorated by a deluge of luxury goods— expensive cars and watches, sumptuous villas—and has given rise to a vapid mass culture that wraps itself in pretty veneers while it deals in illusions of prosperity. The selling of this mass culture dominates the cultural marketplace and has itself become a highly profitable enterprise. The triviality and philistinism of popular consumer culture fits perfectly with the shrill brayings of official injunctions. The authoritarian system actively indulges a hedonist culture in which crassness and barbarity can do as they like.

Fourth, the Party has ruthlessly silenced all dissenting opinion, cracking down especially hard on any social group that dares to organize.

People who have no connection with the Party or a government work unit can enjoy reasonable latitude in their private activities, but such people cannot organize or help to shape an independent civil society. They remain atomized, scattered, and isolated. They can form no independent group of any kind, let alone a group that might compete with the centralized, powerful, and high-organized apparatus of the state.

Fifth, the Party has bought off the intellectuals.

The intellectual elite played a key role in the 1989 pro-democracy movement, and the Communists used two methods to be sure they stopped doing such things. First they terrorized them with a bloody crackdown, then they seduced them with material rewards. After a few years the intellectuals had been transformed into a pack of complacent cynics. In their hearts, many of them still reject the regime's ideology and feel contempt for its actions. But the lure of material benefit on one side and the threat of political persecution on the other have channeled them into alignment with the regime. This leaves them openly professing their support for the status quo and cozying up to the power elite, grasping every opportunity to see if some of the money or status can fall to them. They no longer feel embarrassed at defending what the power elite does, and are often willing to serve as cosmeticians for the new capitalist-Communist regime. The result is a three-way alliance of intellectuals, officials, and capitalists, and for intellectuals this has offered a fast track into the moneyed elite.

## Social Costs

In sum, China's economic transformation, which from the outside can appear so vast and deep, in fact is frail and superficial. Its watchword has been the expansion of quantity, not the raising of quality.

The "miracle" has done nothing for the general quality of personal ethics or social life. Moral standards, intellectual vitality, social concern, and political participation are all far behind where they were in the 1980s. China is on the road to the worst kind of crony capitalism. The power elite brazenly divvies up Party assets (which once were called "public assets"), and the intellectuals shamelessly whitewash what goes on.

The combination of spiritual and material factors that spurred political reform in the 1980s—free-thinking intellectuals, passionate young people, private enterprise that attended to ethics, dissidents in society, and a liberal faction within the Communist Party—have all but vanished. In their place we have a single-barreled economic program that is driven only by lust for profit.

This is what lies behind the economic miracle: the "miracle" of systemic corruption, the "miracle" of an unjust society, the "miracle" of moral decline, and the "miracle" of a squandered future. The damage—to the economy, to human rights, to the entire society—is incalculable. Will we ever be able to recover? If so, *that* will be the miracle.

*Originally published by the British Broadcasting Company, November 4, 2008*
*Translated by Josephine Chiu-Duke*

# BEHIND *THE RISE OF THE GREAT POWERS*

◆ ◆ ◆ ◆ ◆

*During the early years of the twenty-first century, an initiative toward "great power diplomacy" clearly became one of the objectives of the Chinese government under Hu Jintao and Wen Jiabao. The phrase "rise of a great power" entered the official language and was promoted in the state-run media, in part in connection with a spectacular television series. Eventually the phrase took hold in much popular thinking in China, leading Liu Xiaobo to a number of concerns about the idea.*—Ed.

## A Big Hit on China Central Television: *The Rise of the Great Powers*

No list of the major topics in public discussion in China during 2006 can omit the blockbuster production by China Central Television (CCTV) called *The Rise of the Great Powers*. From November 13 to November 24, CCTV's channel 2 broadcast, with great fanfare, a 12-part documentary of that name, and an eight-volume set of books by the same name was published to coincide with the television shows. The theme of this massive project, which was three years in the making, is the history of the rise and fall of great world powers. To get it done, seven separate Chinese production teams were sent to nine different nations that had once vied for preeminence on the world stage: Portugal, Spain, Holland, Great Britain, France, Germany, Japan, Russia, and the United States. The teams did on-site filming and conducted interviews in order to document the 500-year history of the risings and fallings of these "great nations."

The group that planned and designed the project included many Chinese scholars who work within the political system but hold values that are liberal and open-minded. The group also interviewed more than a hundred scholars from China and abroad, so the series can be seen as a genuine cooperative effort between academics and CCTV television producers. It largely avoids the propaganda colorations of the past in favor of a relatively objective and neutral narrative voice, and presents the nine world powers in fairly rich historical contexts. It puts special emphasis on Great Britain and the United States, two democratic countries that have had major impacts on world history, and accords a certain affirmation to the value of modern institutions from the West such as free trade, market economies, and constitutional democracy.

A significant point in the genesis of the project is that, according to Ren Xuean, the chief editor of the series, the earliest impetus for its creation came from the very top of the Communist Party of China. On November 24, 2003, Party leader Hu Jintao presided over his Party Politburo's "ninth collective study session," the topic for which was "An Historical Investigation of the Development of the World's Main Powers since the Fifteenth Century." Two Chinese specialists lectured at that session on the history of the rise and decline of the nine powers in question. Ren Xuean remembers his reaction when he heard about it: "I was listening to the radio one morning on my way to work when I heard that the Politburo was going to study the history of world powers since the fifteenth century—nine great powers over 500 years. There I was, in the noisy, jammed traffic of Beijing's Third Ring Road, and a voice was coming at me out of the hoary past. It was exciting!"

Foreign media reported that after the Politburo's study session was over, the top leaders issued instructions that Party and government officials at all levels study this period of Western history. CCTV's goal in producing the huge project was to spread the theme from within the Party to the whole of society, to expand the Chinese people's awareness of the issue, and to prepare them psychologically for China's own rapid rise. Some of the foreign media speculated that the move was a sign that the top leaders were preparing to initiate political reform.

One would have expected to see a series as important as this aired on CCTV-1, the higher-rated of the CCTV channels. Maybe the authorities put it on CCTV-2 just to try to keep the controversy down, but in any case the series was a major production, appeared on the Party's main television outlet, and in so doing broke the long-standing policy in the official media of keeping issues of major public concern off the air. It provided the Chinese people, with their pent-up longings to participate in public discussion of *any* kind, an excuse to speak up, and the torrent of heated comments that gushed forth as soon as the series aired should not, therefore, surprise us. Whether or not the series clearly explains the history of the rise and fall of world powers is of course a matter of individual opinion. What we know of the reactions of the viewing public—whether we speak of netizens or scholars, Chinese or foreigners—can only be summed up as "mixed."

The people who worked on the production and the inside-the-system scholars who consulted about it all gave it high praise, tinged with a bit of superficial self-congratulation. Mai Tianshu, the chief producer of the series, told the *China Youth Daily* in interview:

> The series adopts the method of emphasizing historical facts with comparatively little by way of value judgment. For that reason it tells a story that differs somewhat from what we are familiar with from our textbooks, and this difference has created a certain tension and excitement that makes people suspect that some major policy change may be on the way. This reaction just shows how fragile the psychology of our society is. A society as big as ours?—And we think some huge turn-around is going to happen just because of a television series? That belittles and underestimates our society.

Mai went on to claim three major virtues of the series: (1) it allowed the public to understand what "historical reason" is; (2) it called for a "spirit of compromise" that Chinese history lacks; and (3) it made clear the key role of a strong central power in a country's rise. On the latter point Mai Tianshu was clearly putting in a plug for authoritarianism.

China's "New Left" launched a fierce attack on the series, saying such things as "it's nothing but a re-run of *River Elegy*" [the famous 1988 television series that suggested that the Communist Party was hidebound and "feudal," while China's salvation lay in tides from abroad—Ed.]; or it "caters to the right-leaning views that have dominated the last twenty years," or "praises the development of the United States to high heaven," or "will stimulate the U.S. and other enemy forces to mount a new high tide in their efforts to hold China back," and so on. The New Left, freshly clothed in its stylish Western Marxism, continues to get nowhere fast. All the foreign ink they have imbibed has done little to dilute the Maoist wolf's milk that still fills their stomachs. They continue to "raise questions to the political level"—letting theory determine what the facts are—and speak of "class struggle" as if we hadn't already been down that disastrous path. One New Left commentary, written under the pen name Li Yang, made an accusation that could send the program producers to prison if taken seriously. "*River Elegy* brought social turmoil," Li Yang wrote, but "*The Rise of the Great Powers* wants regime change." The comment can be seen as a sequel to the New Left's recent campaign to oppose the efforts of people like He Weifang, Peking University's distinguished professor of law, to move China toward liberal democracy. Another of the New Left, writing as Zuo Ke ("the Left will conquer"), posted on the Internet "An Open Letter to the Communist Party Committee of Peking University—You Must Deal Seriously with the Anti-Party Speech of He Weifang!" [In the Mao era, "anti-Party speech" was a crime punishable by a prison sentence or execution.—Trans.]

Evaluations of *The Rise of the Great Powers* from intellectuals called "the liberals" have been more balanced: there have been affirmations as well as some sharp criticisms. The views of Yuan Weishi, a famous professor of history at Sun Yat-sen University, can be taken as representative. In Yuan's view, "the series offers a comparatively objective narration of historical realities and does a pretty good job in its selection of facts. Through its narration of the facts it gives a fairly clear picture of why these countries rose and declined, and it can help the Chinese people to understand the worldwide process of modernization."

But Professor Yuan also pointed out a number of major deficiencies in the series. Foremost of these was its "undue emphasis on 'wealth and power.' Wealth and power have indeed been the long-term goals of many countries," Yuan wrote, "but in order to get there, a country needs to build an appropriate institutional infrastructure. Without the security that such institutions provide, jumping straight into economic growth and into science and technology can lead to dangerous unforeseen results, such as, for example, a state that is rich and a people who are poor, or a state that invades and plunders other countries. The examples are legion." Yuan was most critical of the final episode in the series, the one that was supposed to sum up the lessons of history. This should have been the place, Yuan felt, "to point out the key elements that led to the rise of the great powers, and yet there was no mention at all of the factors that have been critical in determining whether countries can experience long-term stability and enduring peace: things like democratic systems, constitutions, the protection of individual property rights, and guarantees of individual freedom." Another liberal scholar, Dang Guoying, from the Research Institute of the Chinese Academy of Social Sciences, counted the number of times the commentary in *The Rise of the Great Powers* mentioned the word "democracy." He found exactly twelve among the twelve segments and noted that "most of them occur as parts of proper names. There is no serious discussion of the meaning of democracy."

Whatever the authorities intended by broadcasting *The Rise of the Great Powers*, what matters is that the immense power of television brought about more enlightenment than they had in mind. One netizen commented: "Excellent series! I can't believe CCTV made it! I'm stunned, and just hope it won't be banned, because its contents are at odds with China's political system at every turn. It talks about fairness, human rights, democracy, laws, market economy . . ."

If the frenzy of public comment over *The Rise of the Great Powers* is a result of its sponsorship at the very highest level of the Communist Party, it is also an expression of the increasingly virulent nationalism that has gripped our country in recent years. Once patriotism became an absolute form of "political correctness," a slogan like "peaceful rise"—as the Hu Jintao regime put it—was bound to draw notice from many quarters. When I searched *The Rise of the Great Powers* on the Baidu search engine on December 12, 2006, I got 1,820,000 hits. On Google I got 3,000,000. Amazing.

## Official Great Power Diplomacy

China's rapid economic growth in such a large economy is unique in the world today. China's foreign exchange reserves, already more than US $1 trillion in 2006, are number one in the world, and its military power has shot up as well. Communist Party potentates shower the globe with cash, buying influence, and Chinese tourists spend lavishly. Chinese goods are everywhere. China has more cell phones than any place else, and its number of Internet users grows faster than anywhere else as well. In the late years of the Jiang Zemin era (the early 2000s), with victories like the successful Olympics bid and entrance to the World Trade Organization, the low-profile diplomacy of the Deng Xiaoping era—"concealing one's strengths and biding one's time"—gradually gave way to the high-sounding rhetoric of "great power diplomacy," and the traditional notion of China as "the center of all under heaven" reemerged. Jiang Zemin's appetite for showing off personally all over the world was a telltale sign of his desire to rise in the ranks of world leaders. The reasons the Jiang regime beefed up its military, embraced Kazakhstan, Kyrgyzstan, Russia, Tajikistan, and Uzbekistan in the "Shanghai Cooperation Organization," and was generous toward countries that the United States had called "evil states" was not just to bring pressure on Taiwan, but much larger than that: it was to replace the former Soviet Union as the main contender with the United States for world power.

It took Hu Jintao less than three years after coming to power to completely embrace this Jiang Zemin–type great-power diplomacy, and the Hu regime's attitude toward Taiwan, Japan, and the United States grew increasingly hard-line. In blustering rhetoric, Hu announced an "Anti-Secession Law" (2005) that could authorize war with Taiwan; toward Japan, his regime not only engineered the largest outpouring of anti-Japanese sentiment since the reform era began, but also announced a five-year suspension of visits between Chinese and Japanese heads of state; and as for the U.S., after Hu felt snubbed during his U.S. visit after becoming China's president, he set out to unite America's adversaries around the world, from Cuba to Venezuela, from rogue states like North Korea and Iran to the increasingly dictatorial Russia, and they all became close allies of the Hu regime. Hu Jintao and Vladimir Putin issued a "united declaration" as a warning to the U.S., although without mentioning it by name; large-scale Sino-Russian military exercises were also meant as a warning to the U.S. During the same period Hu Jintao, Wen Jiabao, and other high Chinese officials launched a campaign of dollar diplomacy through Latin America, the Middle East, Africa, and Asia. The "Beijing Summit on Chinese-African Cooperation" on November 4–6, 2006, seemed almost to mark a return to the Third World diplomacy of the Mao Zedong era. The regime spent a huge amount of money to bring forty-eight African heads of state to Beijing to gather around Communist Party chief Hu Jintao, rather like the myriad stars of the heavens clustering around the Big Dipper.

### Elites, the Media, and "Angry Youth" Fan the Flames of Emotion

In their efforts to "guide public opinion," government-mouthpiece intellectuals as well as the New Left group in China have been stoking chauvinism of an unseemly sort. Big talk like "the great revival of the Chinese nation is upon us," "The twenty-first century is China's century," "China is destined to replace America as the world's superpower in fifty years," and so on pervades the official media and appears in the pronouncements of many in the elite. Well-known economists observe that China's GNP is on track to exceed Japan's, and some, like Hu An'gang, have even calculated that, measured by per capita purchasing power, China's economy might even surpass that of the U.S. within twenty years and leap to the position of number one in the world. The most conservative voice in this group, Lin Yifu, still calculates that China will outstrip the U.S. by 2050.

When nationalist passion against the U.S., Japan, or Taiwan independence pours out, it often has a bloodthirsty flavor. Whenever conflicts arise between China and the U.S., between China and Japan, or across the Taiwan Straits, voices shouting for killing and beating are sure to ring out on the Internet. Some of the so-called experts join this chorus as it hoots for war. A military specialist warns that "war between China and the U.S. is a certainty"; a foreign affairs expert declares that "it is time to give up the policy of concealing our strengths while biding our time." A People's Liberation Army general even raves that "if the U.S. attacks Chinese territory with guided missiles, I think we can only use nuclear weapons to counterattack . . . we Chinese are prepared for the destruction of all of our cities east of Xi'an, [but] the U.S., of course, must be prepared for the destruction by China of one hundred, two hundred, or even more of its West coast cities."

Any time the achievements of a Chinese person, be it mainlander or overseas Chinese, draws attention in the West, the Chinese state media ballyhoo the achievements for chauvinist effect. Achievements in sports, in particular, are used to try to throw off the "sick man of East Asia" complex that Chinese have inherited from the past. When Wang Junxia took first place in 10,000- and 5,000-meter races in 1993, setting new world records and winning the Jesse Owens Prize, which symbolizes the highest achievement in track and field—and again following her sterling performance at the 1996 Atlanta Olympics—China's state media trumpeted that "the speed and endurance of the East is conquering the world!" When Yao Ming became the starting center for the Houston Rockets, the media cried that "Chinese height subjugates the U.S.!" When Liu Xiang won a gold medal at the Athens Olympics in 2004 for the 110-meter hurdles, the Chinese media saw this as "Chinese speed surpassing the world!" When the Taiwanese-American film director Ang Lee won the "best director" Oscar in 2005 for his film *Brokeback Mountain,* the mainland media called it "a matter of pride for all Chinese" that will "make the world see Chinese film directors in a new light."

Superficial pride of the kind that bespeaks inner insecurity is evident in the frequent repetition of the theme that "we were once rich." Television series highlight the majesty and prosperity of the Han (206 BCE–220 CE) and Tang (618–917) periods and the flourishing eras of the early Qing emperors Kangxi (r. 1661–1722) and Qianlong (r. 1735–1796). In addition to highlighting China's former wealth, the spotlight shines as well on its glorious history of territorial expansion: the great Martial Emperor of Han tramples the Xiongnu barbarians; Genghis Khan gallops across Asia and Europe; Zheng He takes to the seas in the fifteenth century and reaches the Western Pacific; Kangxi and Qianlong expand China to include Taiwan, Mongolia, and Xinjiang; and so on. All this not only feeds nationalist vanity; it also revives the traditional Chinese worldview of China "at the center of all under heaven."

China's rise has become a steady refrain in the Western world as well. Comments from the West like "a formidable China is on the rise" and "the sleeping giant has re-awoken" ring constantly in the ears. This Western talk about China's rise, added to the chorus of Western politicians and pundits expressing their wonderment, and to the stream of pro-China reports from prestigious international agencies, all does much to stimulate Chinese nationalism. Chinese people really begin to think of themselves as "a huge soaring dragon" or "a sleeping giant re-awoken."

## The Other Side of China's Rise

China's diplomatic and military power in the world of course is greater than it used to be. In fact, though, China remains far behind the free world in both hard power and soft power, and talk of its "surpassing the U.S. in twenty years" to become the world's hegemon is nonsense. Westerners sometimes stir up the "China threat" as a way to warn themselves, but in terms of the actual world situation such a view is unnecessarily alarmist. China's infatuation with its "rise as a great nation" is primarily a recoil from its feelings of extreme inferiority in earlier times, and it reflects only a superficial grasp of what the West actually is.

What is clear beyond question is only this: an autocratic regime has hijacked the minds of the Chinese populace and has channeled its patriotic sentiments into a nationalist craze that is producing a widespread blindness, loss of reason, and obliteration of universal values. The nationalist craze has already become standard stock for the dictatorship's claims to hegemony, and that ancient mindset—that ignorant and frightening idea—of "China ruling all under heaven" is on its way back. Through these moves the regime has again led the nation to the brink of peril, causing a part of the Chinese population to lose the most minimal standards of critical thought and to mistake the illusions spun by the dictatorial regime for reality. The result is that our people are infatuated more and more with fabricated myths: they look only at the prosperous side of China's rise, not at the side where destitution and deterioration are visible; they listen only to the praise that comes from Western countries, not to any of the criticisms. They will not face squarely the two great bottlenecks that hobble China's development—its political system and its need for resources—and will not acknowledge the huge gap in both soft and hard power that still stands between China and the countries in the world's mainstream.

The huge costs that China has paid in order to buy economic growth under the constraints imposed by its authoritarian political system have no match in what other nations, during their rises, had to pay. China's economic boom is driven by the export of inexpensive products that are made in sweatshops where workers have no unions, no insurance, no legal recourse, in short no rights; the "maximum output whatever the cost" approach of the bosses creates massive waste of energy and wanton pillage of the environment.

Behind the Communist Party's huge foreign purchase orders, including orders for sophisticated military equipment from Russia, lies the regime's monopoly control of the hard-won wealth that properly belongs to the people of the nation as a whole, but it is wealth the regime can squander as it likes. Behind the spending sprees of Chinese tourists all around the world lies the extreme polarization of wealth that has resulted from the plunder of "collective" and "state" resources by a corrupt power elite. Behind the seemingly rock-solid stability of the social order lies increasingly bitter antagonism between officials and the people as well as the ever-growing pressure of rights-defense efforts that appear now here, now there, but never go away.

Most depressing is this: behind the superficial, arrogant nationalism lies a national ethic that is disconnected from civil values. It is more nearly a primitive jungle ethic of master and slave. In front of the strong, people act like slaves; in front of the weak, like masters. Feeling very bad when utterly bereft, they feel much better in the secure status of slave; then, after prospering as slaves, they have no time for anyone else, but borrow the mantle of their masters to assume airs of superiority. With this sort of national mentality, it will be most difficult for us Chinese, "risen" in the world, actually to become an independent and self-respecting people. We will be fit only to receive the indoctrination, deceit, and threats of our rulers—rather like children, alternately wheedled and deceived by words that their parents use to keep them in line. We will lack our own minds, dignity, and character, and have no way to walk or to think independently. The rulers will bribe us with small favors, threaten us with the lash, entertain us with songs and dances, and use lies to poison our souls.

The great powers in human history that rose as dictatorships—Napoleon's France, Hitler's Germany, the Meiji Emperor's Japan, and

Stalin's Soviet Union—all eventually collapsed, and in doing so brought disaster to human civilization. The rises of Britain and the United States exhibit different patterns: these two countries, based on liberal constitutional governments, were able to avoid the turmoil of sharp ups and downs and to become great powers that enjoyed stability and national security over long periods of time. The British empire depended on colonialism, and with the fall of colonialism Britain reverted to the status of one country among others. The case of the U.S. is different. The U.S. rose in the twentieth century without relying on the occupation and plunder of colonial territory, but was built by supporting freedom, democracy, and national independence around the world, including independence from colonial rule.

Will China's rise today take the German, Japanese, and Soviet Russian road of "the rise of a dictatorship," or will it pattern itself more after the British or American "rise of a democracy"?

In China today, wide and growing differences of opinion on many issues between the government and people in society leave this question of how China will "rise" in deep uncertainty. The very rapid growth of the market economy and a broad awakening of people's awareness of private property rights have generated enormous popular demand for more freedom. On the other hand, the government's jealous defense of its dictatorial system and of the special privileges of the power elite has become the biggest obstacle to movement in the direction of freedom. No matter how long China's economic growth can keep going, no matter how many Chinese cities come to resemble modern international metropolises in their outward appearances, and no matter how luxurious and modern a lifestyle the Chinese power elite can show off, as long as China remains a dictatorial one-party state, it will never "rise" to become a mature civilized country.

The international community ignores at its peril the fact that the contest today between Chinese Communist dictatorship and the free world is very different from the earlier one between the free world and the Soviet Communists. The Chinese Communists have abandoned their ideology and are not pursuing global military confrontation in the way the Soviets did. They are concentrating on economics, seeking to make themselves part of globalization, and are courting friends internationally precisely by discarding their erstwhile ideology. At home, they defend their dictatorial system any way they can, explicitly combating the "peaceful evolution" about which Western leaders have expressed hope and sometimes confidence. They use their bulging purse to buy "friendship" in dollar diplomacy throughout the world. Already they have become a blood-transfusion machine for a host of other dictatorships. Meanwhile they use the carrots and sticks of trade deals, and the lure of the huge market they control, to manipulate and divide the world's major democracies. When the "rise" of a large dictatorial state that commands rapidly increasing economic strength meets with no effective deterrence from outside, but only an attitude of appeasement from the international mainstream, and if the Communists succeed in once again leading China down a disastrously mistaken historical road, the results will not only be another catastrophe for the Chinese people but likely also a disaster for the spread of liberal democracy in the world. If the international community hopes to avoid these costs, free countries must do what they can to help the world's largest dictatorship transform itself as quickly as possible into a free and democratic country.

At home in Beijing, December 17, 2006

*Originally published in* Ren yu renquan *(Humanity and Human Rights), January 2007*
*Translated by Josephine Chiu-Duke*

# TO ST. AUGUSTINE

*For Xia, who likes* The Confessions

St. Augustine
it was at the altar that I came to know you
I had to gaze up at the bishop's red gown
to feel the majesty of the ages

And again in my neighbor's pear garden
I met you
I spied a thieving child
and knew the joy of risk

Facing the silence of time
building the City of God
wanton in the embrace of women
exotic positions in endless number
completely immersed in worldly pleasures
you then fell headlong into the arms of God

There is no reason to doubt your confession was sincere
and every reason to accept your disdain of the flesh
but that child stealing pears and that youngster stealing love
also have the most instinctual reasons for human guilt
wild lust for wickedness and danger

I imagine you look down upon the grandeur of earth
mulling over your humility when you knelt in reverence
and I wonder if saints and gamblers
are really any different at heart
I hear God's an expert at playing dice
so why, after all of your sensual indulgence,
did you choose sainthood over the bettor's life?

Maybe you were the first to discover
the cruelty and mystery of time
and so feared to enter our brief human world
everyone longs for eternal life
and the desire for it may have crushed you, too

I wonder if confession truly makes one tremble
and if the road to atonement is really that long
in God's stage drama people know how
to perform offerings of solemnity
does God like watching plays?
if God is just a tedious theater-goer
then the creation myth is nothing but a
crude practical joke
luckily, in your soul
there is another stage and a few puppets

But be silent
this is the only virtue of saints
stones have seen great ruin and are speechless
the sky looks down over all and is speechless
the earth buries all things and is speechless
the meaning of poems, faith, logic
silver-tongued humanity is a waste
believing in language is believing Judas's promise

December 26, 1996

*Translated by Nick Admussen*

# HATS OFF TO KANT

*For Xia, who has never read Kant*

I am so far away from that little German town
like a eunuch deep in a palace's inner chambers
I can only peer at you through millennia of trash
see all the townspeople proceeding toward the church
hear all the churchbells ringing as one
just to mourn the death of a wise old recluse
there was none among them who could grasp the
    thing-in-itself
or follow the categorical imperative

When you were young you too were headstrong
you sought a rod to hold you up
charged with passion you created a world
the mystery of the night drew suddenly down
to threaten the infinity
which made you tremble
the meek tremble and are great
the great tremble and are meek
therefore, you understand
how humans must kneel in awe
of the infinite, the profound, the divine—

A fatal boundary
made knowledge bow its proud head
the break with tradition is bloodless
yet blanches the spirit terribly
as when God cast out humanity's first ancestor
the tree heavy with its fruit of worldly sin
the crack reaches deep into the marrow
a wound almost impossible to perceive
but never healing, always fresh
and you, inscrutable bachelor
you turned philosophy into salt

I know you never married
how with the mischievous mind of a boy
you stayed up late nights wondering whether when you die
you'd still be a child
I imagine you approached the question as scrupulously
as you questioned the limits of knowledge
did the blade of knowledge castrate you
or did your body's blade castrate knowledge
I know how you entered the sanctum of reason and
    experience
firm in your belief that critical philosophy
was like Columbus's ship approaching the New World
how under the infatuated gaze of women
you paced your hermit's room, self-deploring, alone

God chose you
to reveal the categorical imperative
your decrees oppressed humanity
and oppressed you
if Freud had been born two centuries earlier
beneath his mesmeric stare, your virginity
would have split into dreams of every color
spirits endowed with every poison
yet you were born too early

you escaped that fate
I do not know whether, for you
that was good fortune or ill

You stood in awe of the divine
yet you never evangelized or repented
walking into church was like opening an old book
playing child's games with a grown man's knowledge
laying out those indecipherable figures
behind you sky, clouds, sun
before you only darkness, bright as day

So much erudition and mystery
So much experience and clarity
heaped upon your grave
a bloodless murder
your hands spotless
your body, eroded by the refuse of thought
into a dubious monument
posterity gazes up through the smoke of its genocides
at those days of contemplation and perception
a broken language resurrected
this jetsam of syntax and vocabulary
reflecting you warping you hiding you revealing you
holding you aloft
a black hole at the center of the sun

December 17, 1996

*Translated by Isaac P. Hsieh*

# THE COMMUNIST PARTY'S "OLYMPIC GOLD
MEDAL SYNDROME"

◆   ◆   ◆   ◆   ◆

IN THE SEVEN YEARS between Beijing's successful bid to host the Olympics in 2001 and the opening of the Games in 2008, the government ran a nationalistic publicity campaign that emphasized "the Hundred-Year Olympic Dream." In the final year, as the countdown to the Games entered the home stretch, this campaign went into a sprint. The mainland media were saturated with PR about the Olympics. Once the Games started, a tidal wave of patriotic sentiment first focused on the lavish, dreamlike opening ceremony, then switched to an obsession with the gold-medal count.

Chinese state television—local stations as well as China Central Television (CCTV)—began tallying gold medals right from the first one that a Chinese team won. China led continuously in the gold medal count, and all channels kept constant track of the total. In the on-air commentary and in all of the reporting on the Chinese athletes, the impression that gold medals were everywhere dazzled the eyes and ears. In the tone of voice and expression of the announcers, and in the questions that reporters saw fit to ask of the gold medal winners, there was a constant sense that everyone was high on the opium of gold-medalism. Other than gold medals and the flag there were, well—gold medals and the flag! All of Beijing was resplendent in red and yellow! It was hard, by comparison, to sense anyone's appreciation for the brilliant athletic performances themselves, and harder still to find any traces of the "Olympic spirit" or human values.

245

In the light-heavyweight boxing competition, when the Chinese boxer Zhang Xiaoping defeated the Irishman Kenny Egan to win the gold, CCTV anchorman Han Qiaosheng burst out with: "Our Zhang Xiaoping has knocked his opponent silly! His blows show the glory of Chinese manhood! We can talk with our fists, and in any contest can fight with brawn as well as brains! A legend is born! China soars! The Chinese dragon takes flight!"

Even now, weeks after the Games have ended, the Chinese state media continue with a steady mantra of "number one in gold," intruding the message into the lives of Chinese everywhere, including in Hong Kong and Macao. CCTV and local sports channels are *still* counting and recounting the gold medals, reviewing how each was won, praising once more each Chinese champion, and harping on the idea that China has risen to become a gold medal colossus. Sina.com, the huge state-sponsored Internet portal, has set up a site where, under the heading "Boundless Glory: The Rise of a Great Nation," viewers "can take one more look at how each of China's gold medals was won." NetEase, another major portal, offers a similar opportunity under the heading "A Perfect End to the Beijing Games: China's Haul of 51 Gold Medals Makes History."

After the Games were over, a delegation of gold-medal winners, led by Party sports official Liu Peng, descended upon Hong Kong and Macao to wow the locals with the mainland's gold-medal luster. At a press conference in Hong Kong, Liu Peng and his fellow officials could hardly have been more overbearing. Their tone and demeanor seemed to be telling the people of Hong Kong: "These gold medalists are heroes of the people. No disrespect will be tolerated!" Whenever a politically sensitive question was directed to any of the athletes, they cut the athlete off and answered themselves, and each answer was obviously scripted.

The love of gold medals among Party officials and the patriotic set has reached a point that we can call pathological. They are like some of our country's new millionaires, who adore counting the gold in their pockets, and to whom the clink of coins is the loveliest music in the world and their glitter the most dazzling of the world's light.

The Beijing Olympics were always a top priority for the Hu-Wen regime in its program to channel popular nationalism into support of its dictatorship. In preparing for the Olympics, Chinese officials pitched in at all levels, the whole nation was mobilized, enormous sums of money were spent, a wild surge of nationalism resulted—and all of this happened on scales that were unprecedented in the hundred-year history of the modern Olympics. Moreover, in China, winning or losing international sports contests had become so thoroughly politicized and so steeped in nationalism that the gold medals of the Beijing Olympics had taken on the added burden of the Great Country dream—the playing out of the "overtaking-the-West" complex that Mao Zedong had planted in the popular Chinese mind fifty years ago when he promised that China's "Great Leap Forward" would see it "overtake" the developed world in fifteen years.

I do not know whether other countries love gold medals as much as China does, but I do know that there is no way any other country could marshal such vast resources in pursuit of a "Gold Medal Great Leap Forward." Before the Olympics, Party boss Hu Jintao issued a proclamation. "The Beijing Olympics," he said, "should demonstrate the superiority of the socialist system by showing how it concentrates strength in order to manage great undertakings." Hu's enthusiasm echoed Mao and the Great Leap Forward about "surpassing" Britain and America. Mao had targeted iron and steel production, and Chinese at the time were led to be fanatical about producing iron and steel, even in their own backyards. Then, the slogan was "The Whole Nation Is One Big Steel Mill." Now, it was "The Whole Nation Does the Olympics." The goal was different; the madness was similar.

China's rulers, after making gold-medalism the core of their Olympic strategy, and after fueling the Olympic effort with the kind of massive investment that only the authoritarian government of a large country could make, did indeed achieve steady increases in the number of gold medals at successive Olympic Games. In Atlanta in 1996, China took fourth place; in Sydney in 2000, third place; in Athens in 2004, second place: with each Olympics, it was one step up. After the Athens Games, to reach first place in the gold-medal count became *the* goal for the Beijing Games. And in the end the regime got its wish: it supplanted America as Mr. Big at the gold-medal table. The first-place finish gave China bragging rights before the world.

When Liu Xiang won the 110-meter hurdles at the Athens Games in 2004, his time was 12.91 seconds, a new Olympic record and an equal of the world record. Liu was the first Asian athlete ever to win such an honor. When the race concluded, the CCTV announcer went crazy on the live broadcast, positively howling, and Liu Xiang himself descended into histrionics when he accepted the medal. In a later interview he said, "No worries, Asia; no worries, China: you've got *me* on your side!" Overnight he became "a hero of the people," and Chinese fans grew giddy as they celebrated that "a New China has emerged in competition." Liu Xiang became the country's new "Soaring Man" (punning on his given name *xiang* 'soar'), and simultaneously a symbol for all of Chinese athletics as well as the single Chinese athlete upon whom the greatest of hopes were pinned.

In the run-up to the Beijing Games, the halo of nationalism hovering over Liu Xiang shined all across China. His image was on posters everywhere—in both city and countryside, along broad avenues and tucked into narrow alleys. Even more over-the-top, this: the number on his track suit, No. 1356, symbolized the 1.3 billion people of China and their 56 ethnic nationalities. All eyes were anticipating his performance in the dazzling new stadium called the Bird's Nest, and the gold for the 110-meter hurdles became the number-one gold medal in the popular mind. For some fans, it was only Liu Xiang's hurdles that drew them to the Bird's Nest.

Then, when Liu had to withdraw from the event because of an injury, in the process quashing hopes for the Chinese track team's sprint to the gold, "the people's hero" instantly lost his luster, inflicted keen disappointment upon the "patriotic" set, and brought forth a tidal wave of gossip among the public.

In Olympic history there have been many instances of great athletes needing to withdraw from competition because of injury. Never, though, has there been a public howl the size of what we heard after Liu Xiang's withdrawal. China was already well ahead of the U.S. in the race to be Mr. Big in gold medals, so that was not the point. The outcry over Liu Xiang's withdrawal exposed something deeper; it showed the defensive mentality, the aberrant vanity, of an insecure country that "cannot afford to lose." With so many people—officials and ordinary citizens alike—so in a tizzy over gold medals, the guardians of "patriotism" could be as oppressive toward Liu Xiang as they liked; they could invoke the sacred cows of "national honor" and "the interests of the state" to force him to bow his head. Amid all the hue and cry the superhero "soaring man" finally crumbled. He had to come out before the whole nation and apologize.

I think that only a centralized sports machine like China's could generate such a fixation on gold medals, and only that fixation could have necessitated the absurd spectacle of an athlete apologizing to his fellow citizens for an injury. The real absurdity, though, is that—given what the Chinese system is—the demands for an apology actually did make a kind of sense. Liu Xiang's achievements were the result of training for which the Party-state had paid; his crown as a "hero of the people" was also something that the Party-state, and the "patriotic masses," had given to him. Therefore his success or failure was much more than his personal gain or loss; it involved the interests of the State and the honor of the nation. The number 1356 on his back meant that his fate was the fate of 1.3 billion people: a win from him was glory for the Party-state and the people; a loss was their collective shame. *Of course* he had to apologize if he didn't deliver the goods.

The gold-medalism of China's centralized sports machine arose after the Los Angeles Games of 1984, when China won its first gold medal, and since then has cost Chinese taxpayers dearly. Now, after coming in first in gold medals in Beijing, the machine will feel the added burden of pressure from high expectations. As soon as the Beijing Games were over, the Chinese media descended into endless rounds of spectacular boasting, and they made much of praise that appeared in foreign media. When Jacques Rogge, president of the International Olympic Committee (IOC), said that the Games were "truly exceptional," China's state media trumpeted the phrase and, in their translation, promoted it to "beyond compare." The excitement that gripped the whole country at being number one in gold seemed to forecast a brilliant prospect of China's overtaking America in every other respect and becoming the number one nation in the world. It is this implied mission of the centralized sports machine that causes it to fall into the gold-medal syndrome and to create so much anxiety.

The gold-medal syndrome generates at least the following four crises:

1. Sports in China have come to be divided into two broad categories, the Olympic elite and everybody else, and the two groups are grossly

unequal in their access to resources. The Olympics machine is the biggest among the projects that the Party-state uses to manufacture face for itself. No amount of either money or manpower is too great to spend on it. In the seven years before the Beijing Olympics, elite athletes got nothing but the best in support and equipment, while ordinary people often got nothing at all. The gold-medal athletes in the Olympics machine lived in a lonely world all their own, high in the clouds, lavishly supplied with both money and glory, while ordinary athletes, by the same two measures, were poverty-stricken. Just as China's lopsided economic reforms have given rise to a singular worship of GDP and have divided China between a heaven where the power elite can get rich overnight and a hell where the powerless constantly lose out, the gold-medal obsession of the centralized sports machine similarly—no, inevitably—creates a heaven for elite athletes and a hell for ordinary athletes.

China's number one place in gold medals depended on huge investments. Leaving aside the incalculable costs in money and manpower of the worldwide "torch relay," and without counting the costs for all the Olympic security, the official on-paper outlays for the Olympics reached 43 billion U.S. dollars. This is more than four times the $9.7 billion that China spent in 2007 on public health and medical care, and nearly three times the $15.7 billion spent on education. (Huang Wei, advisor to the Beijing Olympic committee, at one point disclosed an even higher figure: 520 billion yuan, or more than $70 billion U.S.) Such extravagance for "gold-medal sports" is not only unprecedented in developing countries; it would be lavish even in developed nations. The scale of the Chinese Party-state's outlays probably exceeds anything in Olympic history and may never be matched again. It will be impossible for London, four years from now, to invest more money or to mobilize more manpower than Beijing did. To sponsor events in which money is no object is something that lies within the reach only of dictatorships that can disregard the interests of their own people. They can simply mandate that taxpayers foot the bill.

In sharp contrast to China's massive spending, the IOC, right after the Beijing Games, announced a plan to "trim costs." IOC president Rogge, while praising Beijing's spectacular show, saw a danger that the Beijing example might put pressure on future host countries and frankly stated that the Olympics need to undergo some "changes." "Olympic gigantism" was imposing heavy burdens on host countries. The Games should be "trimmed down" and not staged on this kind of scale again.

2. Gold-medal obsession obliges China's athletes to pay enormous prices in personal dignity and in normal human relations. For the sake of Olympic gold, Chinese athletes, right from childhood, enter government-run sports schools where they live in special dormitories, are completely cut off from the outside world, and submit to training that is almost military in nature. They not only lose their freedom but must make sacrifices in love and affection as well. In the words of a Party sports official, "to win Olympic glory for the Motherland is a sacred mission entrusted to us by Party Central." This "sacred mission" can be a cruel thing. It can obstruct even the love between a mother and daughter. Xian Dongmei, winner of the gold in judo, was the only mother on China's Olympic team. In order to train for the Games, she had to leave her 18-month-old daughter and didn't see her for a whole year. Cao Lei, who won the gold in weightlifting, was sealed off even from the news of his mother's death, and did not attend her funeral.

Athletes hand over their entire personal lives in full-bore preparation for the Games. Chen Yibing, the gymnast who won the gold in the flying rings, was candid in an interview: "You've got no control over your own life. The coach is always right there with you. Someone is always watching you, even the physicians and the cooks in the cafeteria. You've got no choice: you have to submit to the training. You can't let others down."

The coercion in the centralized sports machine exacts another price from China's athletes: their health. Prospective Olympic divers are selected for training as young as 5 or 6, even though health professionals know that to start diving at this age, before the eyes have fully developed, can do permanent harm. The force of impact when a diver enters the water is enough to damage a child's retina. Gold medalist Guo Jingjing, who had been recruited for the diving team at age 6, has sustained serious eye damage. His vision is now so bad that he has trouble making out the diving board, and he could go blind at any time. Li Fenglian, the doctor for China's Olympic diving team, told a journalist that a research report she published last year showed that 26 of the 184 members of the team had suffered damage to their retinas.

3. Gold-medal obsession increases both the power and the cynicism of "all-pervasive politics" under the rule of China's Party-state. Once the Olympics were declared the highest national interest, they naturally also became the highest political mission, and that meant that they trumped everything else. From then on, everything had to be either "for the Olympics" or "out of the way of the Olympics." Party, government, military, civilians, business, the academy—*everybody*—fell in line to pursue the overriding political goal. No expense was spared—in money, materials, or manpower—to build first-class stadia and service facilities. Staff, security personnel, and volunteers working on the Games not only broke an Olympic record in their numbers; they had to be politically reliable, too. They all went through a multistage screening process and were closely observed during training. Their task was to envelop foreign reporters and tourists in comfort and amiability, offering them VIP treatment and charming smiles, reducing friction to a minimum.

In the name of the exalted interests of state, "omnicompetent politics" could, moreover, use absolutely any means it chose—from brazen fakery like the dubbed singing and fake footprints at the opening ceremony* to the falsified ages of some of the athletes to the inauthentic smiles of the trained volunteers. Meanwhile a heavy hand obliterated every trace of dissent. The media had guidelines of "zero criticism" when speaking for itself and "only praise" in selecting material from the foreign media. Foreign protesters were expelled from China, and the three parks that were reserved for domestic protesters produced, as expected, "zero criticism."

Only its unlimited power could allow the Party-state to flaunt a report card for such smooth logistics and such first-rate stadia and facilities. And only a government of this kind could throw a ring of steel around Beijing to assure security. Silently missing from the report card was the Party-state's cynical abandonment of its promises about human

---

* At the opening ceremony, *Ode to the Motherland* was sung by the 7-year-old Yang Peiyi, but at the insistence of an official who deemed her insufficiently photogenic she was replaced on camera by the 9-year-old Lin Miaoke. Fireworks in the sky appeared as "footprints," but, because these could not be captured on camera, their image had to be artificially added to the video feed.—Trans.

rights. The dream-come-true of winning the gold-medal derby must be weighed against a citizens' nightmare of utterly dismal human rights.

4. The worst consequence of the gold-medal obsession has been that it has strengthened the forces blocking reform. The Olympics "success" has confirmed the Communist regime's confidence in its style of authoritarian control and has deepened the delusion of many citizens that China, thanks to the efficiency of the Party's dictatorship, is on the verge of becoming the number one country in the world. Zhang Yimou, the famous film director who agreed to design Beijing's opening ceremony, said in an interview that "the ceremony combined opulent extravagance with precise regularity of movement and a grand narrative, and this required tremendous resources—human, material, and financial. In today's world, the only countries that could pull this off are China and North Korea."

In other words, the Olympics have served to delay the reform of a rotten system, and indeed have helped it to gain strength that might keep it going longer than it otherwise would. This is, in any case, how the Party-state itself sees the matter. As soon as the final tallies in the gold-medal derby were clear, Party sports officials were quick to credit China's success to the centralized sports machine. Wei Jizhong, senior advisor to the Beijing Olympic Committee, said at a press conference that forty-five gold medals demonstrated the efficacy of the "whole nation system." He cited the fate of sports programs in the former Soviet Union after the collapse of central authoritarian rule there as proof that China had been wise to stick to its ways.

After the Games, *People's Daily* published an interview with Liu Peng, director of the State General Administration of Sports, under the headline "Sports Must Persist with the Whole Nation System." Liu was candid in saying that China needs a system of centralized control in sports not only because the country is so large but for political reasons. He said:

> Sports themselves are not political, but they have important political functions. The close connection between sports and national identity takes different forms in different countries at various stages of development, and in China it has special significance. The phrase "a weak country has no sports" has

particularly painful associations for Chinese people [owing to
China's nineteenth-century image as "The sick man of Asia"—
Trans.]. For sports to keep pace with the general progress of a
nation is not only right and proper in itself but serves as an
inspiration to the people; as inspiration it extends beyond the
domain of sports to heighten national confidence, pride, and
cohesion in a broader sense . . . [this is why] we shall continue
to rely on the approach of centralized command. It is one of
our fine traditions, it sums up our efficient model, and it works
to bring our people together and to get them moving. Our po-
sition on the "whole nation system" is clear: we will retain it
and we will continue to perfect it.

Liu went on to remark with satisfaction, "I hear that many countries
today are looking at China's system and trying to learn from it."

This kind of vain pride in power and in ethnic identity has exerted a
distorting pressure on Chinese sports "not to lose at any price." The pop-
ular uproar after Liu Xiang withdrew became a burden on him so heavy
that humiliating apology was his only way out. The Chinese athletes
who will head to London in 2012 will have to carry the further burden of
"top dog in gold medals," and, if China pulls down fewer than 51 gold
medals in London, or worse, slips from its number one position, I don't
want to think about the hysteria that will ensue back home.

When sports have become so commercialized and so deeply colored
by nationalism, a gold medal no longer stands for an athletic achieve-
ment alone. At the same time, a gold-medal count has become an unre-
liable indicator of a nation's strength or its degree of civilization. During
the Cold War era, the Soviet Union often won more Olympic medals,
including gold medals, than any other country. At the Seoul Games in
1988, it won 132 medals, a record, and 55 of them were gold, also a record.
East Germany, too, was once a mighty Olympic power. In Montreal, Mos-
cow, and Seoul, East Germany ranked number two in the world in the
medal haul. But what did these titanic achievements do for the authori-
tarian systems that produced them, when finally it came time for those
systems to collapse?

The record shows that gold-medal nationalism is even more corro-
sive to sports culture than commercialization is, and this is especially

true when an authoritarian country is playing host. "Whole nation systems" in such countries can indeed allow them to tower over others in a medal count, but these systems do nothing to promote human values in the country. On the contrary they can do disastrous harm: sport can turn into a tool for the self-promotion of despots, and the spirit of sports, which originally was a universal value, can be pressed into the service of narrow nationalism. The gleam of the gold can help a dictatorial regime to tighten its grip on power and to fan flames of nationalism that it can use for other purposes.

If Chinese officials and people continue to use a sports machine to pursue gold-medal glory, and continue to bask in the comments of foreigners who say we are "beyond compare" (or something like that, depending on our "translation with Chinese characteristics"), then sports in China can only go farther and farther down the road of a radical disjunction between ordinary sports for ordinary citizens and a super-politicized, super-extravagant elite gold-medalism. A nation obsessed with gold medals will never turn into a great civilized nation.

At home in Beijing, September 18, 2008

*Originally published in* Zhengming *(Cheng Ming Monthly), September 2008*
*Translated by A. E. Clark*

# HONG KONG TEN YEARS AFTER THE HANDOVER

◆　◆　◆　◆　◆

THE UPCOMING TENTH ANNIVERSARY of Hong Kong's handover from London to Beijing is a splendid occasion for the regime in China but a sorrowful one for the people of Hong Kong.

On July 1, the day of the anniversary, China's President Hu Jintao will visit Hong Kong to accept the tribute of its pro-Beijing faction and to flaunt the might of his dictatorship. Meanwhile, the people of Hong Kong will continue their ten-year struggle for democracy by greeting their mainland overlord with yet another expression of their aspirations. They have planned a protest march for this day to demand "twin general elections," by which they mean one-person-one-vote elections for (1) the chief executive and (2) the legislature.

It is well known that the British legacy of freedom and the rule of law is the wellspring of Hong Kong's economic prosperity. Yet the Beijing regime, despite its vaunted policy of "one country, two systems," has been steadily eroding Hong Kong's liberties ever since the handover.

The most glaring casualty has been freedom of the press. The Hong Kong media have become largely self-censoring in response to Beijing's two-pronged approach of economic inducements plus political bullying. Another example is Beijing's pretty-sounding policy of "free travel" between Hong Kong and the mainland. In fact this is a right only to semi-free travel, limited to things like tourism and shopping, and moreover is granted only to those who do not cause trouble for Beijing. It is denied to Hong Kong democracy advocates and to opposition journalists even if they are traveling for personal reasons. Beijing has revoked the Home Visit Permits of blacklisted pro-democracy figures like Szeto Wah, Martin Lee, and the editors of well-known Hong Kong political magazines.

### Bribery Cannot Silence the July 1 Protest Movements

There is no doubt that China's steady economic ascent since the June 4 Tiananmen Square crackdown eighteen years ago has bolstered the regime's grip on the mainland. The Beijing regime, having seen how distorted reforms that favor the wealthy can have the effect of producing a surface stability inside China, has applied similar techniques of subornment in Hong Kong and invested in Hong Kong's economic revival with the goal of silencing dissent. The policy of "free travel" that I just referred to is but one example. Never mind the political discrimination in the policy; it brings *money* to Hong Kong. Wealthy mainlanders who travel to Hong Kong inundate local hotels and gratify merchants with their lavish spending.

An unintended positive side effect of the travel policy has been to allow information-starved mainlanders access to accurate information. It has whetted their appetites for books and magazines that are banned on the mainland—especially exposés of Chinese Communism. Indeed, some sightseers from the mainland, intrigued by Hong Kong's protest marches, demonstrations, and mass meetings, time their visits so that they can participate in the annual July 1 protest marches or June 4 candlelight vigils in Victoria Park. For mainland intellectuals, long closed off from the world, this political awakening is far more significant than the consumer aspects of travel.

Right from the start, Beijing has been doing what it can to backtrack on its original promise to Hong Kong of "one country, two systems" and has alternated between tactics of bribery and coercion in pursuit of the goal. Beijing insisted, for example, that Hong Kong's first chief executive, Tung Chee-hwa, follow its model of repression by forcing the passage of an antisubversion law known as Article 23. In order to counter a protest against Article 23 that Hong Kong people had planned for July 1, 2003, Premier Wen Jiabao arrived in Hong Kong in late June bearing monetary gifts like the "Closer Economic Partnership

Arrangement." Posing as a benefactor of Hong Kong and staging displays of solicitude, Wen hoped to win popular support for his regime's dictatorial plans and to weaken the protest march.

But Beijing had miscalculated. It had relied on the self-serving advice of sycophants in Hong Kong who promised that Hong Kong runs on economics alone, and had badly underestimated the courage and commitment to freedom of the Hong Kong people. Half a million protesters came out for the July 1 march against Article 23, showing Wen Jiabao and the entire world that the ordinary people of Hong Kong were above the temptations of money and that Hong Kong remained a luminous "Pearl of the East." The common people turned out to be the ones who possessed the true wealth: political wisdom and high principles. The tycoons who had been selling out to Beijing to line their own pockets have reduced themselves to the level of pawns and showed their moral bankruptcy.

The whole world witnessed the massive July 1 protest march, which hamstrung the Beijing regime and its puppet, Chief Executive Tung Chee-hwa. Hu Jintao and Wen Jiabao, forced to pragmatism, had to accede to Hong Kong popular opinion: Tung Chee-hwa tabled Article 23, following which high officials on the mainland made outward shows of "respecting the decision of the Hong Kong government." Everyone knew that the only reason for this concession was that awkward public promise of "one country, two systems" that the regime had made.

### "Patriotism": A Bludgeon in the Hands of Scoundrels

In its search for ways to squelch freedom in Hong Kong, the Beijing regime has promoted a twisted definition of patriotism: "Love of Hong Kong is love of China." Armed with this tool, the regime has incited its toadies and their media hacks in Hong Kong into a savage mudslinging campaign that accuses democracy advocates of a lack of "patriotism." Their tactics have descended into ad hominem attack and character assassination and might be called "hooligan-patriotism." Such abuse of the term "patriotism" has nothing to do with any ethical principles; on the contrary, it is a bludgeon in an assault on common human values.

While acknowledging that the vast majority of people who took part in the 2003 protest march were patriotic, the regime has singled out a small number as treacherous rabble-rousers. This reminds me of the regime's distorted characterizations of the Tiananmen Square protests of 1989, when it claimed that although the vast majority of protesting students were patriotic, a few "black hands" lurking behind the scenes had instigated "turmoil" and "rioting." This is one of the regime's favorite tactics in trying to build "united fronts." In a speech about the 2003 demonstration, Liu Yandong, vice chair of the Party's Political Consultative Conference, put it plainly: "Consolidate the majority and isolate the handful."

Intense political pressure and economic appeasement are both manifestations of the extreme arrogance of a dictatorial system. Sometimes the display is personified in a high-handed, abusive tyrant, like Jiang Zemin when he excoriated Hong Kong journalists in 2000. At other times it shows itself in the image of the enlightened despot who poses as a benefactor of the common people. This was the case with Wen Jiabao and his show of solicitude during his 2003 visit.

### Wu Bangguo's Arrogant Proclamation

Emboldened by the burgeoning Chinese economy, China's rulers have in recent years been chasing the pipe dreams that have been suggested in the television documentary called *The Rise of the Great Powers* [see pp. 228–239]. This month, on the eve of the tenth anniversary of the Hong Kong handover, Beijing delivered an unprecedented and arrogant statement at a conference on the first ten years of experience with Hong Kong's constitutional document known as the Basic Law. Wu Bangguo, chair of the Standing Committee of China's National People's Congress, declared at the conference:

> The high degree of autonomy enjoyed by the Hong Kong Special Administrative Region is not intrinsic, but is granted by the central government. China is a single country, united under one system. Hong Kong will have only as much power as the central government grants to it, and no more. Furthermore, Article 20 of the Basic Law is unambiguous on the issue of so-called "residual powers": it stipulates clearly that additional powers that have not been specified may be granted only by the central government. In sum, the Basic Law is solely about the center's granting of powers.

This declaration—a seeming death-knell for Hong Kong's democratization and the "one country, two systems" policy—stimulated much comment in Hong Kong and around the world. Former prime minister Margaret Thatcher of Britain and a former governor of Hong Kong, Christopher Patten, both lambasted Beijing for trying to shelve Hong Kong's democratization. Hong Kong democracy advocates Anson Chan, Martin Lee, Szeto Wah, James To, Albert Ho, Joseph Zen, Jackie Hung, and others all challenged Wu Bangguo's claim. Even the mild-mannered senior journalist Lam Shan Muk published an article in the *Hong Kong Economic Journal* saying that Wu's speech meant that China expected Hong Kong to move from "two systems" to "one country" and that Beijing's tenth-anniversary "gift" to Hong Kong was but an attempt to enslave it.

Hong Kong's democrats answered Wu Bangguo by launching a prolonged legislative campaign that called for "twin general elections" by 2012. The Democratic Party organized a conference to study the progress of democratization in Hong Kong, and the Civil Human Rights Front began to plan another march for July 1 so that Hu Jintao could hear the people's voice during his tenth-anniversary visit. Surveys show that a majority in Hong Kong want these "twin general elections" and that their faith in Beijing has declined.

From my vantage point here on the mainland—still living under dictatorship—Hong Kong's June 4 candlelight vigils and July 1 demonstrations are a heartening and rousing sight. To me, the eighteen years since the Tiananmen Square crackdown have passed like a single day, but have been illuminated continuously by the brilliance of Hong Kong's candles. They burn with the determination of its people to treasure their freedom, uphold righteousness, and resist tyranny.

Looking back on the huge demonstration of July 1, 2003, the protest that brought down the iniquitous Article 23, it is clear that the people of Hong Kong achieved a political miracle for themselves and for all who seek freedom. It was a people's victory over their Hong Kong puppet government and the dictatorial Chinese Communist Party, and it was achieved through a potent combination of organization, popular will, and momentum. A free political system is and will be the best protection that Hong Kong people can have for their personal freedoms; their own determination is their strongest weapon against tyranny; and world opinion is and will be on their side.

In the long run, there are two main projects that Hong Kong people must pursue in order to preserve their freedoms and to avoid being engulfed by the mainland. First, they must work together for the democratization of the Hong Kong government, especially the direct election of a chief executive. Second, they must promote political reform in mainland China, working indirectly but by every means possible. Preserving Hong Kong's democracy should be the sacred responsibility of everyone in China, not just Hong Kong people; similarly, promoting political reform in all of China should be the sacred responsibility of people on both sides of the Hong Kong border. This is because the two sides are inextricably connected in the overall quest for freedom. Hong Kong will have no guarantee of freedom until the people of the mainland are free as well.

At home in Beijing, June 18, 2007

*Originally published in* Kaifang *(Open Magazine), July 2007*
*Translated by Eva S. Chou*

## SO LONG AS HAN CHINESE HAVE NO FREEDOM, TIBETANS WILL HAVE NO AUTONOMY

◆　◆　◆　◆　◆

*In March 1959, the People's Liberation Army of China crushed a popular rebellion in Tibet, an event that has made March 10, the day the rebellion had begun, a "sensitive" day in Tibet ever since. On March 10, 2008, about 400 Buddhist monks in the Tibetan capital of Lhasa took to the streets demanding freedom of religion and a reduction in the migration of Han Chinese into Tibet. The monks had strong popular support among the Tibetan populace, and protests continued until March 14, when scuffles between young Tibetans and Chinese plainclothes police turned into what Tibetans called "resistance" (with the admixture of some provocateur activity) and what the government called "riots."*

*During the next few days, martial law was put in force, Tibetan neighborhoods were searched door to door, many people were beaten, more than a hundred were killed, and more than 2,000 were arrested. The foreign media were expelled from Tibet, while Chinese television showed repeatedly—all across China—images and accounts to back the government claim that Tibetan rioters, in an operation "plotted, planned, and organized" by the Dalai Lama, a "wolf in sheep's clothing," had attacked Han Chinese. The events were costly to the Chinese government's image at the beginning of its "Olympic year."—Ed.*

As of today, April 10, the crisis in Tibet has held the attention of the world for one month. If the regime of Hu Jintao and Wen Jiabao cannot come up with some acceptable responses, Tibetan resistance as well as the censure of the international community will likely extend through this summer's Beijing Olympics and the world may very well take a dim view of the Games. The protests that have accompanied the Olympic Torch relay along its route outside of China already show how this can happen.

Within China's borders, the regime of course can quell Tibetan resistance by force and can stimulate Han chauvinism to draw popular support to itself. The regime's tactics so far—replaying some carefully edited video footage of riot damage in Lhasa on March 14, finding a few errors in Western media coverage and blowing them out of proportion, mobilizing public opinion with a call to "Oppose Splittism and Protect the Sacred Torch," and protecting its one-sided account of events by enforcing a strict blackout of news reporting from Tibet—have already been very successful in stimulating a frenzy of Han nationalism. A confrontation between freedom and dictatorship has been made to look like a clash between ethnicities.

But such tactics can do nothing to extinguish the resistance of Tibetans who live outside of China and nothing to earn support from the international community. Moreover, the regime is helpless to remove the root causes of the troubles in Tibet, just as it is helpless to eradicate the deep-seated crisis that grips China as a whole. The advantages that it gains from its tactics in Tibet are only short-term expediencies; they help to buy more time for dictatorship, but are useless in promoting peaceful governance of a multi-ethnic China in the long run.

It has been reported that, before the present crisis in Tibet arose, a special emissary of the Dalai Lama had met six times for "dialogue" with Beijing officials. Perhaps they were making some progress. But now, as the Hu-Wen regime sees it, a brouhaha in their Olympic year "smashes their stage" and ruins the glamour of their "big international party." Beijing's distrust, even hatred, of the Tibetan government in exile thereby deepens, and any resolution of the Tibetan question becomes ever more distant.

We must be clear that the roots of the crisis in Tibet are the same as the roots of the crisis in all of China. The conflict between central rule and the "high level of autonomy" that Tibet is seeking is in essence a conflict between dictatorship and freedom. The greatest hazard in the ongoing crisis in Tibet is not that it might exacerbate conflict and hatred between the Han and Tibetan peoples but that it uses ethnic conflict to mask a struggle between two political systems. If we just look at the existing Chinese system and the policies of the Hu-Wen regime, it is obvious, crisis or no crisis, that there is no way that regime would ever accept the Dalai Lama's "middle way" of "seeking only autonomy, not independence." For the regime to consent to a "high level of autonomy" for Tibet would mean conceding political powers to Tibet, creating something like the "one country, two systems" arrangement in Hong Kong. This would be hard for the Hu-Wen regime to accept.

The Tibet problem is different from Hong Kong, and differs even more from Taiwan.

In Taiwan, political power has been separate from central Chinese governments for a hundred years. Not even the Chinese Communists, who wrested control of the mainland in 1949, managed to govern in Taiwan. Taiwan enjoyed diplomatic and military independence after the Nationalists arrived in 1949, and, until Chinese-American diplomatic relations began in 1979, also held membership in the United Nations. Today Taiwan has completed the transition of its political system. Its people enjoy basic human rights and an ever-improving democracy. The Taiwan president is directly elected by the voting public among 23 million Taiwanese. Such changes make it harder for Beijing to interfere in Taiwan's governance, diplomacy, and military affairs.

In Hong Kong, political power always rested with the British. The 1997 handover to China was a handover of sovereignty only, as the independence of Hong Kong's governance continued to be guaranteed by the principle of "one country, two systems." The city's economic, political, and legal systems today are all extensions of what the British left behind. It is true that the Hong Kong chief executive needs to be approved by Beijing, but this person has to be a Hong Kong person, and the government of the Special Administrative Region still governs independently in most ways. Furthermore, unlike the mainland, Hong Kong has a free market economy, an independent judiciary, and a free press.

Tibet is different. Up until the Communist suppression of the Tibetan rebellion in 1959, at least a portion of political power in Tibet remained in the hands of the Dalai Lama and the 200-year-old ruling council known as the Kashag, and this arrangement did bear some resemblance to "one country, two systems." But after 1959 Tibet completely lost the right to govern itself. The fourteenth Dalai Lama was forced into exile, the tenth Panchen Lama was placed under house arrest in Beijing, and the Communist Party seized political power by force. Party Central dispatched Party secretaries to Tibet to exercise this political power. From 1959 on, the Tibetans were like the Han: they had to submit to the Communist Party's dictatorship and they suffered the same kinds of human rights disasters that the Han suffered.

The catastrophes that Tibetan culture and the Tibetan people endured during the Cultural Revolution were by no means less than what Han culture and Han people experienced. In Tibet, living Buddhas, the aristocracy, merchants, artists, and practitioners of Tibetan medicine were taunted, ostracized, paraded through the streets, beaten, imprisoned, and sometimes persecuted to death—just as Han people were in the rest of China. The tenth Panchen Lama was imprisoned for nearly ten years, just as "capitalist roaders" and other prominent Han figures were.

After the "reform and opening" that began in 1978, both Hans and Tibetans have lived through the high hopes of the 1980s, the tragedy of bloodshed in 1989, and the forcible pacification and buying-off of elites from the 1990s until now. Today, even though both Hans and Tibetans have seen important economic growth and improvements in the material life of common people (an end, at least, to the widespread struggles of the Mao era to eke out the bare minimum), everyone still lacks basic human rights. The freedoms that the Tibetans lack are also missing for the Han. The exiled Dalai Lama cannot go home, just as Han dissidents who were exiled after the 1989 Tiananmen massacre cannot go home. The tactics that the regime uses against the Dalai Lama are the same that it uses against the Falungong and other popular religions among the Han. Authorities force Tibetans to denounce the Dalai Lama, just as they force Falungong believers to denounce their leader Li Hongzhi.

In short, to cast the current Tibetan crisis as a conflict between Hans and Tibetans is misleading and superficial. The real and deeper issue is a conflict between dictatorship and freedom. During the current crisis, Han people have gone onto the Internet to do a lot of verbal spitting on the Dalai Lama. This is silly; it only obscures the real situation of both the Han and the Tibetan people, which is that everyone is prisoner to the same dictatorial system. So long as Han people live under dictatorship, it will be unthinkable that Tibetans precede them in gaining freedom. And so long as people in China proper are denied authentic self-rule, self-rule for Tibetans and other minorities will remain a pipe dream.

This is why the resolution of the Tibet question depends fundamentally on the question of the form of government that China will have in the future. Democratization for all of China is the necessary condition for any solution, whatever its form, to the Tibet issue. Whether or not genuine peace talks can begin between the Dalai Lama and the Hu-Wen regime and, if they do begin, whether or not there will be any concrete results will depend neither on how relations between the Beijing government and the Tibetan government in exile are defined nor on external pressures that Western nations might exert. These questions will depend upon the progress of political change inside the mainland. Only when the democratization of Chinese politics truly begins can negotiations between Beijing and the Dalai Lama also truly begin.

*Originally published in* Guancha *(Observe China), April 11, 2008*
*Translated by Eva S. Chou*

# ONE MORNING

*For Xia, who went to Tibet alone*

One morning
yawning, dispirited morning
I suppose
that between you and the high plateau
the sky seems inconceivably
deep and distant
no wind no clouds no mist
transparent blue, deeply perplexing

When you left
I was calm
when your receding figure disappeared
my longing was born, off in the distance
like how inside the lines of a child's palm
another person walks
passing through my body, circuitously
looking for a unique word

The flight of word needs no wings
just as scent can lead a spirit
rays of morning light tremble, ill at ease
the feeling's a bit alien

as when, for this long journey
you bought a pair of new shoes

This shaken time
has left my dreams pregnant and unmarried
the oxygen-poor, snowy peaks
greedily suck in
the steam of your first exhalation

July 14, 1993

*Translated by Nick Admussen*

# DISTANCE

*For Xia*


My emptiness has been filled by distance
for the first time I have known
those sweeping vistas
another world is growing within me
horizon and dawnlight
by turns transfiguring distance
entrusting life to love
beyond the limits of distance

A trembling violin
broken by distance
such deep pain
just to reach out through the distance

Everything I am has been revealed by distance
living, loving, standing, reaching
you are distance, tender distance
like a strand of hair tossed into the sea
sucking gold out of azure
those who drowned of despair
rise quietly and dance


January 28, 1997

*Translated by Isaac P. Hsieh*

# OBAMA'S ELECTION, THE REPUBLICAN FACTOR, AND A PROPOSAL FOR CHINA

◆　◆　◆　◆　◆

*Liu Xiaobo, like many Chinese, was impressed when American voters chose an African American to be president of the United States. In the following piece, written the day after the election of Barack Obama, he gives his view of the genesis and significance of the event, then follows with a startling suggestion of how a fundamental principle that he sees in the Obama victory might be applied to China.—Ed.*

THE SIGHT OF THE OBAMA FAMILY waving to the people in their new role as the next occupants of the White House sparked long-dormant political enthusiasm in America and around the world.

The eyes of the entire world were on this election because the status of the United States as a superpower and as the leading nation in the free world makes its president the most powerful man on earth. People even jokingly refer to him as "the President of the World."

People were watching this election with some problems in mind as well. The financial crisis and the quagmire in Iraq had drastically eroded support for the Bush administration both at home and abroad. The Wall Street crisis had had worldwide repercussions, and the Iraq war seemed to be undermining the international counterterrorist effort. Mainstream opinion in many places was looking forward to "change" in the U.S.

Barack Obama, an African American who sprang from the grass-roots, had no weighty political pedigree, not much of a political track record, and not even much administrative experience. His credentials as a state senator and a U.S. senator seemed meager compared to those of other candidates. People were surprised when such a dark-horse candidate defeated Hillary Clinton, a white Democrat from the establishment, in the primary elections. As the election day face-off between him and John McCain approached, there was concern that racist backlash might block an Obama victory, but, just as in the primaries, he defeated his highly qualified opponent by a wider margin than had been seen in years.

My view as a Chinese is that Obama's elevation to the position of 44th president of the United States underscores the greatness of the American system. What interests me most is not whether Obama will be able to handle the crises he faces, but the obvious evidence of how the American democratic system can correct itself. Every four years, the United States can, if it wants, turn itself around by means of a general election that is open to all. It sometimes does this, especially at moments of great crisis. Despite its democratic traditions, America is a predominantly white nation with a problem of racism that pervades its 200-year history. The election of Obama, a man of Kenyan descent, is a remarkable sign of a more tolerant America in the twenty-first century.

Obama was born in 1961, in an era still marked by racial segregation in the U.S. In 1964 the burgeoning civil rights movement led by Dr. Martin Luther King Jr. achieved some landmark victories: Congress passed the Civil Rights Act, outlawing racial discrimination and segregation and guaranteeing blacks equal rights under the law; and Dr. King won the Nobel Peace Prize, one of the most prestigious honors in the world. But bigotry remained rampant, as evidenced most dramatically when a racist assassinated Dr. King on April 4, 1968, and then again when riots occurred in Los Angeles in 1992.

Obama's election as the first black president is the culmination of a 200-year-long story. His victory grows out of the fertile soil of democracy, the spontaneous struggle of his black brethren, the support of upstanding whites, and the concerted efforts of the Republican and Democratic parties. Obama of course should appreciate what the Democrats have done. But perhaps he should thank his opponents, the Republicans, even more. I say this not only because the Democratic victory was the result of Republican administrative failures. In a much broader sense, the systemic changes that Republicans instituted at earlier points in history did much to lay the groundwork for Obama's election.

The Democrats, and others who oppose racial discrimination, have made historic contributions to the long struggle for racial equality in America. John Brown's nineteenth-century insurrection set the stage for the abolition of slavery. President Lyndon Johnson, who signed the Civil Rights Bill in 1964, was a Democrat. The Democrats' strong opposition to racial discrimination is evident, for example, in the left-leaning culture of American academe, where racial equality has become "politically correct" to the point where it has led even to charges of "reverse discrimination."

But Republicans have also made enormous contributions to the cause of racial equality. Abraham Lincoln, a colossus in American history, was a Republican. It was he who issued the Emancipation Proclamation in 1863, legally abolishing slavery, and this paved the way for the ratification in 1868 of the Fourteenth Amendment to the U.S. Constitution, which granted citizenship rights to African Americans. These measures, which were the first steps in African American liberation, became the legal foundations for the twentieth-century civil rights movement. Without the Emancipation Proclamation in the nineteenth century, there would have been no Civil Rights Act in the twentieth.

Moreover it was Ronald Reagan, the preeminent American president of the late Cold War era, who designated the third Monday in January of each year as Martin Luther King Day, a national holiday. Only three people have received this rare honor in the U.S.: Columbus, who is recognized on the second Monday in October for his discovery of America; George Washington, the first American president, who is honored on President's Day, the third Monday in February; and Dr. Martin Luther King Jr., martyr to the cause of civil rights.

The Republican administration of George W. Bush, despite the predicaments it put the country in at home and abroad, made significant contributions to the advancement of African Americans in the highest echelons of power. In his eight years in office, Bush achieved some "firsts" in this respect: he appointed the first black secretary of state in American history, Colin Powell, and later replaced him with Condoleezza Rice, the first black woman ever to hold this position. These appointments did a great deal to raise the status of African Americans and energized American minorities politically. The media buzz over whether either Rice or Powell might run for president as a Republican did much to prepare the American public for the emergence of an African American presidential candidate.

Regardless of how well Obama does in handling America's problems, America definitely now has a new image in the world. America's new first family is black—and that fact has more symbolic power than any campaign promises. On the television news, I watched how the whole world—including Obama's ancestral land of Kenya—hailed his election.

In its historical context, Obama's victory should be called an "American miracle" rather than "Obama's miracle." It reminds the world of the greatness of the American melting pot, and inspires us again to look beyond the material aspects of the American dream: its pinnacle is in the White House, not on Wall Street. From now on, the ranks of high-achieving African Americans can include not only Michael Jordans, but Barack Obamas as well.

Obama expressed this idea in his victory speech: "If there is anyone out there who still doubts that America is a place where all things are possible; who still wonders if the dream of our founders is alive in our time; who still questions the power of our democracy, tonight is your answer."

These reflections make me think of proposals for solving China's ethnic conflicts that have come from my friend Wang Lixiong. Wang argues that, as soon as possible, substantive high-level negotiations should take place between the Chinese Communist Party and the Dalai Lama. Such talks could be advantageous to both sides if they happen while the moderate, nonviolent Dalai Lama is still in good health, and while China is still able to maintain peace in Tibet.

In fact, the Chinese Communist regime could resolve the entire issue with one bold display of political savvy: it could invite the Dalai Lama back to China to serve as our nation's president, our Barack Obama. Such a move would make best use of the Dalai Lama's stature in Tibet and around the world; it could also bring into play a spirit of tolerance among Han Chinese, who have recently been converting to Buddhism in increasing numbers.

Symbolism aside, a great deal of concrete good could result from such a move. In Tibet, the Dalai Lama is a god and his word is law. If he came back to China, he could marginalize radical Tibetan separatist groups by convincing Tibetans to allow Tibet to remain part of China as an autonomous region. With his worldwide prestige, he could also do a huge amount to improve China's international image. In addition to all of that, a peaceful resolution of the Tibet question could be a model for solving the Taiwan problem as well as problems with other Chinese minority groups, thereby averting the very real danger that ethnic strife might escalate into large-scale separatist movements.

The Dalai Lama, a sagacious man, has a vision for an autonomous, democratic Tibet in which church and state are separate. The vision is grounded in a system that has worked well for many years in the Tibetan government in exile in Dharamsala, India. He has an excellent track record for implementing experiments in democracy similar to those of Chiang Ching-kuo in Taiwan in the 1980s. Such experiments could serve as models for the political transformation of China as a whole. The dawn of true political reform in China can arrive as soon as Chinese authorities sit down at the negotiating table with the Dalai Lama.

At home in Beijing, November 5, 2008

*Originally published in* Guancha *(Observe China), November 5, 2008*
*Translated by Paul G. Pickowicz*

# PART IV

# DOCUMENTS

# THE JUNE SECOND HUNGER STRIKE DECLARATION

◆ ◆ ◆ ◆ ◆

*On June 2, 1989, near the end of the spring demonstrations for democracy at Tiananmen Square in Beijing, Liu Xiaobo and three friends—Zhou Duo, Hou Dejian, and Gao Xin—announced that they were beginning a three-day hunger strike to support the student protesters and to promote the democratization of China. At the same time they issued a Declaration, translated below, one of whose points was to warn the government to "correct its mistakes right now, before it is too late." The point is poignant, because their hunger strike itself was cut short by a bloody military crackdown that the government began about 30 hours later.—Ed.*

WE ANNOUNCE A HUNGER STRIKE. We protest, we implore, and we repent.

We seek not death, but to live true lives.

Faced with violent and irrational military repression of the kind that the Li Peng government is currently applying, Chinese intellectuals must end our thousands-of-years-old traditions of standing in docility before power. We can no longer use words alone while taking no action. We must, through action, resist martial law, declare the birth of a new political culture, and repent the mistakes to which our long-term weakness has given rise. All of us must bear responsibility for the backwardness in China today.

## 1. The Goals of Our Hunger Strike

The Democracy Movement that we see today is unprecedented in Chinese history. It has consistently used legal, nonviolent, rational, and peaceful methods in its pursuit of freedom, democracy, and human rights. The Li Peng government, in contrast, has chosen to muster several hundred thousand troops to repress unarmed students and citizens by force. Our hunger strike is not a "petition" to the authorities; it is a protest of their actions.

We advocate the spread of democracy in China through peaceful means and we oppose violence in any form. At the same time, we are unafraid of violence. Our aim is to show through peaceful means how the iron resolve of Chinese people who want democracy will in the end demolish an undemocratic order that maintains itself with bayonets and lies. The almost unimaginable stupidity of using martial law troops to repress students and citizens who are protesting peacefully has set an utterly deplorable precedent in the history of The People's Republic of China. It brings tremendous shame to the Communist Party, the Chinese government, and the army, and it wrecks in a single blow ten years of "reform and opening."

Thousands of years of Chinese history are filled with instances of hatred between adversaries and the use of violence to battle violence. By the dawn of the modern era an "enemy mentality" had taken root in Chinese political thinking, and after the Communist victory in 1949 slogans like "Take class struggle as fundamental" pushed the traditional hate psychology, enemy mentality, and battling of violence with violence to new extremes. The current martial law is a manifestation of "class struggle" thinking. By our hunger strike we appeal to our fellow Chinese to begin immediately to move away from, and eventually to completely abandon, the enemy mentality, hate psychology, and "class struggle" political culture. Hatred leads only to violence and dictatorship.

We must begin to build democracy in China in a spirit of tolerance and with conscious cooperation. A democratic society is not built on hatred and enmity; it is built on consultation, debate, and voting that are carried out on a basis of mutual respect, tolerance, and willingness to compromise. Li Peng, in his role as China's premier, has made major mistakes. He should be held accountable for these mistakes through democratic procedures, and then should resign. But Li Peng is not our enemy. And even after he leaves office he should continue to enjoy the rights of a citizen, including, if he chooses, the right to continue to advocate his mistaken policies. We appeal to everyone—government and ordinary citizen alike—to let go of the old political culture and to embrace a new one. We call upon the government to cancel the martial law order immediately, and we appeal to both government and students to resolve their current standoff by reopening peaceful consultation, negotiation, and dialogue.

The current student movement has earned sympathy, understanding, and support from the whole of Chinese society in a way that is unprecedented, and the declaration of martial law only solidified this pervasive support. Still, we need to recognize that, for most people, support of the students has sprung from simple human sympathy for them and from a dislike of the government. It has not derived from modern consciousness of the political responsibilities of a citizen. This is why we are calling upon everyone in society to move away from the relatively simple role of sympathetic bystander and into the role of engaged citizen. The first rule for a citizen is the principle of equality. Every citizen should be confident that his or her own political rights are the same as those of the country's premier. The second rule is that a citizen does not just "feel sympathy" or "sense injustice"; to be a citizen is to have a rational awareness of the responsibility to participate in politics. We call upon all our fellow citizens to exercise their rights, to participate in building democracy, and to be aware that each citizen shares responsibility for what the political decisions of a society will be. If these decisions are rational and legal, every citizen should share the credit; if they are irrational and illegal, each citizen should get part of the blame. It is the natural duty of every citizen to participate consciously in the politics of his or her society. Our fellow Chinese must realize that in democratic politics everyone is a citizen first, and only after that is a student, a professor, a worker, an official, a soldier, or something else.

For several thousand years, Chinese society has been caught in the vicious cycle of tearing down an old dynasty in order to set up a new one. History has shown, however, that the exit of a leader who has lost popular confidence and his replacement by a leader who has gained it is not a formula that can address China's fundamental political needs.

What we need is not the ideal savior but an ideal democratic system. That is why we are calling:

First, for the establishment throughout society of popular self-governing organizations that can gradually give shape to popular political forces that will serve as counterbalances to the central governing authority. We need this because checks and balances are the heart of democracy. We should prefer to see ten devils working within a system of checks and balances than to see one angel operating with unchecked power.

Second, for the gradual establishment of a system of recall of officials who have seriously abused their power. The questions of who enters office and who leaves it are not as important as the questions of how the enterings and leavings are determined. Undemocratic procedures lead inevitably to dictatorship.

Both the government and the students have made mistakes during the course of the current movement, and this is why we are calling upon both sides in the current standoff to take a square look at themselves.

The main mistake of the government has been to cling to the "class struggle" mentality in how it views the protesting students and citizens; this mentality casts the protesters as enemies and has led to continual escalation of the confrontation. Instead, the government could draw some painful but much-needed lessons from the fact that such a large democracy movement has arisen. It could learn to listen to what people are saying, to accept their constitutional rights to express themselves, and to learn techniques of democratic rule. The democracy movement could actually be the government's teacher as it learns how to govern a society using democracy and rule of law.

The students' mistakes have been mostly in the less-than-ideal internal workings of their organizations. Their efforts to build an edifice of democracy have used too many undemocratic bricks. For example, their theory is democratic but their handling of actual problems is not; and ends are democratic but means and procedures are not; effort is wasted because cooperation is poor. These problems have led to confusion in policy, jumble in finances, and material waste. Too many decisions are based in sentiment, not reason, and there is too much emphasis on special privilege, not equality.

In the end, though, there can be no question that the government's mistakes have been the greater of the two. Marches and hunger strikes are entirely legal and rational ways for citizens to express their will; these tactics in no way constitute "turmoil," and yet that is what the government, stuck in its autocratic thinking and ignoring citizens' rights that are inscribed in our constitution, has declared such actions to be. From this mistake the government has gone on to make a whole series of related ones, repeatedly stimulating the student movement to further action and deepening the antagonism between the two sides. These government mistakes are the true seeds of "turmoil" (just as they were, by the way, during Mao's Cultural Revolution). It is thanks only to self-restraint by the students, plus some powerful appeals from reasonable people in society (including people in the Party, the government, and the military) that we have avoided major bloodshed so far. It is imperative that the government recognize and correct its mistakes right now, before it is too late.

The struggles of the Chinese people for democracy over the last hundred years have stayed largely at the level of theory and slogans. They have focused on ideals, not practical techniques, and on goals rather than means, processes, and procedures. In our view the true realization of democracy will come only when means, processes, and procedures become the heart of the matter. We call upon our fellow Chinese to set aside democracy as expressed in slogans, or in goals alone, or in a simple ideological vision, and instead to pursue the democracy of process, means, and procedures; and then, by focusing on each concrete issue as it comes up, to turn a democracy movement that has centered on theoretical ideals into a movement of democratic processes in action. This is also why we call upon the students to take a second look at how they can better implement democracy in Tiananmen Square.

One of the government's more eye-catching mistakes has been its description of the protesting students as "a tiny minority." By our hunger strike, we want to make it clear to China and the world that the "tiny minority" includes us. We are not students. We are citizens who feel a political responsibility and who have joined a broad social movement in which students have taken a lead. Everything that we have done is rational and legal. Our aim is to use our thinking and our actions to bring the government to reflect upon and to repent what it is doing. Such repentance could arise in officials from their political culture, from personal character, or from moral principles, and it could lead to public acknowledgment of, and correction of, the government's mistakes. Our other hope is that the students will run their organizations more democratically.

We should recognize that all Chinese citizens are strangers to the matter of running a country on democratic principles. All the Chinese people, including the top leaders of the Party and state, need to learn these principles from the beginning. As the learning proceeds, there are bound to be many mistakes among populace and officialdom alike. The key will be to recognize mistakes when they happen, to correct them, and to learn from them. If we proceed in this way, mistakes can be turned into good things. Through continual correction of errors we can learn, step by step, how to govern our country democratically.

## 2. Our Basic Watchwords

1. We have no enemies. We must not let hatred or violence poison our thinking or the progress of democratization in China.

2. We must reflect on our ways. China's backwardness is everyone's responsibility.

3. We are citizens before we are anything else.

4. We are not seeking death. We are seeking to live true lives.

## 3. Location, Time, and Rules of the Hunger Strike

1. Location: the base of The Monument to the Heroes of the People, Tiananmen Square

2. Time: from 4:00 p.m. on June 2 to 4:00 p.m., June 5, 1989

3. Rules: no food; boiled water only, and nothing with nutrition (sugar, starch, fat, or protein) in the water

## 4. The Hunger Strikers

Liu Xiaobo: Ph.D. in Chinese literature; lecturer in the Department of Chinese of Beijing Normal University

Zhou Duo: former lecturer, Sociology Research Institute, Peking University; currently Director of General Planning, The Stone Company

Hou Dejian: famous songwriter

Gao Xin: editor of *The Normal University Weekly,* member of the Communist Party of China

*Original text available at http://www.ngensis.com/june4/june4a.htm*
*Translated by Perry Link*

## YOU · GHOSTS · THE DEFEATED

*For my wife*

My dear
all day you wander among tombs
and spirits of the dead in the wind
facing them in silence
you peer deep into each other
freezing the other's blood
these, the completely defeated
have left no name, no history

At nightfall, the wine in your cup
gets tipsy and becomes a bonfire
for the lost spirits
you illuminate a small space
where they can tell of their lives
you listen well to their sufferings
and both sides are serene
like the two hands
of a child deep in sleep

From the treetop of the dream
again the tortoise-shell vine pushes out soft leaves
its suicide never succeeds
and you

this woman infatuated with the defeated
are yourself never defeated
because from the grins of corpses
you've learned
that it is only death
that never fails

Walking alone on a rainy night
without a shadow to talk to
and lies decorating the sunshine
everything glistens with rot
the day is even crueler than the night
and nobody can fix it

My dear
don't close yourself off
don't stay alone
envying the despair of the defeated
throw open your door
see defeat in me too and take me in
make of me
one of the miserable reasons that keep you going
and let undisturbed smoke
rise between the two of us

October 9, 1998

*Translated by Nick Admussen*

# A LETTER TO LIAO YIWU

◆　◆　◆　◆　◆

*Liao Yiwu, a master writer on the lives of China's common people (see* The Corpse Walker, *Pantheon, 2008), wrote a poem called "Massacre," and a sequel called "Requiem," following the Tiananmen Massacre in 1989. In February 1990 he was detained and sent to prison for four years, during which time he wrote an account, called* Testimony, *of the horrible prison conditions he experienced and witnessed. He finished a draft in 1997 and in 1999 showed it to his friend Liu Xiaobo, who wrote him the following letter on January 13, 2000. Liao, who shaves his head, was wearing a beard at the time.—Ed.*

DEAR BALDIE (or is it Beardie?):

Liu Xia and I have been reading your *Testimony* every night. She can take in ten lines at a time, but I have to chew on every word. Without prejudging how dumb you might be in the future, at least you know whom you're hitting the hardest.

Compared with your years in prison, my three prison stints were pretty mild. During the first, at Qincheng [Beijing's prison for elite prisoners, where Liu stayed from June 1989 to January 1991—Ed.], I had my own cell, and my living conditions were better than what you had to endure. Sometimes I was deathly bored, but that's about it. In my second stint—eight months inside a large courtyard at the base of the Fragrant Hills outside Beijing—I got even better treatment. There, except for my freedom, I had just about everything. During the third—three years at the reeducation-through-labor camp at Dalian—I was again singled out for special handling. My three elite-prisoner experiences can't compare in any way to your suffering; I probably shouldn't even say mine were imprisonments, compared to yours.

Let's face it, the only way to live in dignity, inside this depraved society that we inhabit, is to resist. That being so, to go to prison is really nothing more than to maintain simple human dignity; it's really nothing to brag about. What we should be afraid of is not prison but the danger, when we get out of prison, of an uppity feeling that because the society owes us a blood debt we have the right to start ordering people around.

It has always bothered me that so many of the ordinary citizens who were arrested after the Tiananmen Massacre received heavier sentences than what we "famous" ones got, and that their prison conditions must be unthinkably squalid. But for me, until I read your *Testimony*, these were only things that I could imagine. *Testimony* put me in touch with the living pulse of those victims. Words cannot express the shame that I feel, and that shame is the reason I want to devote the second half of my life to those lost souls, those nameless victims. Everything else can pass, but the blood and tears of those innocent people are like stones that weigh incessantly in my heart. They are cold, heavy stones, and have sharp edges.

Your poem "Requiem" is a masterpiece, even better than "Massacre."

In *Testimony* you offer a lot of critical observations about the people around you, and sometimes it's hard for a reader to see the difference between objective criticism and personal complaint. Perhaps you were still too close to things; your personal pain may have colored your writing too much. Maybe you should reconsider those passages. To write "exactly as things were" is an impossible ideal, of course, but our writing should always have the inner strength to go as far in that direction as we can get it.

Compared to people in other nations that have lived under the dreary pall of communism, we resisters in China have not measured up very well. Even after so many years of tremendous tragedies, we still don't have a moral leader like Václav Havel. It seems ironic that in order to win the right of ordinary people to pursue self-interest, a society needs a moral giant to make a selfless sacrifice. In order to secure "passive freedom"—freedom from state oppression—there needs to be a will to do *active* resistance. History is not fated. The appearance of a single martyr can fundamentally turn the spirit of a nation and strengthen its moral fiber. Gandhi was such a figure. So was Havel. So, even more, was that humble boy born in a manger two thousand years ago. Human progress is the result of the accident of birth of people such as these.

We can't expect a society's conscience to spring automatically out of ordinary life. A moral exemplar is needed to articulate principles of conscience so that these will catalyze the consciences of ordinary people. In China our need for this kind of exemplar is especially strong. For us the power of an ethical model could be immense; a single symbol could tap large reservoirs of moral sentiment. This could have happened in 1989, for example, if Fang Lizhi had come out of the U.S. embassy [where the dissident astrophysicist was staying during the months after the massacre—Ed.], or if Zhao Ziyang [the Party general secretary who sympathized with the students at Tiananmen—Ed.], after he was sacked, could have continued in open resistance, or if major intellectual leaders had not fled overseas. One main reason for the silence and amnesia that enshrouded China in the years after the massacre is that no inspiring moral leader stepped forward to be a symbol.

It is natural to expect kindness and grit from people, not so natural to anticipate evil or cowardice. Every time a disaster occurs, I am surprised when the evil and the cowardice appear. Why am I not equally surprised when kindness and grit are absent?

Language gets its beauty from making truth glow in the darkness. Beauty is concentrated truth; noise and gaudiness obscure truth. You and I, in this clever world, count as fools. We qualify only to drift about on the open sea, like those medieval Europeans in their Ship of Fools, adopting the first lump of land they collide with as their home. We live for that lonely trace of pain in the heart that somehow still survives. This heart pain that we carry causes extreme blindness and extreme clarity at the same time. Blindness because it makes us look past all of the insipid bustle of the numb world around us and still cry out, like fools; clarity because, while the rest of the world forgets, it helps us still to see the blood and tears on those knives. A line in one of my poems to Liu Xia says, "Your footstep is stayed at the weeping of an ant."

I never met your sister Feifei, but have already fallen in love with the woman who emerges from your pages. To dance with lost souls, with the defeated, is the only true dance in this world. If you can, please lay a wreath for me, next time you visit her grave.

Xiaobo

*Originally published on Boxun, http://blog.boxun.com/hero/liuxb*
*Translated by Perry Link*

# FEET SO COLD, SO SMALL

*For my Icy Little Toes*

'Tis a long road you travel, so far, so far
to Winter's iron door
so long a journey for such little feet
such chilly toes, to stub against a cold iron door
and all to catch a glimpse of me, the convict

A bleak road blurs with the fading of memory
a tattered sail graces the gray sea
home at dusk, out at dawn
weary beneath a load of books
your footprints cross the convict's dreams

And at each setting-out, you comb with care
those buoyant, queenly tresses
the wind may blow, but not a hair astray
at times weighed down, you need to pause
but then keep going, not a hair astray

And with your toes you'll smash this iron door
and with one hair you'll saw these iron bars
and your tenacity, transcending any faith
shall bridge the void between us

make each fleeting moment
live forever in your footprints

In the labor camp, December 9, 1996

*Translated by A. E. Clark*

# USING TRUTH TO UNDERMINE A SYSTEM BUILT ON LIES

## Statement of Thanks in Accepting the Outstanding Democracy Activist Award

◆　◆　◆　◆　◆

*Each year since 1986, the Chinese Democracy Education Foundation in San Francisco has presented awards for outstanding activism in the promotion of Chinese democracy. One of its awards for 2002 went to Liu Xiaobo, but government authorities denied Liu permission to leave China to attend the award ceremony, which was held in May 2003. Liu sent the following "statement of thanks" to the Foundation in lieu of an acceptance speech.—*Ed.

MY LITERARY LIFE BEGAN when I was an "educated youth" in the 1970s. It was an era of revolutionary fervor when empty slogans and blind passions, including the lies in *Quotations of Chairman Mao,* ran rampant. As a young man I embraced all of them as the absolute truth. Then, in the 1980s, when my writings began to receive some public recognition, I saw myself with equal confidence as having outgrown Mao-era language and as now grounding my writings in a quest for human dignity and the living of an honest life. Like someone who strikes it rich overnight, I exulted in a new world that seemed to have no limits.

Then that bloody dawn in 1989, fourteen years ago, showed me how shallow and self-centered I still was, taught me to recognize the warmth and the inner strength of love, and gave me a new appreciation of what is most important in life. I knew that from that time on I would forever be living with the guilt of the survivor and in awe of the souls of the dead. I began to feel mortified at my shallowness in the 1970s and my bravado of the 1980s. Indeed, it is only now, in looking back carefully, that I realize that my entire youth was spent in a cultural desert and that my early writings had all been nurtured in hatred, violence, and arrogance—or, alternatively, in lies, cynicism, and loutish sarcasm. These poisons of "Party culture" had permeated several generations of Chinese, and I was no exception. Even in the liberal tides of the 1980s, I had not been able to purge myself of them entirely. I knew at the time that Mao-style thinking and Cultural Revolution–style language had become ingrained in me, and my goal had been to transform myself from the bone marrow out. Hah!—Easier said than done. It may take me a lifetime to rid myself of the poison.

### Respectfully Received in the Name of the Souls of the Dead

I receive this award today, May 31, 2003, only four days before the anniversary of that bloody morning in June fourteen years ago. I do not know whether my work has been worthy of the people who died and cannot claim to deserve this award. I can understand the honor only as a tribute to those who continue to speak the truth inside a system built on lies and as an offering to the souls of the dead, delivered through me, of memory that refuses to be erased.

I feel that those who perished that day are looking down on me from above. They look down on a person privileged still to be alive. They have been looking down for fourteen years now. I was a participant in the 1989 movement and observed how, in that dark night and early dawn, it was sliced by bayonets, pierced by bullets, and crushed by tanks. The glinting tips of the bayonets still stab in the recesses of my memory. As one of the survivors, I see before my eyes two things—the souls of those who died for a free China and the violence, the lies, and the bribery of the killers—and I am haunted by the grave responsibility of being still alive. I do my best to make every word from my pen a cry from the heart for the souls of the dead. I use my memory of their graves to combat the Chinese government's pressure to erase memory; my searing desire to atone for having survived helps me resist the temptations to join the world of lies.

We may feel contempt for a regime that kills people and disgust when it lies to explain its killing, but we can feel only despair if a nation makes allowances for such a regime and forgets the people who were killed. How much more is this the case when the killings were on open display to the world and when the physical deaths of the victims have so well proven the moral deaths of the killers?

The crimes of the Communist dictatorship are many, and the victims whom we do not know about are far, far too numerous—both the souls of the dead from killings and the prisoners of conscience who remain behind bars. One way to compensate for their suffering is to be sure that we reflect upon it scrupulously in memory, and one of the moral preconditions of honest memory is that we utterly refuse the regime's indoctrination and refuse as individuals to repeat its lies. We fortunate survivors, and anyone who lives outside the regime's metal bars, must, each of us as an independent person, hold fast to memory of the victims and refuse to sell out to the material comforts that participation in the official lies can bring. To do anything less is to surrender the meaning of life, to sell one's personal dignity, and to lose sight of what it means to be a human being. Nothing can substitute for individual responsibility.

## Refusing to Lie Can Undermine a Tyranny

All of us, obviously, are ordinary people, and we all have our weaknesses. We all seek security and at least a modicum of worldly comfort. With global modernization and the cultural and social changes that have come with it, the world has softened the standards that it applies to people. There is less emphasis on classic heroism or martyrdom and more acceptance of human weakness and the human desire for material comfort. We no longer need to declaim high-sounding principles or to emulate the ideals of the Hungarian poet Sándor Petőfi (1823–1849), who wrote:

Life is precious
Love yet more;
But for freedom
Both can be flung away.

We do not need to match this standard. We need not demand of our-selves any extraordinary courage, nobility, conscience, or wisdom; we need not ask ourselves to risk prison or to go on hunger strikes or carry out self-immolations. All we need to do is to eliminate lies from our public speech and to give up the use of lies as a tactic in dealing with the threats and the enticements of the regime.

Moral prohibitions against lying are fundamental in the ancient texts of all the world's cultures. For the people in this world who still live under dictatorships, resistance to lies continues to be the first step in the pursuit of freedom from fear and coercion, which is something every human being yearns for. Dictatorships need lies and violence in order to maintain the coercion and fear upon which they depend. They need both—violence alone is not enough; it needs the veneer that lies pro-vide. No single person, of whatever status, can fight back against regime violence alone, but the refusal to participate in lying is something that every person can accomplish. To refuse to lie in day-to-day public life is the most powerful tool for breaking down a tyranny built on mendacity.

This tactic can be especially effective in today's post-totalitarian China, where conditions are ripe for a transition. Worldwide trends and the desires of the Chinese people are both clearly moving toward more openness and democracy; the appeal of Party rhetoric, as well as its sedative effects, are getting weaker by the day. Society is moving to-ward much more diversity in both its economic activities and its values, and these trends constantly eat away at the old, rigid, unitary political system. In this situation, the post-totalitarian dictatorship finds that lies are just about the only tools of argument left to it. Its position is so weak that it no longer even bothers to ask that people be sincere in their self-abasement. The regime understands that people do not believe in it and have no wish to praise it, so it compromises: just be cynical, just *pretend* that you recognize and support us, and that will be enough!

## Why People Participate in the Lying

The regime has learned from the Mao era and the Tiananmen Massacre that use of brute violence has its costs. In order to extract even the su-perficial appearance of submission and support from the populace, the preferred method is neither bamboozlement by ideology nor repression by brute force, but the soft tactic of buying people off. "Spend money to buy stability" has become the regime's primary governing strategy. Any stability or public support that can be bought without use of bayonets or prisons is bought; violent repression is reserved for the very few who cannot be bought.

And so it happens that for people living in this post-totalitarian system, and especially for the notable figures in the intellectual elite, the main reason for going along with official mendacity is not a passive one—not a fear of meeting with violence—but an active, willing submission to the temptations of material gain. We can even say that what the autocrats at the top fear most is not violent uprisings, which they can put down (so long as these are not too large, and we should be wary of wishing for full-scale violent revolution, which might only bring a new dictatorship); their worst nightmare is a situation in which every person, beginning with intellectuals and the other notables who speak in public, is able to ignore material inducements and begins to refuse to utter lies. Even to say nothing, even just to remain silent, would be enough, so long as no lies are repeated and everyone agrees to stop living off the telling of lies. The system would choke.

### Single Truths, Drop by Drop, Can Form a Flood That Washes Away Tyranny

Today the risks involved in truth-telling in China are much less than they once were. Statements that during the Mao era would have brought disaster to entire families can now be heard in informal contexts everywhere. Prominent figures who speak out today do feel pressure, but this falls miles short of what happened to people like Zhang Zhixin [tortured and raped in prison for six years, 1969–1975, and her throat slit prior to her 1975 execution to prevent her from shouting final words — Ed.], and does not amount to much, either, when compared to the prices that Democracy Wall activists paid. [Wei Jingsheng was sent to prison for fourteen years in 1979—Ed.]. The imprisonment of people like journalist Yang Zili [from 2001 to 2009] and Internet writer Liu Di [see "From Wang Shuo's Wicked Satire to Hu Ge's *Egao*," pp. 177–187] shows that today relatively unknown people still sometimes pay a heavy price for speaking out. This makes the path taken by social scientist Li

Shenzhi (1923–2003) during his final years—especially in his very honest essay called "Perils and Panics of Fifty Years," written on the fiftieth anniversary of the beginning of Communist rule in China—all the more important as a model for prominent figures in our society to emulate. When society honors a person with the bestowal of high position, that person owes society a measure of responsibility that matches the honor bestowed; a famous public figure owes something that a Yang Zili or Liu Di does not owe. When prominent people speak in public, their fame is their greatest resource. When they speak truth to power, they not only bring greater moral pressure to bear than others can; they also help to expand the space for public discourse, thereby encouraging more people to emerge from silence.

We must note that speaking truth to power has rewards as well as costs. People who dare to speak out about major public events may not receive tangible benefits, but they receive the very considerable reward of high moral reputation among fellow Chinese as well as in the international community. They can emerge from civil society to become figures who carry substantial influence of their own. After the Tiananmen Massacre, for example, a single sentence of truth from Professor Ding Zilin punctured the Communist Party's sky-covering lies about the events and brought worldwide sympathy and support to the professor. She was then able to create a durable movement, called the Tiananmen Mothers, and she has received many international human rights awards, including this award of Outstanding Democracy Activist.

Dr. Jiang Yanyong is another recent example of how a word of truth from a citizen can collapse a big lie of the government. Dr. Jiang's letter last month to two television stations exposing the official cover-up of China's SARS epidemic led to worldwide condemnation of the government's lies. Jiang's act of courage not only sent the regime running to shut the barn door after the horses were out; it also gave the Chinese people new hope that they could defeat the SARS epidemic, and—perhaps most important—established another precedent for how truth can undermine dictatorship. Predictably, the Party-controlled media inside China bottled up what Dr. Jiang had done, but news of it spread around the world on the Internet, including back into China, and he received a flood of messages of support, praise, and congratulations from both China and abroad. There could be no better reward for China's voices of conscience than the recent popular clamor for greater freedom of the press in China.

These examples make it plain that if every person were to speak just one sentence of truth on major issues that affect society, the dictatorship would fail, no matter how brutal it might be. As resistance to public mendacity builds among the people, drop by drop, eventually the drops will come together to form a flood, and a dictatorship that needs lies in order to maintain itself will find it hard to continue.

### Encouragement for Speaking Truth to Power

I should emphasize that for people like me, who live inside a cowardly dictatorship, which is a prison of its own kind, every little bit of good-hearted encouragement that springs from the human nature of people who live in other places—even when the encouragement is small and expressed only privately—causes us to feel gratitude and awe. The Chinese Democracy Education Foundation's award is neither small nor private. The Foundation has been ceaseless in its encouragement of people who speak out against China's dictatorial regime, and its annual "Outstanding Activist" award is playing a distinctive role in China's political transition. The award is encouragement to people who are working under very difficult conditions; it helps them to pursue their goals, whether this is simply the quest to maintain dignity as a human being or the huge cause of bringing freedom to all of China. I trust that the Foundation will continue to use its Award to encourage those who speak truth to power until the day comes when China is absorbed into the mainstream of human civilization and truly becomes a land where freedom of speech is protected.

I remain acutely aware that I am the lucky and undeserving survivor of a massacre in the waning years of a dictatorship, and that I cannot speak for souls of the dead. What I can express, if indirectly, are my feelings of remorse and my wishes to atone. Please allow me to conclude with some lines I wrote on June 4, 1999, the tenth anniversary of the massacre, during my confinement in a reeducation-through-labor camp:

Gripping the prison bars
this moment

I must wail in grief
for I fear the next
so much I have no tears for it
remembering them, the innocent dead,
I must thrust a dagger calmly
into my eyes
must purchase with blindness
clarity of the brain
for that bone-devouring memory
is best expressed
by refusal

At home in Beijing, May 2003

*Originally published in* Zhengming *(Cheng Ming Monthly), June 2003*
*Translated by Eva S. Chou*

# CHARTER 08

* * ◆ ◆ ◆

*During the summer and fall of 2008, Chinese activists who were part of a loose association called Chinese Human Rights Defenders drafted Charter 08, a manifesto for human rights, democracy, and rule of law that they had conceived in conscious admiration of Charter 77, a document that had appeared in Czechoslovakia more than three decades earlier. The drafters of Charter 08 never called it a "petition," because their point was not to acknowledge the superiority of the authorities and ask them for favors; the point was to approach fellow citizens with shared ideals.*

*By November 2008 Liu Xiaobo had become a main sponsor of Charter 08 and was doing more than anyone else to gather signatures for it. When it was formally unveiled on December 9, 2008, the Charter had 303 signatures—not only of the drafters and other intellectuals, but of leaders of workers' and farmers' groups, and some government officials as well. The organizers posted the Charter on the Internet, and soon more than 12,000 others had signed. In the months that followed, the government cracked down, expunging the Charter from the Internet inside China and pursuing a program of harassing, detaining, and in other ways trying to intimidate its supporters.*

*The main reason for anger among the rulers appears to be that the Charter calls not just for ameliorative reform of the current political system but for an end to some of its essential features, including one-party rule.*

*Police came to Liu Xiaobo's Beijing apartment late at night on December 8, 2008, and took him away to an undisclosed location for what they called "residential surveillance" (even though it was not at his resi-dence) until June 23, 2009, when they formally arrested him on "suspi-cion of instigating subversion of state power." On December 23, 2009, a court in Beijing found him guilty, and Charter 08 served as the main piece of evidence against him. On December 25, the court announced a prison sentence of eleven years.—Ed.*

## I. Foreword

A hundred years have passed since the writing of China's first constitu-tion. 2008 also marks the sixtieth anniversary of the promulgation of the Universal Declaration of Human Rights, the thirtieth anniversary of the appearance of the Democracy Wall in Beijing, and the tenth of China's signing of the International Covenant on Civil and Political Rights. We are approaching the twentieth anniversary of the 1989 Tian-anmen Massacre of pro-democracy student protesters. The Chinese people, who have endured human rights disasters and uncountable struggles across these same years, now include many who see clearly that freedom, equality, and human rights are universal values of hu-mankind and that democracy and constitutional government are the fundamental framework for protecting these values.

By departing from these values, the Chinese government's approach to "modernization" has proven disastrous. It has stripped people of their rights, destroyed their dignity, and corrupted normal human inter-course. So we ask: Where is China headed in the twenty-first century? Will it continue with "modernization" under authoritarian rule, or will it embrace universal human values, join the mainstream of civilized nations, and build a democratic system? There can be no avoiding these questions.

The shock of the Western impact upon China in the nineteenth century laid bare a decadent authoritarian system and marked the be-ginning of what is often called "the greatest changes in thousands of years" for China. A "self-strengthening movement" followed, but this aimed simply at appropriating the technology to build gunboats and other Western material objects. China's humiliating naval defeat at the hands of Japan in 1895 only confirmed the obsolescence of China's sys-tem of government. The first attempts at modern political change came with the ill-fated summer of reforms in 1898, but these were cruelly crushed by ultraconservatives at China's imperial court. With the revolution of 1911, which inaugurated Asia's first republic, the authoritarian imperial system that had lasted for centuries was finally supposed to have been laid to rest. But social conflict inside our country and external pressures were to prevent it; China fell into a patchwork of warlord fiefdoms, and the new republic became a fleeting dream.

The failure of both "self-strengthening" and political renovation caused many of our forebears to reflect deeply on whether a "cultural illness" was afflicting our country. This mood gave rise, during the May Fourth Movement of the late 1910s, to the championing of "science and democracy." Yet that effort, too, foundered as warlord chaos persisted and the Japanese invasion [beginning in Manchuria in 1931—Ed.] brought national crisis.

Victory over Japan in 1945 offered one more chance for China to move toward modern government, but the Communist defeat of the Nationalists in the civil war thrust the nation into the abyss of totalitarianism. The "new China" that emerged in 1949 proclaimed that "the people are sovereign" but in fact set up a system in which "the Party is all-powerful." The Communist Party of China seized control of all organs of the state and all political, economic, and social resources, and, using these, has produced a long trail of human rights disasters, including, among many others, the Anti-Rightist Campaign (1957), the Great Leap Forward (1958–1960), the Cultural Revolution (1966–1969), the June Fourth [Tiananmen Square] Massacre (1989), and the current repression of all unauthorized religions and the rights-defense movement. During all this, the Chinese people have paid a gargantuan price. Tens of millions have lost their lives, and several generations have seen their freedom, their happiness, and their human dignity cruelly trampled.

During the last two decades of the twentieth century the government policy of "Reform and Opening" gave the Chinese people relief from the pervasive poverty and totalitarianism of the Mao Zedong era, and brought substantial increases in the wealth and living standards of many Chinese as well as a partial restoration of economic freedom and economic rights. Civil society began to grow, and popular calls for more rights and more political freedom have grown apace. As the ruling elite itself moved toward private ownership and the market economy, it began to shift from an outright rejection of "rights" to a partial acknowledgment of them.

In 1998 the Chinese government signed two important international human rights conventions; in 2004 it amended its constitution to include the phrase "respect and protect human rights"; and this year, 2008, it has promised to promote a "national human rights action plan." Unfortunately most of this political progress has extended no further than the paper on which it is written. The political reality, which is plain for anyone to see, is that China has many laws but no rule of law; it has a constitution but no constitutional government. The ruling elite continues to cling to its authoritarian power and fights off any move toward political change.

The stultifying results are endemic official corruption, an undermining of the rule of law, weak human rights, decay in public ethics, crony capitalism, growing inequality between the wealthy and the poor, pillage of the natural environment as well as of the human and historical environments, and the exacerbation of a long list of social conflicts, especially, in recent times, a sharpening animosity between officials and common people.

As these conflicts and crises grow ever more intense, and as the ruling elite continues with impunity to crush and to strip away the rights of citizens to freedom, to property, and to the pursuit of happiness, we see the powerless in our society—the vulnerable groups, the people who have been suppressed and monitored, who have suffered cruelty and even torture, and who have had no adequate avenues for their protests, no courts to hear their pleas—becoming more militant and raising the possibility of a violent conflict of disastrous proportions. The decline of the current system has reached the point where change is no longer optional.

## II. Our Fundamental Principles

This is a historic moment for China, and our future hangs in the balance. In reviewing the political modernization process of the past hundred years or more, we reiterate and endorse basic universal values as follows:

*Freedom.* Freedom is at the core of universal human values. Freedom of speech, freedom of the press, freedom of assembly, freedom of association, freedom in where to live, and the freedoms to strike, to demonstrate, and to protest, among others, are the forms that freedom takes. Without freedom, China will always remain far from civilized ideals.

*Human Rights.* Human rights are not bestowed by a state. Every person is born with inherent rights to dignity and freedom. A government exists for the protection of the human rights of its citizens. The exercise of state power must be authorized by the people. The succession of political disasters in China's recent history is a direct consequence of the ruling regime's disregard for human rights.

*Equality.* The integrity, dignity, and freedom of every person—regardless of social station, occupation, sex, economic condition, ethnicity, skin color, religion, or political belief—are the same as those of any other. Principles of equality before the law and equality of social, economic, cultural, civil, and political rights must be upheld.

*Republicanism.* Republicanism, which holds that power should be balanced among different branches of government and that competing interests should be served, resembles the traditional Chinese political ideal of "fairness in all under heaven." It allows different interest groups and social assemblies, and people with a variety of cultures and beliefs, to exercise democratic self-government and to deliberate in order to reach peaceful resolution of public questions on a basis of equal access to government and free and fair competition.

*Democracy.* The most fundamental principles of democracy are that the people are sovereign and the people select their government. Democracy has these characteristics: (1) Political power begins with the people, and the legitimacy of a regime derives from the people. (2) Political power is exercised through choices that the people make. (3) The holders of major official posts in government at all levels are determined through periodic competitive elections. (4) While honoring the will of the majority, the fundamental dignity, freedom, and human rights of minorities are protected. In short, democracy is a modern means for achieving government truly "of the people, by the people, and for the people."

*Constitutional Rule.* Constitutional rule is rule through a legal system and legal regulations to implement principles that are spelled out in a constitution. It means protecting the freedom and the rights of citizens, limiting and defining the scope of legitimate government power, and providing the administrative apparatus necessary to serve these ends.

## III. What We Advocate

Authoritarianism is in general decline throughout the world; in China, too, the era of emperors and overlords is on the way out. The time is arriving everywhere for citizens to be masters of states. For China the path that leads out of our current predicament is to divest ourselves of the authoritarian notion of reliance on an "enlightened overlord" or an "honest official" and to turn instead toward a system of liberties, democracy, and the rule of law, and toward fostering the consciousness of modern citizens who see rights as fundamental and participation as a duty. Accordingly, and in a spirit of this duty as responsible and constructive citizens, we offer the following recommendations on national governance, citizens' rights, and social development:

*1. A New Constitution.* We should recast our present constitution, rescinding its provisions that contradict the principle that sovereignty resides with the people and turning it into a document that genuinely guarantees human rights, authorizes the exercise of public power, and serves as the legal underpinning of China's democratization. The constitution must be the highest law in the land, beyond violation by any individual, group, or political party.

*2. Separation of Powers.* We should construct a modern government in which the separation of legislative, judicial, and executive power is guaranteed. We need an Administrative Law that defines the scope of government responsibility and prevents abuse of administrative power. Government should be responsible to taxpayers. Division of power between provincial governments and the central government should adhere to the principle that central powers are only those specifically granted by the constitution and all other powers belong to the local governments.

*3. Legislative Democracy.* Members of legislative bodies at all levels should be chosen by direct election, and legislative democracy should observe just and impartial principles.

*4. An Independent Judiciary.* The rule of law must be above the interests of any particular political party, and judges must be independent. We need to establish a constitutional supreme court and institute procedures for constitutional review. As soon as possible, we should abolish all of the Committees on Political and Legal Affairs that now allow Communist Party officials at every level to decide politically sensitive cases in advance and out of court. We should strictly forbid the use of public offices for private purposes.

*5. Public Control of Public Servants.* The military should be made answerable to the national government, not to a political party, and should be made more professional. Military personnel should swear allegiance to the constitution and remain nonpartisan. Political party organizations must be prohibited in the military. All public officials, including police, should serve as nonpartisans, and the current practice of favoring one political party in the hiring of public servants must end.

*6. Guarantee of Human Rights.* There must be strict guarantees of human rights and respect for human dignity. There should be a Human Rights Committee, responsible to the highest legislative body, that will prevent the government from abusing public power in violation of human rights. A democratic and constitutional China especially must guarantee the personal freedom of citizens. No one should suffer illegal arrest, detention, arraignment, interrogation, or punishment. The system of "reeducation through labor" must be abolished.

*7. Election of Public Officials.* There should be a comprehensive system of democratic elections based on "one person, one vote." The direct election of administrative heads at the levels of county, city, province, and nation should be systematically implemented. The rights to hold periodic free elections and to participate in them as a citizen are inalienable.

*8. Rural–Urban Equality.* The two-tier household registry system must be abolished. This system favors urban residents and harms rural residents. We should establish instead a system that gives every citizen the same constitutional rights and the same freedom to choose where to live.

*9. Freedom to Form Groups.* The right of citizens to form groups must be guaranteed. The current system for registering nongovernment groups, which requires a group to be "approved," should be replaced by a system in which a group simply registers itself. The formation of political parties should be governed by the constitution and the laws, which means that we must abolish the special privilege of one party to monopolize power and must guarantee principles of free and fair competition among political parties.

*10. Freedom to Assemble.* The constitution provides that peaceful assembly, demonstration, protest, and freedom of expression are fundamental rights of a citizen. The ruling party and the government must not be permitted to subject these to illegal interference or unconstitutional obstruction.

*11. Freedom of Expression.* We should make freedom of speech, freedom of the press, and academic freedom universal, thereby guaranteeing that citizens can be informed and can exercise their right of political supervision. These freedoms should be upheld by a Press Law that abolishes political restrictions on the press. The provision in the current Criminal Law that refers to the crime of "incitement to subvert state power" must be abolished. We should end the practice of viewing words as crimes.

*12. Freedom of Religion.* We must guarantee freedom of religion and belief, and institute a separation of religion and state. There must be no governmental interference in peaceful religious activities. We should abolish any laws, regulations, or local rules that limit or suppress the religious freedom of citizens. We should abolish the current system that requires religious groups (and their places of worship) to get official approval in advance and substitute for it a system in which registry is optional and, for those who choose to register, automatic.

13. *Civic Education.* In our schools we should abolish political curriculums and examinations that are designed to indoctrinate students in state ideology and to instill support for the rule of one party. We should replace them with civic education that advances universal values and citizens' rights, fosters civic consciousness, and promotes civic virtues that serve society.

14. *Protection of Private Property.* We should establish and protect the right to private property and promote an economic system of free and fair markets. We should do away with government monopolies in commerce and industry and guarantee the freedom to start new enterprises. We should establish a Committee on State-Owned Property, reporting to the national legislature, that will monitor the transfer of state-owned enterprises to private ownership in a fair, competitive, and orderly manner. We should institute a land reform that promotes private ownership of land, guarantees the right to buy and sell land, and allows the true value of private property to be adequately reflected in the market.

15. *Financial and Tax Reform.* We should establish a democratically regulated and accountable system of public finance that ensures the protection of taxpayer rights and that operates through legal procedures. We need a system by which public revenues that belong to a certain level of government—central, provincial, county, or local—are controlled at that level. We need major tax reform that will abolish any unfair taxes, simplify the tax system, and spread the tax burden fairly. Government officials should not be able to raise taxes, or institute new ones, without public deliberation and the approval of a democratic assembly. We should reform the ownership system in order to encourage competition among a wider variety of market participants.

16. *Social Security.* We should establish a fair and adequate social security system that covers all citizens and ensures basic access to education, health care, retirement security, and employment.

*17. Protection of the Environment.* We need to protect the natural environment and to promote development in a way that is sustainable and responsible to our descendants and to the rest of humanity. This means insisting that the state and its officials at all levels not only do what they must do to achieve these goals, but also accept the supervision and participation of nongovernmental organizations.

*18. A Federated Republic.* A democratic China should seek to act as a responsible major power contributing toward peace and development in the Asian Pacific region by approaching others in a spirit of equality and fairness. In Hong Kong and Macao, we should support the freedoms that already exist. With respect to Taiwan, we should declare our commitment to the principles of freedom and democracy and then, negotiating as equals and ready to compromise, seek a formula for peaceful unification. We should approach disputes in the national-minority areas of China with an open mind, seeking ways to find a workable framework within which all ethnic and religious groups can flourish. We should aim ultimately at a federation of democratic communities of China.

*19. Truth in Reconciliation.* We should restore the reputations of all people, including their family members, who suffered political stigma in the political campaigns of the past or who have been labeled as criminals because of their thought, speech, or faith. The state should pay reparations to these people. All political prisoners and prisoners of conscience must be released. There should be a Truth Investigation Commission charged with finding the facts about past injustices and atrocities, determining responsibility for them, upholding justice, and, on these bases, seeking social reconciliation.

China, as a major nation of the world, as one of five permanent members of the United Nations Security Council, and as a member of the UN Council on Human Rights, should be contributing to peace for humankind and progress toward human rights. Unfortunately, we stand today as the only country among the major nations that remains mired in authoritarian politics. Our political system continues to produce human rights disasters and social crises, thereby not only constricting

China's own development but also limiting the progress of all of human civilization. This must change, truly it must. The democratization of Chinese politics can be put off no longer.

Accordingly, we dare to put civic spirit into practice by announcing Charter 08. We hope that our fellow citizens who feel a similar sense of crisis, responsibility, and mission, whether they are inside the government or not, and regardless of their social status, will set aside small differences to embrace the broad goals of this citizens' movement. Together we can work for major changes in Chinese society and for the rapid establishment of a free, democratic, and constitutional country. We can bring to reality the goals and ideals that our people have incessantly been seeking for more than a hundred years, and can bring a brilliant new chapter to Chinese civilization.

*This translation by Perry Link originally appeared in the* New York Review of Books,
*vol. 56, no. 1, January 15, 2009.*

## Postscript: A Partial Chronology of the Immediate Aftermath of the Charter's Appearance

*December 6, 2008 (three days before the Charter's formal announcement): Police in Hangzhou, in eastern central China, detained Wen Kejian, a writer and primary drafter of the Charter, and questioned him for about an hour. They told Wen that Charter 08 was "different" from earlier dissident statements, and "a fairly grave matter." They said there would be a coordinated investigation in all cities and provinces to "root out the organizers" and advised Wen to remove his name from the Charter. Wen declined, answering that he saw the Charter as possibly a turning point in Chinese history.*

*December 8: Police in Shenzhen, just north of Hong Kong, called on Zhao Dagong, a drafter and signer of the Charter, for a "chat." They told Zhao that the central authorities were concerned about the Charter and asked if he was the organizer in the Shenzhen area.*

*December 8, at 11 p.m.: Police in Beijing came to the home of Liu Xiaobo, confiscated books, notes, and computers, detained Liu, and took him away.*

*December 8, also 11 p.m.: About twenty police entered the Beijing home of Zhang Zuhua, one of the Charter's main drafters. A few of them escorted Zhang to the local police station, where they held him for twelve hours, questioning him in detail about Charter 08 and Chinese Human Rights Defenders. The others remained in the apartment and, as Zhang's wife watched, searched the home, confiscating books, notebooks, Zhang's passport, all four of the family's computers, and all of their cash and credit cards. (Zhang later learned that his family's bank accounts, including those of both his and his wife's parents, had been emptied.)*

*December 9: Beijing police summoned a number of people who had signed the Charter, including the rights lawyer Pu Zhiqiang and the physicist and philosopher Jiang Qisheng, for "chats" aimed at extracting information about the organization of the Charter effort.*

*December 10: Police in Hangzhou again came to the home of Wen Kejian, and this time were more threatening. They told Wen he would face severe punishment if he wrote about the Charter or about Liu Xiaobo's detention. "Do you want three years in prison?" they asked. "Or four?"*

*December 11: Beijing police interrogated the journalist Gao Yu and the Internet writer Liu Di ("the stainless steel mouse") about their signing of the Charter. Police also visited the rights lawyer Teng Biao, but Teng declined on principle to speak with them.*

*December 12 and 13: There were reports of interrogations in many provinces—Shanxi, Hunan, Zhejiang, Fujian, Guangdong, and others—of people who had seen the Charter on the Internet, found that they agreed with it, and signed. With these people the police focused on two questions: "How did you get involved?" and "What do you know about the drafters and organizers?"*

*December 10–14: Chinese living outside China signed a letter of strong support for the Charter. The eminent historian Yu Ying-shih, the astrophysicist Fang Lizhi, writers Ha Jin and Zheng Yi, and more than 160 others were original signatories.*

*December 12: The Dalai Lama published a letter of support for the Charter, writing that "a harmonious society can come into being only when there is trust among the people, freedom from fear, freedom of ex-*

*pression, rule of law, justice, and equality" and calling on the Chinese government to release prisoners "who have been detained for exercising their freedom of expression."*

—Perry Link, December 18, 2008

# MY SELF-DEFENSE

◆　◆　◆　◆　◆

*At his trial on December 23, 2009, Liu Xiaobo presented the following written response to the government's charges that he was guilty of "inciting subversion of state power." The six articles that Liu refers to in the first paragraph include "To Change a Regime by Changing a Society" (pp. 21–29 above) and "A Deeper Look into Why Child Slavery in China's 'Black Kilns' Could Happen" (pp. 94–106). The other four were "The Authoritarian Patriotism of the Communist Party of China" (Epoch Times, October 4, 2005); "Who Says the Chinese People Deserve Only 'Democracy by Party Rule'?" (Observe China, January 6, 2006); "The Many Faces of Communist Party Dictatorship" (Observe China, March 13, 2006); and "How a Rising Dictatorship Hurts Democracy in the World" (the BBC Chinese website, May 3, 2006).—Ed.*

CRIMINAL INDICTMENT Number 247 of Branch One of the Beijing Prosecutor's Office for the year 2009 lists six of my articles plus Charter 08, quotes about 330 characters from them, and uses these quotations as its bases to charge that criminal responsibility should be determined for my having violated the stipulations of Article 105, Section 2, of the Criminal Law of the People's Republic of China regarding "incitement of subversion of state power."

The statements in the Indictment that follow the phrase "after [he] solicited more than 300 signatures" contain some factual inaccuracies.

Other than that, I have no objection to the factual statements that are made. The six articles indeed are mine, and I did contribute to Charter 08. I was, however, able to collect only about 70 signatures for it (not "more than 300," as the Indictment says). The other signatures were not collected by me.

I cannot accept the claim that I have broken the law. Throughout the time of my detention, slightly more than a year, I have consistently maintained my innocence before every police interrogator, prosecutor, and judge whom I have met. Now, basing myself on China's constitution, on human rights conventions of the United Nations, on my ideals for political reform, and on the trends of world history, I am once again presenting a claim of "not guilty."

1. One of the more important fruits of "reform and opening" has been the steadily rising awareness of human rights among our fellow Chinese and the sporadic but increasing incidents in which their demands for rights have pressed the government to progress in its own thinking on this topic. In 2004 the National People's Congress, in amending China's constitution to include the phrase "the state respects and guarantees human rights," made this guarantee a constitutional principle for the governance of our country by rule of law. The human rights that the government is now bound to respect and guarantee are the various rights of citizens that are listed under Article 35 of China's constitution. Freedom of speech is one of those fundamental rights. Because my expression of dissenting political opinion is an exercise by a Chinese citizen of rights to freedom of expression granted by the Chinese constitution, the Chinese government is therefore not only bound not to limit or to arbitrarily remove the right; it is bound, on the contrary, to respect and guarantee it. It is not my words but those of the Indictment that infringe upon China's most fundamental law. They are an excellent example of treating words as crimes, which itself is an extension into the present day of China's antique practice called "literary inquisition." This practice deserves our moral censure in addition to prosecution for violation of the constitution. Article 105, Section 2, of the Criminal Law itself seems clearly to violate the constitution and should be referred to the National People's Congress for a review of its constitutionality.

2. The Indictment quotes a few paragraphs from my articles as its basis to charge that I have used "rumor-mongering and slander to incite subversion of state power and overthrow of the socialist system." The charges are specious. "Rumor-mongering" means to invent or fabricate falsities that harm the interests of others. "Slander" means to use invented material to sully a person's reputation. Both charges depend on the question of truth and falsity and on the question of harming of others or not—either their reputations or their interests. All of my articles, however, fall into the category of commentary; they express my thinking, viewpoints, and value judgments. They are not judgments of fact, and none has harmed the interests of any person. They do not come near to either "rumor-mongering" or "slander." Criticism is not rumor-mongering, and opposition is not slander.

3. Citing a few excerpts from Charter 08, the Indictment charges that I have slandered the ruling party and "have plotted to incite subversion of the current government." The selection of excerpts in the Indictment has been made with a view to serving the preconceived goals of the prosecutors. It completely ignores the basic position of Charter 08 and the overall viewpoint that my articles consistently express. Let me illustrate.

> The "human rights disasters" to which Charter 08 refers are all facts of recent Chinese history. The Anti-Rightist Campaign wrongly labeled more than 500,000 people as "rightists." The Great Leap Forward led to more than ten million unnatural deaths. The Cultural Revolution produced a national calamity. The June Fourth [Tiananmen] Massacre brought death to many and prison terms to many more. All of these facts are well-known "human rights disasters" that have been recognized for bringing crises to China—thereby, as Charter 08 says, not only "constricting China's own development but also limiting the progress of all of human civilization." What Charter 08 says about abolishing one-party rule is simply a call upon the ruling party to carry out reforms that will return power to the people so that we might establish a free nation "of the people, by the people, and for the people."

Charter 08 avows certain values and advocates certain structures that are aimed at building a free and democratic federated republic in the long term. It lists nineteen specific reform measures and recommends that they be pursued gradually and peacefully. The purposes of these measures are to correct the many abuses in China's current system of crippled reforms and to press the ruling party to convert its program of crippled reforms into a healthier model in which political and economic reforms move forward in tandem. At another level the Charter's aim is to bring popular pressure to bear on officialdom to return power to the people as soon as possible. Popular pressure from below can induce political reforms from above and lead to a healthful symbiosis between people and officials that can bring us nearer than ever to the dream of constitutional government that our countrymen have been cherishing now for about a hundred years.

Over the past two decades, from 1989 to 2009, I have consistently held that China's political reform should be gradual, peaceful, orderly, and under control. I have always opposed the notion of sudden radical leaps, and have opposed violent revolution even more stoutly. My preference for a gradual approach to reform is set forth in my essay "To Change a Regime by Changing a Society" [pp. 21–29] where I make it clear that I look to things such as the spread of rights consciousness in society, increased numbers of rights-advocacy projects, greater autonomy at the popular level, and the gradual expansion of civil society as ways to build pressure from below and eventually to compel officialdom to make reforms. This pattern is what in fact has been happening during the last thirty years of reform in China in any case: the record shows that every one of the changes that has made a significant difference in our system was, in its earliest inception, something that began spontaneously among the people. Only after the popular innovations achieved a certain identity and influence did authorities adopt them and turn them into top-down policies.

In sum, my keywords for China's political reform are *gradual, peaceful, orderly,* and *controllable,* and I favor a symbiosis of bottom-up and top-down efforts. I hold this view because I see it as having the greatest benefits at the lowest costs. I am aware, as are most people, that orderly and controllable social change is always superior to disorderly and uncontrollable change and that order under a bad government is still better than chaos under no government at all. From this it should be clear that my opposition to dictatorial government and power monopoly is not the same as "inciting subversion of the current government." Opposition is not the same as subversion.

4. An ancient Chinese proverb says "The arrogant lose while the modest gain," and a similar maxim from the West says "Pride comes before a fall." I am aware of my own limits, and know that my public statements cannot have been perfect. Especially in my commentaries on current events, I have sometimes fallen into slipshod argument, excessive emotion, factual error, and sweeping conclusion. But none of these errors has anything to do with crime, and cannot be valid evidence in a criminal trial. This is because the right to free speech includes not just the right to say correct things but also the right to say incorrect things. Correct statements and majority views must be protected, but incorrect statements and minority views need equal protection. The familiar statement from the modern West that "I may disagree with your view but insist on protecting your right to express it in public, even if it is incorrect" captures the essence of free speech. China's ancient traditions contain the same wisdom, for example in the famous "24-character ditty" that says, "Say all you know, in every detail; a speaker is blameless, because listeners can think; if the words are true, make your corrections; if they are not, just take note." How is it that this ditty could be passed down through the ages in China, staying alive on the tongues and in the ears of so many people? This happened because the words capture the essential meaning of free speech. In my view the line "a speaker is blameless, because listeners can think" could well serve as watchword for anyone who listens to criticisms of him- or herself. All the more should the ruling authority heed it when dealing with political dissidence.

5. Another reason I cannot be judged guilty is that the charges against me are in violation of human rights agreements of the international community. As early as 1948, China, as a permanent member of the United Nations Security Council, participated in drafting the UN's Universal Declaration of Human Rights. Fifty years later, in 1997 and 1998, the Chinese government again undertook solemn understandings

with the international community by signing two agreements on human rights that had been drafted at the United Nations [the International Covenant on Economic, Social and Cultural Rights, signed in 1997 and ratified in 2001; and the International Covenant on Civil and Political Rights, signed in 1998 but not yet ratified—Ed.]. One of these, the International Covenant on Civil and Political Rights, lists freedom of speech among the most fundamental of universal human rights and calls upon every member state to respect and guarantee it. As a member of the UN Human Rights Council, and as a permanent member of the UN Security Council, China should feel a duty not only to honor its own commitments to UN human rights covenants but, beyond that, to be a model for others in showing how rights should be guaranteed. This is the way, indeed the only way, in which the Chinese government can assure the human rights of its own citizens as well as make its contribution, as a great nation should, to the project of advancing human rights globally.

6. Treating speech as crime not only runs counter to the modern trends in world history, but, more deeply, abuses humanism and human rights in a fundamental moral sense. This is true regardless of whether we are speaking of ancient times or modern, of China or the world. In the annals of Chinese imperial history from the third century BCE to the early twentieth CE, wherever punishment of scholars for their words has been noted, those events have come to be viewed as black marks on the records of the regimes that imposed them and as embarrassments to the Chinese nation. The First Emperor of Qin (259–210 BCE) is credited with unifying China, but is also eternally attached to phrase "burning of books and live burials of scholars." Emperor Wu of the Han (156–87 BCE) did many great things, but they have been overshadowed over the centuries by his cowardly decision to castrate Sima Qian, the Grand Historian. High Qing saw "the splendid era of Kang Xi and Qian Long" (1662–1796 CE), but the harsh censorship of those times has also left a legacy of opprobrium. On the other hand, Emperor Wen of the Han period, in abolishing the "crime of slander," has been praised ever since for inaugurating the enlightened "era of Wen and Jing [Wen's son]."

And so it has been in modern times. One fundamental reason why the Communist Party of China was able to grow stronger in its early years, and eventually to defeat the Guomindang government, was that its calls to "oppose dictatorship and demand freedom" had deep appeal to the public. Before 1949, Communist Party newspapers like *New China Daily* and *Liberation Daily* were constantly criticizing the Chiang Kai-shek regime for its repression of free speech and often issued loud appeals on behalf of persecuted voices of conscience. Mao Zedong and other communist leaders expounded upon freedom of speech and other basic human rights at length. After 1949, however, from the Anti-Rightist Campaign of 1957 to the Cultural Revolution of the late 1960s, from Lin Zhao's death by firing squad (see pp. 134–136) to the slicing of Zhang Zhixin's throat to prevent her from crying out before she was shot, freedom of speech disappeared while the entire country fell into a tawdry chorus of enforced uniformity. During the reform era following the death of Mao, the ruling party's tolerance of different political opinion has greatly increased, and the scope for public expression has steadily expanded. Speech crime is much less common than before, but the tradition of using the tool has not died out. From April Fifth [1976, when police using billy clubs drove thousands of protesters from Tiananmen Square—Ed.] to the June Fourth Massacre of 1989, from Democracy Wall to Charter 08, cases of treating words as crimes have remained common. My own case, before you today, is but the latest item in this line.

Today, in the twenty-first century, awareness of freedom of speech is already well established among the people of our country, and the idea of treating words as crimes is widely condemned. Whether power-holders like it or not, "blocking people's mouths is harder than blocking a river," as the proverb says, and no prison walls are high enough to cut off free expression. Suppressing dissident opinion cannot buy legitimacy for a regime, and political prisons will not bring lasting peace or harmony. Problems of the pen can be solved only by the pen; to answer pens with guns only leads to human rights disasters. Only when the practice of treating speech as crime is fundamentally uprooted from our system can citizens across our great land finally be assured that the freedom of speech guaranteed by our constitution will be a living reality for them. This guarantee will require institutional change.

In sum, the treatment of words as crimes is inconsistent with the provisions on human rights in China's constitution, violates UN covenants on human rights, and runs counter to the tides of history as well as universal moral principles. I hope that the court, by accepting my plea of "not guilty," will allow its ruling on this case to stand as a precedent in Chinese legal history, a precedent able not only to meet the human rights standards in the Chinese constitution and in United Nations' covenants, but also to withstand moral scrutiny and the test of history.

My thanks to all.

December 23, 2009

*Original text available at http://blog.boxun.com/hero/liuxb*
*Translated by Perry Link*

# I HAVE NO ENEMIES

## My Final Statement

◆ ◆ ◆ ◆ ◆

*Liu Xiaobo prepared the following statement for presentation at his trial on December 23, 2009. His reading of it was cut off after fourteen minutes when the presiding judge declared that the defendant could use no more time than the prosecutor, who had used only fourteen minutes to present the state's case against Liu.—Ed.*

June 1989 has been the major turning point in my life, which now is just over one half century in length.

Until June 1989, I had an academic career and it was flourishing. I was part of the class of 1977, the first group of students to enter university after the national entrance examinations were reinstated in the post-Mao era. After college I went on to M.A. and Ph.D. degrees and then was offered a teaching position at my alma mater, Beijing Normal University, where my teaching was well received by students. Beyond the classroom, my books and articles provoked quite a bit of comment, and by the end of the 1980s I had become a "public intellectual." I received invitations to give talks all around our country as well as invitations to Europe and America as a visiting scholar. Through all of this my essential demands upon myself were only that, both as a person and as a writer, I be honest and responsible, and that I live in dignity.

At the June 1989 turning point, I had chosen to return to China from the U.S. to join the protest movement, and then was thrown into prison for "the crime of spreading and inciting counterrevolution." I found myself separate from my beloved lectern and no longer able to publish my writing or give public talks inside China. Merely for expressing different political views and for joining a peaceful democracy movement, a teacher lost his right to teach, a writer lost his right to publish, and a public intellectual could no longer speak openly. Whether we view this as my own fate or as the fate of a China after thirty years of "reform and opening," it truly is a sad fate.

Come to think of it, my most dramatic experiences since 1989 have come inside a courtroom. My only two chances to state my views publicly—once in January 1991 and once again today—have come as parts of trials at the Beijing Intermediate Court. The names of the crimes I have faced in the two instances are different, but their substance is the same: they are speech crimes, both.

Twenty years have passed since 1989, but the aggrieved ghosts of those who were massacred that year are still watching us. It was that massacre that put me on the road to political dissidence, but later, when I got out of prison in 1991 and found myself unable to speak publicly inside China, my only public voice, of necessity, was through the foreign media. This expression led to further consequences: continual police monitoring, a stint under house arrest (May 1995 to January 1996), and a term of "reeducation-through-labor" (October 1996 to October 1999). Today the regime, with its "enemy mentality," has once again pushed me into the defendant's dock.

I wish, however, to underscore something that was in my "June 2nd Hunger-Strike Declaration" of twenty years ago: I have no enemies, and no hatred. None of the police who have watched, arrested, or interrogated me, none of the prosecutors who have indicted me, and none of the judges who will judge me are my enemies. There is no way that I can accept your surveillance, arrests, indictments, or verdicts, but I respect your professions and your persons. This includes Zhang Rongge and Pan Xueqing, the two prosecutors who are bringing the charges against me today. As you interrogated me on December 3, I could sense your respect and sincerity.

Hatred only eats away at a person's intelligence and conscience, and an enemy mentality can poison the spirit of an entire people (as the experience of our country during the Mao era clearly shows). It can lead to cruel and lethal internecine combat, can destroy tolerance and human feeling within a society, and can block the progress of a nation toward freedom and democracy. For these reasons I hope that I can rise above my personal fate and contribute to the progress of our country and to changes in our society. I hope that I can answer the regime's enmity with utmost benevolence, and can use love to dissipate hate.

It is well known that "reform and opening" brought development to our country and change to our society. In my view the key to "reform and opening" has been the abandonment of the Mao-era policy of "taking class struggle as fundamental" and replacing class struggle with economic development and more social harmony. Since the abandonment of Mao's "struggle philosophy" we have seen a weakening of the enemy mentality and of the psychology of hatred. The noxious "wolf's milk" that seeped into our nature and caused us to be predatory upon others is slowly draining away—and that process, in turn, has created an environment, both inside China and in our foreign relations, in which reform and opening can flourish. There is now some soft turf within which people's care and sympathy for one another can grow, and where differing interests and values can coexist in peace. This sort of environment stimulates the creativity of our citizens and restores their compassion for others. In sum, reform and opening could never have worked if "class struggle" at home and "anti-imperialism plus anti-revisionism" in foreign relations had continued.

Our market economy, our newfound cultural variety, and our progress toward rule of law all owe something to the decline of the enemy mentality. Even in political matters, where progress has been the slowest, a weakening of the enemy mentality has turned the ruling regime toward greater tolerance of pluralism in society and considerably less use of force in the persecution of dissidents. The official term for the 1989 protest movement has softened from "rioting" to "political disturbance." Moreover the regime has gradually come to accept the universality of human rights. By 1998 the Chinese government had made commitments to the world in two major United Nations human rights covenants, the signing of which marked the Chinese government's acceptance of universal standards of human rights. In 2004 the National People's Congress amended the Chinese constitution to write into it, for the first time, that "the state respects and guarantees human rights." This move made human rights now officially part of China's law. Meanwhile the regime's announcement of slogans like "Putting people first" and "Creating a harmonious society" showed some progress at the rhetorical level in the Communist Party's philosophy of government.

These recent changes at the macro level have been noticeable in my own personal experience.

Even as I have insisted, throughout the year and a bit more since I lost my freedom, that I am innocent and that the charges against me are unconstitutional, none of the people who have been charged with handling me has been disrespectful, has exceeded any time limits, or has tried to force a confession. I have been held at two different locations and have dealt with four pretrial police interrogators, three prosecutors, and two judges, and all of them have been reasonable and moderate in manner. They have often shown goodwill. On June 23, 2009, police moved me from a location where I had been kept under "residential surveillance" to the Number One Detention Center of the Beijing Public Security Bureau. It was a new facility, and just within my six months there I have been able to observe progress in prison management.

In 1996 I spent time at the old Number One, at Banbuqiao, and compared to that one, the new one is a huge improvement both in its facilities (its "hardware") and its management style (its "software"). The more humane policies at the new Number One, which do better to respect the rights and integrity of detainees, trickles down to the words and deeds of correctional staff in daily life. One can also sense new policies in the "soothing broadcasts" that the loudspeakers provide, the "repentance magazines" that carry articles by and for the inmates, and the music that is played before meals, before bed, and upon rising. These management techniques give detainees a certain feeling of dignity and warmth, encourage them to support prison order, and help them to resist bullying by other inmates. They create not only a more humane physical environment but also a much better mental environment for detainees as they prepare to face trial. I have had close and extended contact with Liu Zheng, the warden in charge of my cell, and can say that his respectful care for detainees is visible in every detail of his work, in every word and deed, and that it does create feelings of warmth. Perhaps it was just my good fortune to get to know this sincere, honest, conscientious, and kind correctional officer at Number One.

If our politics can grow from beliefs and behavior of this kind, we can be confident that political progress will continue. I feel thoroughly optimistic about the prospects for a free China in the future. No force can block the thirst for freedom that lies within human nature, and some day China, too, will be a nation of laws where human rights are paramount. I also hope that progress of this kind might be reflected in the present trial, in a just verdict—a verdict that can stand the test of history—delivered by the officers of this court.

If one were to ask what my most fortunate experience of the past twenty years has been, I would need to say that it has been the selfless love that I have received from my wife, Liu Xia. She was not allowed to come to court to hear me today, yet I feel a need to address her directly, so will: I feel confident, my dear one, that there cannot possibly be any change in your love for me. For several years now, as I have been in and out of prison, external factors have forced bitterness upon our love, and yet, as I look back, the love still seems boundless. I have been held in tangible prisons, while you have waited for me within the intangible prison of the heart. Your love has been like sunlight that leaps over high walls and shines through iron windows, that caresses every inch of my skin and warms every cell of my body. It has bolstered my inner equanimity while I try to stay clearheaded and high-minded; it has infused with meaning every minute of my stays in prisons. My love for you, on the other hand, is burdened by my feelings of guilt and apology. These are so heavy that they sometimes seem to make me stagger. I am like a stone on a barren plain, whipped by fierce winds and driving rain, so cold that no one dares touch me. Yet my love is rock-solid and sharp. It can pierce any barrier. Even were I ground to powder, still would I use my ashes to embrace you.

Armed with your love, dear one, I can face the sentence that I am about to receive with peace in my heart, with no regrets for the choices that I have made, and filled with optimism for tomorrow. I look forward to the day when our country will be a land of free expression: a country where the words of each citizen will get equal respect; a country where different values, ideas, beliefs, and political views can compete with one another even as they peacefully coexist; a country where expression of both majority and minority views will be secure, and, in particular, where political views that differ from those of the people in power will be fully respected and protected; a country where all political views will be spread out beneath the sun for citizens to choose among, and every citizen will be able to express views without the slightest of fears; a country where it will be impossible to suffer persecution for expressing a political view. I hope that I will be the last victim in China's long record of treating words as crimes.

Free expression is the base of human rights, the root of human nature, and the mother of truth. To kill free speech is to insult human rights, to stifle human nature, and to suppress truth.

I feel it is my duty as a Chinese citizen to try to realize in practice the right of free expression that is written in our country's constitution. There has been nothing remotely criminal in anything that I have done, yet I will not complain, even in the face of the charges against me.

I thank you all.

December 23, 2009

*Original text available at http://www.liuxiaobo.eu/*
*Translated by Perry Link*

# THE CRIMINAL VERDICT

Beijing No. 1 Intermediate People's Court
Criminal Judgment No. 3901 (2009)

◆ ◆ ◆ ◆ ◆

PROSECUTING ORGAN: Branch No. 1 of the People's Procuratorate of Beijing

DEFENDANT: Liu Xiaobo, male; 53 years of age (born December 28, 1955); Han nationality; born in Changchun city, Jilin Province; Ph.D. education; unemployed; household registry 2-1-2 number 5 Qingchun St., Xigang District, Dalian city, Liaoning Province; current address no. 502, Unit One, Building 10, Bank of China apartments, Seven Sages Village, Haidian District, Beijing City. Convicted in September 1996 of disturbing social order and sent for three years of reeducation-through-labor. Detained for questioning on suspicion of incitement to subvert state power on December 8, 2008. Put under residential surveillance on December 9, and arrested on June 23, 2009. Currently held at the Beijing No. 1 Detention Center.

DEFENSE COUNSEL: Ding Xikui, lawyer, Mo Shaoping Law Firm, Beijing

DEFENSE COUNSEL: Shang Baojun, lawyer, Mo Shaoping Law Firm, Beijing

Branch No. 1 of the People's Procuratorate of Beijing, in its Criminal Indictment No. 247 (2009), has charged defendant Liu Xiaobo with the crime of inciting subversion of state power and on December 10, 2009, delivered its Indictment to this court for prosecution. This court, in accordance with law, assembled a panel of judges to hear the case in open court. Branch No. 1 of the People's Procuratorate of Beijing assigned prosecutor Zhang Rongge and deputy prosecutor Pan Xueqing to prosecute the case, and defendant Liu Xiaobo and his counsel, Ding Xikui and Shang Baojun, appeared in court to participate at the trial. The proceedings are complete.

## The Charges

The Indictment from Branch No. 1 of the People's Procuratorate of Beijing charges that Defendant Liu Xiaobo, because of his dissatisfaction with the People's Democratic Dictatorship and the socialist system in our country, began in 2005 to use the Internet to post subversive articles such as "The Authoritarian Patriotism of the Communist Party of China," "Who Says the Chinese People Deserve Only 'Democracy by Party Rule'?" "To Change a Regime by Changing a Society," "The Many Faces of Communist Party Dictatorship," "How a Rising Dictatorship Hurts Democracy in the World," and "A Deeper Look into Why Child Slavery in China's 'Black Kilns' Could Happen" on foreign websites such "Observe China" and the Chinese service of the BBC and that the articles contain rumor and slander including "the top priority of the Chinese Communist dictators, from the time they took power, has been their grip on power, and human lives have been their lowest," "the official love-of-country that the Chinese Communist dictators promote is an absurdity by which 'Party stands for country' and the actual demands on people are that they love a dictatorial regime, love a dictatorial political party, and love dictators; it usurps the word 'patriotism' to bring suffering and disaster to the nation and its people," "all these measures of the Communist Party of China are stopgaps that dictators use to shore up power to the last, but there is no way they can hold together an edifice that already shows such a vast network of cracks" and incitement including "change a regime by changing a society" and "hope for a free China is placed better with 'new forces' in society than with any 'new policies' from the rulers," and that between September and December, 2008, Defendant Liu Xiaobo colluded with others to draft and concoct Charter 08, which, aiming to incite subversion of state power, put forward proposals such as "abolish the special privilege of one party to monopolize power" and "aim ultimately at a federation of democratic communities of China" and that, after collecting more than 300 signatures on it, Liu Xiaobo used email to send Charter 08 and the signatures for public posting on the foreign websites of Democratic China, Independent Chinese PEN, and other foreign websites.

Following commission of these crimes, Defendant Liu Xiaobo was found, seized, and brought to account.

Branch No. 1 of the People's Procuratorate of Beijing has delivered to this court evidence of the crimes of Defendant Liu Xiaobo including witness testimony, on-scene observation reports, records of investigations, electronic data, and forensic reports. In the opinion of the Procuratorate, Defendant Liu Xiaobo's behavior violates Section 2 of Article 105 of the Criminal Law of the People's Republic of China and constitutes the crime of inciting subversion of state power, and the criminal behavior is severe. It submitted the evidence to this court for judgment according to law.

## Reply

At his trial Defendant Liu Xiaobo argued that he is innocent and was only exercising the right of freedom of speech that the constitution grants to citizens; that his critical opinions did no actual harm to any person, and that he did not incite subversion of state power.

At the trial, defense lawyers for Defendant Liu Xiaobo argued that Charter 08 and the six articles Liu Xiaobo wrote contain no rumor, libel, or slander. They held that the articles Liu Xiaobo wrote were covered by a citizen's rights to free speech and to expression of personal opinion and did not constitute a crime of inciting subversion of state power.

## Findings

At trial, it was determined that Defendant Liu Xiaobo, because of his dissatisfaction with the People's Democratic Dictatorship and the socialist system in our country, between October 2005 and August 2007, at his current address no. 502, Unit One, Building 10, Bank of China apartments, Seven Sages Village, Haidian District, Beijing City, by means of writing and posting articles on Internet sites such "Observe China" and the "BBC Chinese web," on many occasions incited others to subvert the state power and the socialist system of our country. In his published articles "The Authoritarian Patriotism of the Communist Party of China," "Who Says the Chinese People Deserve Only 'Democracy by Party Rule'?" "To Change a Regime by Changing a Society," "The Many Faces of Communist Party Dictatorship," "How a Rising Dictatorship Hurts Democracy in the World," and "A Deeper Look into Why Child Slavery in China's 'Black Kilns' Could Happen," Liu Xiaobo commits slander: "The top priority of the Chinese Communist dictators, from the time they took power, has been their grip on power, and human lives have been their lowest"; "The official love-of-country that the Chinese Communist dictators promote is an absurdity by which 'Party stands for country' and the actual demands on people are that they love a dictatorial regime, love a dictatorial political party, and love dictators; it usurps the word 'patriotism' to bring suffering and disaster to the nation and its people"; "all these measures of the CCP are stopgaps that dictators use to shore up power to the last, but there is no way they can hold together an edifice that already shows such a vast network of cracks" and he incites: "Change a regime by changing a society" and "Hope for a free China is placed better with 'new forces' in society than with any 'new policies' from the rulers."

Furthermore between September and December, 2008, Defendant Liu Xiaobo colluded with others to write the article Charter 08 that promoted many items of incitement such as "abolish the special privilege of one party to monopolize power" and "aim ultimately at a federation of democratic communities of China." After Liu Xiaobo and his group had collected more than 300 signatures, they used email to send Charter 08 and the signatures to it for public posting on the foreign websites of Democratic China, Independent Chinese PEN, and other foreign websites. The articles by Liu Xiaobo noted above were linked to many websites, forwarded to many others, and were accessed by many people.

Following commission of these crimes, Defendant Liu Xiaobo was found, seized, and brought to justice.

## Evidence

This court has determined that the foregoing facts have been substantiated at trial by the following evidence that was presented to the court:

1. The testimony of witness Liu Xia shows: She is the wife of Liu Xiaobo and lived together with him at no. 502, Unit One, Building 10, Bank of China apartments, Seven Sages Village, Haidian District, Beijing City. They had a total of three computers in their home, of which one was a desktop model and two were notepad computers. She understands nothing of computers and never used the computers in their home. Normally it was always Liu Xiaobo who used the computers. Liu Xiaobo used the computers to write articles and go online. Only she and Liu Xiaobo lived in their home, no one else. Guests did not often come to their home. Most of Liu Xiaobo's meetings with others were outside the home. She is not clear about how their computers connect with the Internet. Liu Xiaobo arranged to have the connection done in 2001. The source of livelihood for her and Liu Xiaobo normally was the manuscript fees for the items he wrote. Liu Xiaobo opened a bank account in her name, and manuscript fees arrived in the account at irregular intervals. She went to the bank every month at irregular intervals to withdraw money.

2. A "Certificate of Account Opening" and a "Record of Bank Remittances" supplied by the Beijing Branch and Muxidi Sub-branch of the Bank of China, Limited, show: The bank account of Liu Xia, wife of Liu Xiaobo, shows remittances and withdrawals of foreign funds (in foreign currency).

3. A "Reply about Assistance in Executing an Investigation of Relevant Data" supplied by the Beijing branch of the China United Internet Communications Company, Limited, shows: There are records of Internet use for the ADSL account that Liu Xiaobo used.

4. The testimony of witness Zhang Zuhua shows: At the end of 2008 he and Liu Xiaobo together finished drafting Charter 08. He also collected signatures, after which Liu Xiaobo published Charter 08 on foreign websites.

5. The testimony of witness He Yongqin shows: In early December 2008, he received Charter 08 from Liu Xiaobo by email. Liu Xiaobo

asked him to sign it after he read it. After he read it he replied to Liu Xiaobo by email, saying he agreed to sign.

6. The testimony of witness Zhao Shiying shows: In October 2008 Liu Xiaobo sent him Charter 08 over the Internet, solicited his opinions on revising it, and asked him to look for others to sign it. At one gathering he took out Charter 08 and showed it to more than ten of the gathered people, and four agreed to sign. Liu Xiaobo also asked him, over the Internet, to go to Guangzhou to solicit signatures, and he collected five signatures in Guangzhou.

7. The testimony of witness Yao Bo shows: On one occasion in October 2008, Liu Xiaobo met him and told him about Charter 08. He agreed to add his signature.

8. The testimony of witness Zhou Duo shows: One day in November 2008, Liu Xiaobo came to his home to show him the manuscript of Charter 08 and asked him to help with revisions. After Liu Xiaobo left, he read the manuscript but made no revisions. They did not discuss the matter of signing. But later, when he saw Charter 08 on the Internet, his name was there.

9. The testimony of witness Fan Chunsan shows: At the end of November 2008, while he, Liu Xiaobo, and some others were eating together, Liu Xiaobo took out Charter 08 and showed it to him. Liu Xiaobo asked if he would sign, and he agreed to sign. He knew that Liu Xiaobo published articles on foreign websites such as Boxun and Independent Chinese PEN, and had read them online. The content of Liu Xiaobo's articles was always contemporary political commentary.

10. The testimonies of witnesses Xu Junliang, Zhi Xiaomin, and Teng Biao show: In November and December, 2008, Charter 08 appeared in their email inboxes. They did not know who had sent it. Each signed and returned Charter 08 to the mailbox from which it had come.

11. The testimony of witness Wang Zhongxia shows: He saw Charter 08 on the Internet. He agreed with its content and signed his name. He

later printed some Charter 08 T-shirts. He wanted to wear one himself and give them to others to spread the word of Charter 08.

12. A "Search Record" supplied by Public Security organs and police photographs shows: On December 8, 2008, Public Security organs, as witnessed by eyewitnesses, carried out a search of Liu Xiaobo's residence at no. 502, Unit One, Building 10, Bank of China apartments, Seven Sages Village, Haidian District, Beijing City, where they discovered and confiscated two notepad computers, one desktop computer, and one printer, which were the implements used by Liu Xiaobo to write Charter 08 ("Tentative Text for Soliciting Opinions") and to send it to the Internet.

13. A "Forensic Opinion" supplied by the Center for Electronic Data Forensics of the Internet Trade Association of Beijing City shows: On December 13, 2008, the Center carried out a forensic evaluation of the electronic data recovered from the three computers that were confiscated from Liu Xiaobo, and the evaluation found and recovered electronic versions of "The Authoritarian Patriotism of the Communist Party of China," "Who Says the Chinese People Deserve Only 'Democracy by Party Rule'?" "To Change a Regime by Changing a Society," "The Many Faces of Communist Party Dictatorship," "How a Rising Dictatorship Hurts Democracy in the World," "A Deeper Look into Why Child Slavery in China's 'Black Kilns' Could Happen," and Charter 08. In the data records of the Skype chat software in the computers for November 2008 until December 8, 2008, the Center found and recovered many records of sending Charter 08 and its "tentative text for soliciting opinions."

14. On-site investigation, records of examination, and work descriptions supplied by Public Security organs show:

(1) Between December 19, 2008, and December 23, 2008, Division One of the Department of Supervision of the Public Information Network of the Public Security Bureau of Beijing City discovered on the Internet and downloaded an article that bore the name "Liu Xiaobo" and was entitled "Liu Xiaobo: The Authoritarian Patriotism of the Communist Party of China." The article had appeared on a website at the domain http://epochtimes.com

(The Epoch Times), whose server is outside the country. The posting date of the article was October 5, 2005. As of December 23, 2008, there were links to five websites that had either posted it or reposted it on the Internet.

(2) Between December 19, 2008, and August 3, 2009, Division One of the Department of Supervision of the Public Information Network of the Public Security Bureau of Beijing City discovered on the Internet and downloaded an article that bore the name "Liu Xiaobo" and was entitled "Liu Xiaobo: Who Says the Chinese People Deserve Only 'Democracy by Party Rule'?" The article had appeared on websites at the domain http://epochtimes.com (The Epoch Times) and the domain http://www.observechina.net (Observe China), whose servers are outside the country. The posting dates of the article were January 5, 2006, and January 6, 2006. As of December 23, 2008, there were links to five websites that had either posted it or reposted it on the Internet. The total number of hits was 402.

(3) Between December 20, 2008, and August 3, 2009, Division One of the Department of Supervision of the Public Information Network of the Public Security Bureau of Beijing City discovered on the Internet and downloaded an article that bore the name "Liu Xiaobo" and was entitled "Liu Xiaobo: To Change a Regime by Changing a Society." The article had appeared on websites at the domain http://epochtimes.com (The Epoch Times) and the domain http://www.observechina. net (Observe China), whose servers are outside the country. The posting dates of the article were February 26, 2006, and February 27, 2006. As of December 23, 2008, there were links to five websites that had either posted it or reposted it on the Internet. The total number of hits was 748.

(4) Between December 20, 2008, and August 3, 2009, Division One of the Department of Supervision of the Public Information Network of the Public Security Bureau of Beijing City discovered on the Internet and downloaded an article that bore the name "Liu Xiaobo" and was entitled "Liu Xiaobo: The Many

Faces of Communist Party Dictatorship." The article had appeared on websites at the domain http://www.secretchina.com (Look at China) and the domain http://www.observechina.net (Observe China), whose servers are outside the country. The posting date of the article was March 13, 2006. As of December 23, 2008, there were links to six websites that had either posted it or reposted it on the Internet. The total number of hits was 512.

(5)  On December 20, 2008, Division One of the Department of Supervision of the Public Information Network of the Public Security Bureau of Beijing City discovered on the Internet and downloaded an article that bore the name "Liu Xiaobo" and was entitled "Liu Xiaobo: How a Rising Dictatorship Hurts Democracy in the World." The article had appeared on a website at the domain http://www.secretchina.com (Look at China), whose server is outside the country. The posting date of the article was May 7, 2006. As of December 23, 2008, there were links to seven websites that had either posted it or reposted it on the Internet. The total number of hits was 57.

(6)  Between December 20, 2008, and August 3, 2009, Division One of the Department of Supervision of the Public Information Network of the Public Security Bureau of Beijing City discovered on the Internet and downloaded an article that bore the name "Liu Xiaobo" and was entitled "Liu Xiaobo: A Deeper Look into Why Child Slavery in China's 'Black Kilns' Could Happen." The article had appeared on websites at the domain http://www.minzhuzhongguo.org (Democratic China) and the domain http://www.renyurenquan.org (Humanity and Human Rights), whose servers are outside the country. The posting date of the article was August 1, 2007. As of December 23, 2008, there were links to eight websites that had either posted it or reposted it on the Internet. The total number of hits was 488.

(7)  On December 11, 2008, Division One of the Department of Supervision of the Public Information Network of the Public Security Bureau of Beijing City discovered on the Internet and downloaded an article entitled "Charter 08." The article had

appeared on a website at the domain http://www.chinesepen
.org (Independent Chinese PEN), whose server is outside the
country. The posting date of the article was December 9, 2008.
Its author was listed as a group of citizens. On the same day, on
websites at the domain http://www.boxun.com (Boxun) and the
domain http://www.minzhuzhongguo.org (Democratic China),
whose servers are outside the country, an article entitled "People
from All Parts of Society Come Together to Announce Charter
08" was discovered and downloaded. The posting dates of the
articles were December 8, 2008, and December 9, 2008. For these
articles, as of December 12, 2008, there were links to thirty-three
websites, nineteen of which were websites outside the country,
that had either posted it or reposted it on the Internet. The total
number of hits was 5,154, and there were 158 replies. On Decem-
ber 9, 2009, it was discovered on the front page of a website at the
domain http://www.2008xianzhang.info that, as of December 9,
2009, a total of 10,390 people had signed Charter 08.

(8)  On August 14, 2009, the Department of Supervision of the
Public Information Network of the Public Security Bureau of
Beijing City conducted an examination of the email mailbox
that Liu Xiaobo used and discovered that the mailbox that Liu
Xiaobo used was based outside the country. After using pass-
words to login, the Department verified that the earliest items
in the sent box were dated November 25, 2008, and that thirty
of the sent items were related to the sending out of Charter 08.


15.  Liu Xiaobo's acknowledgment of articles by his signature shows: Liu
Xiaobo has carried out identification of the articles "Liu Xiaobo: The Au-
thoritarian Patriotism of the Communist Party of China," "Liu Xiaobo:
Who Says the Chinese People Deserve Only 'Democracy by Party Rule'?"
"Liu Xiaobo: To Change a Regime by Changing a Society," "Liu Xiaobo:
The Many Faces of Communist Party Dictatorship," "Liu Xiaobo: How a
Rising Dictatorship Hurts Democracy in the World," and "Liu Xiaobo: A
Deeper Look into Why Child Slavery in China's 'Black Kilns' Could
Happen" that departments of supervision of Public Security organs have
downloaded and preserved and of the electronic versions of "The Au-
thoritarian Patriotism of the Communist Party of China," "Who Says

the Chinese People Deserve Only 'Democracy by Party Rule'?" "To Change a Regime by Changing a Society," "The Many Faces of Communist Party Dictatorship," "How a Rising Dictatorship Hurts Democracy in the World," and "A Deeper Look into Why Child Slavery in China's 'Black Kilns' Could Happen," that have been recovered from his computers, and Liu Xiaobo has acknowledged that the identified articles are articles that he wrote and posted on the Internet. The articles that Liu Xiaobo has identified and acknowledged by signature contain language of incitement as determined by the aforementioned facts.

16. The confession of Defendant Liu Xiaobo shows: Liu Xiaobo has confessed that he used computers to write the aforementioned articles and to post them on Internet websites. The confession of Liu Xiaobo and the aforementioned evidence are mutually corroboratory.

17. A case log supplied by Public Security organs shows: The Public Security Bureau of Beijing City detained Liu Xiaobo at no. 502, Unit One, Building 10, Bank of China apartments, Seven Sages Village, Haidian District, Beijing City on the night of December 8, 2008.

18. Criminal Verdict IC no. 2373 (1990) of the former Intermediate People's Court of Beijing City and the Reeducation-Through-Labor Decision JLS no. 3400 (1996) of the Reeducation-Through-Labor Management Committee of the People's Government of Beijing City show: On January 26, 1991, Liu Xiaobo was exempted from criminal punishment for the crime of counterrevolutionary incitement; on September 26, 1996, he was directed to undergo three years of reeducation-through-labor for disturbing social order.

19. Material for certifying identity supplied by Public Security organs shows: the name, address, and other aspects of the identity of Defendant Liu Xiaobo.

## Judgment

It is the judgment of this court that Defendant Liu Xiaobo, with the goal of overthrowing the state power of the People's Democratic Dictatorship and the socialist system of our country, took advantage of the

Internet, with its features of rapid transmission, broad reach, large influence on society, and high degree of public notice, and chose as his means the writing of articles and posting them on the Internet to do slander and to incite others to overthrow state power and the socialist system in our country. His actions have constituted the crime of incitement to subvert state power, have persisted through a long period of time, and show deep subjective malice. The articles that he posted, which spread widely through links, copying, and visits to websites, had a despicable influence. He qualifies as a criminal whose crimes are severe and deserves heavy punishment according to law. The facts adduced by Branch No. 1 of the People's Procuratorate of Beijing in charging Defendant Liu Xiaobo with the crime of incitement of subversion of state power are clear; its evidence is accurate and ample, and its charges are well founded.

With regard to the reply offered at trial by Defendant Liu Xiaobo and the defense arguments of his legal counsel, examination has shown that the facts and evidence verified at this trial already prove overwhelmingly that Liu Xiaobo took advantage of the media characteristics of the Internet and used the means of publishing slanderous articles on the Internet to carry out actions of incitement of subversion of the state power and the socialist system of our country. Liu Xiaobo's actions have exceeded the scope of freedom of speech and constitute crimes. Therefore the aforementioned reply offered at trial by Defendant Liu Xiaobo and defense arguments of his legal counsel both are inadequate and are not accepted by this court.

Based on the facts, nature, circumstances, and degree of social harm of the crimes of Defendant Liu Xiaobo, this court, in accordance with Section 2 of Article 105, Section 1 of Article 55, Section 1 of Article 56, and Article 64 of the Criminal Law of the People's Republic of China, rules as follows:

1. The Defendant Liu Xiaobo has committed the crime of incitement to subvert state power and is sentenced to eleven years in prison plus the deprivation of political rights for two years. The prison term is calculated from the day of sentencing. (Days in custody prior to sentencing reduce the sentence by one day for one day, which means the term extends from June 23, 2009, to June 21, 2020.)

2. The items submitted with this case that Liu Xiaobo used in committing his crimes are confiscated. If the verdict of this court is not accepted, it may be appealed either through this court or by direct application to the High People's Court of Beijing City within ten days of the day following its receipt. Written appeals should be supplied in one original and two copies.

Chief Judge: Jia Lianchun
Associate Judge: Zheng Wenwei
Associate Judge: Zhai Changxi

December 25, 2009

*Original text available at http://news.sina.com.hk.news*
*Translated by Perry Link*

# BIBLIOGRAPHY

## BOOKS BY LIU XIAOBO

*Xuanze de pipan: Yu Li Zehou duihua* [Criticizing choice: A dialogue with Li Zehou]. Shanghai: Shanghai renmin chubanshe, 1987. Republished as *Xuanze de pipan: Yu sixiangjia Li Zehou duihua* [Criticizing choice: A dialogue with the thinker Li Zehou]. Taibei: Taiwan fengyunshidai chubanshe, 1989.

*Shenmei yu ren de ziyou* [Aesthetics and human freedom]. Beijing: Beijing shifandaxue chubanshe, 1988. (A published version of Liu's PhD dissertation.)

*Xingershang xue de miwu* [The fog of metaphysics]. Shanghai: Shanghai renminchubanshe, 1989.

*Chishenluoti, zouxiang shangdi* [Walking naked toward God]. Changchun: Shidai wenyi chubanshe, 1989.

*Sixiang zhi mi yu renlei zhi meng* [The enigma of thought and the dreams of humanity]. Taibei: Taiwan fengyunshidai chubanshe, 1989 and 1990. 2 volumes.

*Zhongguo dangdai zhengzhi yu Zhongguo zhishifenzi* [Contemporary Chinese politics and Chinese intellectuals]. Taibei: Tangshan chubanshe, 1990. Translated and published in Japanese as *Gendai Chūgoku chishikijin hihan* [A critique of contemporary Chinese intellectuals]. Tokyo: Tokuma Bookstore, 1992.

*Mori xingcunzhe de dubai* [Monologues of a survivor of doomsday]. Taibei: Shibao wenhua chubanqiye gongsi, 1992.

*Liu Xiaobo Liu Xia shixuan* [Selected poems of Liu Xiaobo and Liu Xia]. Hong Kong: Xiafeier guoji chubangongsi, 2000.

*Meiren zeng wo menghanyao* [A beauty gives me a knockout drug]. Co-authored with Wang Shuo, with Liu Xiaobo writing under the pen name Lao Xia. Wuhan: Changjiang wenyi chubanshe, 2000.

*Xiang liangxin shuohuang de minzu* [A nation of people who lie to their consciences]. Taibei: Taiwan jieyou chubanshe, 2002.

*Weilai de ziyou Zhongguo zai minjian* [A free China of the future will emerge from the people]. Washington, D.C.: Laogai Research Foundation, 2005.

*Danren dujian: Zhongguo minzuzhuyi pipan* [Single-edged poison sword: A critique of Chinese nationalism]. Flushing, N.Y.: Broad Press, 2006.

*Daguo chenlun: Xie gei Zhongguo de beiwanglu* [The sinking of a great nation: Memorandum for a future China]. Taibei: Yunchen wenhua chubanshe, 2009.

*Niannian liusi: Liu Xiaobo shiji* [June Fourth on my mind: A collection of Liu Xiaobo's poems]. Hong Kong, 2009.

*Liu Xiaobo wenji* [Collected essays of Liu Xiaobo]. Edited by Liu Xia, Hu Ping, and Liao Tianqi. Hong Kong: Xinshiji chubanshe, 2010.

*La philosophie du porc et autres essais* [Philosophy of the pig and other essays]. Edited by Jean-Philippe Béja. Paris: Gallimard, 2011.

*Zhuiqiu ziyou* [Pursuing freedom]. Washington, D.C.: Laogai Research Foundation, 2011.

### BOOKS ON LIU XIAOBO AND HIS WORK

Bei Ling. *Der Freiheit geopfert* [Surrendering oneself for freedom]. Munich: Riva Verlag, 2011.

Chen Kuide and Xia Ming, eds. *Ziyou jingguan: Liu Xiaobo yu Nobeier heping jiang* [A crown of thorns for freedom: Liu Xiaobo and the Nobel Peace Prize]. Hong Kong: Chenzhong shuju, 2010.

Hong Bin, ed. *Liu Xiaobo mianmianguan* [The many sides of Liu Xiaobo]. Hong Kong: Posi chubanshe, 2010.

Li Xiaorong and Zhang Zuhua, eds. *Ling-ba xianzhang* [Charter 08]. Hong Kong: Kaifang chubanshe, 2009.

Link, Perry. *Liu Xiaobo's Empty Chair: Chronicling the Reform Movement Beijing Fears Most.* New York: New York Review of Books eBook Original, 2011.

Liu Yanzi, ed. *Ten'anmon jiken kara '08 kenshō e* [From the Tiananmen incident to Charter 08]. Tokyo: Fujiwara Bookstore, 2009.

Miller, Frederic P., Agnes F. Vandome, and John McBrewster, eds. *Liu Xiaobo*. Beau Bassin, Mauritius: Alphascript, 2010.

Yu Jie. *Liu Xiaobo dabai Hu Jintao* [Liu Xiaobo defeats Hu Jintao]. Hong Kong: Chenzhong shuju, 2010.

Yu Jie. *Liu Xiaobo yu Hu Jintao de duizhi: Zhongguo zhengzhi tizhi gaige wei he tingzhi?* [A standoff between Liu Xiaobo and Hu Jintao: Why has the reform of China's political system stagnated?] Hong Kong: Chenzhong shuju, 2009.

Zheng Wang and Ji Kuai, eds. *Liu Xiaobo qiren qishi* [Liu Xiaobo: The man and his works]. Beijing: Zhongguo qingnian chubanshe, 1989.

Zhongguo xinxi zhongxin. *Ling-ba xianzhang yu Zhongguo biange* [Charter 08 and China's restructuring]. Washington, D.C.: Zhongguo xinxi zhongxin, 2009.

### WEBSITES ON LIU XIAOBO

http://www.liuxiaobo.eu/

http://blog.boxun.com/hero/liuxb/

# ACKNOWLEDGMENTS

I am grateful to Geremie Barmé, Jean-Philippe Béja, Hu Ping, Li Xiaorong, Tienchi Martin-Liao, Joshua Rosensweig, Susan Wilf, and Su Xiaokang for information on Liu Xiaobo, for editorial assistance, and/ or for help in solving puzzles in translation. The *New York Review of Books* kindly granted permission to republish my translation of Charter 08, which originally appeared on its website on December 10, 2008, and in its issue of January 15, 2009 (vol. 56, no. 1). Some of the material in the Introduction appeared in different form in my book, *Liu Xiaobo's Empty Chair*, published by *New York Review of Books* in 2011.

*Perry Link*

# INDEX